Saving Succeeding Generations from the Scourge of War

Nijhoff Law Specials

VOLUME 100

The titles published in this series are listed at *brill.com/nlsp*

Saving Succeeding Generations from the Scourge of War

The United Nations Security Council at 75

By

Niels Blokker

TUTA SUB AEGIDE PALLAS · 1683 ·

BRILL
NIJHOFF

LEIDEN | BOSTON

Cover illustration:
Above: "The Signing of the United Nations Charter, San Francisco on 26th June, 1945, Mary Evans Picture Library Ltd., copyright ANP, The Netherlands".
Below: "New York City, USA – September 26, 2019: A meeting of the UN Security Council on the sidelines of the 74th session of the United Nations General Assembly at the UN headquarters. Valery Sharifulin/TASS; copyright ANP, The Netherlands".

The Library of Congress Cataloging-in-Publication Data is available online at http://catalog.loc.gov

Typeface for the Latin, Greek, and Cyrillic scripts: "Brill". See and download: brill.com/brill-typeface.

ISSN 0924-4549
ISBN 978-90-04-44391-4 (paperback)
ISBN 978-90-04-44392-1 (e-book)

This book is printed on acid-free paper and produced in a sustainable manner.

Dedicated to

Nicolaas Blokker
Gertrude Sophie Blokker–Hafenbraedl
my parents (in dierbare herinnering)

and to

Antonie Jakob Bosman
Aleida Jennigje Bosman–Tharner (in warme herinnering)
much more than parents-in-law

∵

Contents

Tables

Introduction

This year, the United Nations (UN) is celebrating its 75th anniversary. Commemorations and events are organized. Often, such occasions are used to evaluate the work of the UN, to honour its achievements and to criticize its failures. Questions such as 'is the glass half full or half empty?' are asked. Yet it is easier to ask this question than to answer it. The glass is certainly not full. There are too many examples of cases and situations in which the UN ideally would have done much better, in any of its fields of activity. Peace and security, social and economic cooperation, human rights, criminal justice, sustainable development, the list is long. However, neither is the glass empty. There are also many achievements, examples of cases and situations where the UN has made a positive difference, in any of its fields of activity. Peace and security, peacekeeping in particular, social and economic cooperation, human rights, criminal justice, sustainable development, this is also a long list.

The UN's 75th anniversary takes place in an era in which globalization and nationalism struggle for supremacy. One battleground where this struggle becomes notably clear is the ministerial week of the annual regular session of the UN General Assembly. Using the weapons of rhetoric, political leaders of the UN member states emphasize the achievements of multilateral cooperation or criticize globalization. Antagonism seems to prevail.

Globalization and nationalism struggle for supremacy. On the one hand, throughout the last 75 years the world has become more interconnected and integrated. Already in the 1960s, the Canadian communication theorist Marshall McLuhan referred to the 'global village'. The invention of the World Wide Web in 1989 by the British engineer and computer scientist Tim Berners-Lee working at CERN, the European organization for nuclear research, was the beginning of internet.[1] Through the development of smart phones we may be connected to almost anyone at any place at any time, and have access to unprecedented amounts of information. The social medium is the message nowadays. On the other hand, perhaps also due to globalization and the pace of change, there is a revival of nationalism, a reappraisal of national values and national identity. Disadvantages of globalization, including increasing social inequality and a lack of inclusion fuel xenophobia and bring voters to elect nationalist and populist leaders, who campaign to leave international

1 J. Gillies & R. Cailliau, *How the Web was Born – The Story of the World Wide Web* (2000).

 | DOI:10.1163/9789004443921_002

organizations and reclaim national sovereignty. 'We want our country back' is a slogan not only used by Nigel Farage in the days of Brexit.

Globalization and nationalism struggle for supremacy. In 2020, this is also illustrated by the coronavirus (COVID-19) pandemic. The outbreak of this virus in December 2019 in Wuhan, China, resulted in a major global health crisis. The reactions to this crisis underline how much our world is organized in sovereign states. Just as many individuals, many states have been in almost full quarantine. For weeks or months, they were largely isolated from the outside world. Each country took its own political decisions, mainly based on the expert advice of its own national health institutions. In each country, political leaders addressed their own population in historic addresses explaining the challenges, often making comparisons with war. The French President Macron stated on 16 March 2020: "nous sommes en guerre" (we are at war).[2] The German Chancellor Merkel on 18 March: "this is serious. [...] Since German reunification, no, since the Second World War, there has not been a challenge for our country in which action in a spirit of solidarity on our part was so important".[3] Prime Minister Rutte of the Netherlands ended his television address on 16 March by making the following appeal to the Dutch: "despite all the uncertainty, one thing is perfectly clear: the challenge we face is enormous, and all 17 million of us will have to work together to overcome it".[4] The reactions to this health crisis have been intensely national.

At the same time, the global dimensions of this crisis cannot be ignored. Not only this disease has global dimensions, also the fight against it. The fight against this health crisis, and also the fight against the expected post-corona economic recession, cannot be effective without international cooperation and coordination. This is why long ago international organizations such as the World Health Organization and the International Monetary Fund were created, in the common self-interest of the participating states. Global problems

2 See https://www.elysee.fr/emmanuel-macron/2020/03/16/adresse-aux-francais-covid19. More in full, President Macron referred to an invisible enemy: "Nous sommes en guerre, en guerre sanitaire, certes: nous ne luttons ni contre une armée, ni contre une autre Nation. Mais l'ennemi est là, invisible et insaisissable, qui progresse".

3 See https://www.bundeskanzlerin.de/bkin-en/news/statement-chancellor-1732302. In German: "Es ist ernst. [...] Seit der Deutschen Einheit, nein, seit dem Zweiten Weltkrieg gab es keine Herausforderung an unser Land mehr, bei der es so sehr auf unseres gemeinsames, solidarisches Handeln ankommt".

4 See https://www.government.nl/documents/speeches/2020/03/16/television-address-by-prime-minister-mark-rutte-of-the-netherlands. In Dutch: "bij alle onzekerheden die er zijn, is één ding volstrekt duidelijk: de opgave waar we voor staan is heel groot en we moeten dit echt met 17 miljoen mensen doen".

cannot be solved exclusively at the national level. This is as much true for man-made disasters like armed conflicts as it is for (largely) non-man-made disasters like the corona pandemic. Perhaps it is no coincidence that the initiative for the creation of the World Health Organization was taken at the same conference in San Francisco where the United Nations was established.[5]

∴

The United Nations is celebrating its 75th anniversary against this backdrop of the corona pandemic and the struggle for supremacy between globalization and nationalism. Such an anniversary is a proper occasion to reflect on the UN's past activities and future perspectives. This book is a small contribution to such reflections. Because of the vast scope of the work of the UN, it is necessarily incomplete. It will not provide an overall assessment of the work of the UN or sketch its future potential in broad-brush strokes. Neither will it try to give a list of main successes and failures. Rather, the purpose of this book is to focus on the Security Council, the UN body with primary responsibility to "save succeeding generations from the scourge of war", that famous first sentence of the UN Charter. The issues discussed in Chapters Two, Three and Four were hotly debated when the UN was founded, in 1945 in San Francisco, at the UN Conference on International Organization (UNCIO). They have always been highly relevant for the Council's functioning during the last 75 years, and it is likely that they will continue to do so in the future.

However, before this book will focus on the Security Council, Chapter 1 will take a broader look at 'The United Nations at 75'. It will discuss the world organization of which the Security Council forms part and without which it would not be able to perform its functions. Chapter 1 will pay particular attention to issues that are essential for the role and functioning of the Security Council. It will look at developments in UN membership, and at its evolution as an international organization. No United Nations without the Security Council, but also: no Security Council without the United Nations.

When the UN was established, it was widely felt that lessons should be learnt from the League of Nations, coined as a 'Great Experiment' in world organization by Robert Cecil, one of its founding fathers.[6] There was general support for the creation of a mechanism to maintain or restore international peace that should be much stronger than its predecessor. This mechanism

5 This initiative was taken by Brazil and China. See UNCIO, Vol. X, pp. 117–121.

6 R. Cecil, *A Great Experiment* (1941).

should derive its strength, its force from the five most powerful allied powers. They should remain allied after the war; their combined power was now to be embedded in the Security Council within the UN. However, these five powers were only willing to accept this exceptional responsibility if they would receive an exceptional position in the Security Council: permanent membership with the right to veto any decisions other than procedural decisions. This position is exceptional since decision-making by majority vote is the rule in the UN. As Jenks wrote in 1945, "the battle to substitute majority decision for the requirement of unanimity in international organization has now been largely won".[7] The right of veto was the most difficult issue to solve during the UN Charter negotiations. By agreeing to the right of veto for the most powerful five, the other 45 states involved in these negotiations submitted themselves to a considerable degree to these powerful five. Based on the League experience, they exchanged a certain, but less powerful control over their own security for an uncertain, but potentially more powerful control by the Security Council. This had far-reaching implications. The veto has not only been the most difficult issue of the Charter negotiations, it also became the most dominant feature of the functioning of the Security Council during the last 75 years. Chapter 2 will therefore analyse both the Charter negotiations about the veto and how it has been used in practice.

From the outset, the exceptional position of the five permanent members and the strong enforcement powers of the Security Council have raised fundamental questions, both in 1945 and in subsequent practice. If majority voting is the rule, even in the Security Council, why should it be possible for one single member to block decisions that are considered necessary by nearly all other members? Is this not undemocratic? If the United Nations "is based on the principle of the sovereign equality of all its Members" (Article 2(1) of the Charter) as is reflected in the one state one vote rule of the General Assembly, why are five states much more equal than others? Other fundamental questions concern the Security Council's functioning in practice. What prompts the Council (not) to act? It was created as a political organ with strong enforcement powers, but is the exercise of such powers completely governed by (super) power politics, or also by law (and if so, by what rules of law)? For example, is it within the discretion of the Security Council to introduce individual sanctions without any remedial mechanism? Is it within its full discretion to refer the situations in Darfur and in Libya to the International Criminal Court, but not the situation in Syria?

7 C. Wilfred Jenks, 'Some Constitutional Problems of International Organizations', 22 *British Yearbook of International Law* (1945), pp. 11–72, at p. 34.

The common denominator of fundamental questions such as these is the general question whether or to what extent the Security Council is governed by the rule of law. This will be examined in Chapter 3.

When the UN was established and it was agreed that it would have a strong enforcement mechanism, the idea was never that the Security Council would only have the five most powerful allied powers as its members. Since the Council was to perform its peace and security functions on behalf of all UN member states, it should be composed of a number of non-permanent members, in addition to the five permanent members. Following the rapid increase of UN membership, the Council had become less representative. The original number of six non-permanent members was therefore increased to ten, as part of the first amendment of the Charter in 1963. When UN membership continued to increase and now has almost quadrupled since 1945, the need to enlarge the Security Council presented itself again. However, while a second enlargement was agreed for the Economic and Social Council in 1971, this has so far not been possible for the Security Council. After decades of discussions and negotiations, there is only general agreement that a further enlargement is necessary, but not at all how this should be done. Chapter 4 will focus on the need to expand membership of the Security Council. Chapter 5 will present some concluding reflections.

∴

This book will use an institutional legal lens to look at the UN Security Council, in the five above-mentioned chapters. Key chapters within the law of international organizations, the author's field of expertise, are the legal status and powers of international organizations, the composition of international organs, rules of decision-making. Key themes in this field are the relationship between international organizations and their members, and the relationship between law and practice of international organizations. These key chapters and themes of international organizations law provide a useful perspective for Chapter 1 (discussing the UN at 75), and for the more specific analysis of the right of veto in Chapter 2, the rule of law in Chapter 3, and the need for a second enlargement of the Security Council in Chapter 4.

Websites mentioned in footnotes were last visited on 9 July 2020.

∴

I am grateful to dr. Zsuzsanna Deen-Racsmány, to my former students Dorine Nauleau, Anna Smulders and Kseniia Soloveva, as well as to my colleagues and friends professors Rick Lawson and Nico Schrijver, for their willingness to read drafts of (parts of) this book and to give comments and suggestions. I also thank Ms. Lindy Melman from Martinus Nijhoff Publishers, part of Brill Publishers, for her immediate warm support when I first shared the idea to write this book and for her assistance throughout its preparation. This book is dedicated to my parents and my parents-in-law, who belong to the generation that experienced the Second World War and the creation of the United Nations.

CHAPTER 1

The United Nations at 75

The Security Council is not a self-standing institution; it is part of the United Nations. The Security Council is neither an international organization (such as the UN or NATO) nor a treaty organ (such as the Assembly of States Parties to the Rome Statute of the International Criminal Court and the Conference of the Parties of the UN Framework Convention on Climate Change). It is not a specialized agency of the UN – if it was, it would be based on a treaty separate from the UN Charter, having a membership separate (and possibly different) from that of the UN. Instead, it is one of the UN's six principal organs.[1] Therefore, before focusing on the Security Council in the next few chapters, this chapter will first make some observations on the larger institutional structure of which the Council is part and parcel.

The overview of the UN at 75 in this chapter is necessarily brief and incomplete. It will pay particular attention to issues that are essential for the role and functioning of the Security Council. First, paragraph 1 will briefly compare the UN with its predecessor, the League of Nations. Within the League, the organ that best resembled the Security Council was the Council, even though the powers and composition of the two are rather different. Next, paragraphs 2 and 3 are devoted to membership of the UN and its evolution as an international organization. Since the Security Council is not a self-standing institution but part and parcel of the UN, its functioning is closely connected to developments in membership of the UN and to evolutions in its 'organizationship' (i.e. evolutions of the organization of which it forms part). Paragraph 4 offers a few concluding observations.

1 A Comparison with the League of Nations

A comparative perspective is often helpful, but there is not much with which the UN can be compared. If anything, it is its predecessor, the League of Nations. This 'Great Experiment'[2] is considered the first general political world organization.

---

1 UN Charter, Art. 7(1).

2 This is the title of a book by Robert Cecil (*A Great Experiment* (1941)). Robert Cecil was a British politician, closely involved in the creation of the League of Nations. In 1946, Cecil delivered the funeral speech for the League when it was dissolved. The final words of this

 | DOI:10.1163/9789004443921_003

At the UN's 75th anniversary, it is first of all noteworthy that the League's life was much, much shorter than that of the UN. Its formal existence ended in 1946, but *de facto*, its death warrant was signed in 1939, when the Second World War started. This is twenty years after the League of Nations was founded. Twenty years, this is less than one generation.

The word 'generation' is deliberately chosen, because it is also used in that famous first sentence of the UN Charter: "We the peoples of the United Nations, determined to save succeeding generations from the scourge of war, which twice in our lifetime has brought untold sorrow to mankind, [...]". "Twice in our lifetime": this refers to the two World Wars, not to other, smaller scale wars that were fought in the decades before 1945. The ambition in 1945 was not to have another World War for "succeeding generations". If one generation covers 25 to 30 years, we may conclude that this ambition has been achieved for some three generations. This is no mean feat. It is true that, since 1945, there has been a Cold War. There have been a number of international and non-international armed conflicts (in 1945, the UN Charter was primarily written for the former, although it did not exclude UN involvement in the latter). Since 1945, millions of people were killed in wars, genocides and massacres, or died in mass annihilations, for example during the partition of India (1947), in China (during the Great Leap Forward (1958–1962) and the Cultural Revolution (1966 – 1976), in Indonesia (killings of communists in 1965), during the Bangladesh Liberation War (1971), during the Khmer Rouge regime in Cambodia (1975 -1979), in Rwanda (1995), the former Yugoslavia (mid 1990s), North Korea and in various parts of Africa.[3] However, there has not been a World War Three. This is anything but self-evident. If the UN is compared with the League of Nations from this perspective, the glass is therefore at least half full, rather than half empty.

At the same time, while we can say that there has not been another World War during the last 75 years, we cannot say that this is entirely *because of* the United Nations. We do not know what would have happened without the UN or some other world organization. There is no alternative history. Some might say: the main reason why there has not been another World War is the existence of nuclear weapons. In a balance of terror, the possession of nuclear weapons may be an effective deterrent against an attack from outside. Others

speech became famous ('The League is dead, long live the United Nations', emphasizing the continuity in world organization).

3 See A. de Swaan, *The Killing Compartments – The Mentality of Mass Murder* (2015). At p. 87, mass annihilation is defined as killings of human beings who lack any means to defend themselves, on a very large scale (from many thousands to tens of millions), almost always with direct support from the ruling regime.

will disagree with such a proposition. This reasoning suffers the same level of incertitude.

∵

This raises more fundamental questions about the role and effectiveness of international organizations in maintaining or restoring international peace. Can such organizations make a difference, and maintain or restore international peace where this could not be achieved in their absence, by states alone? Or, in times of crisis, is it all about political will, the willingness of states, in particular the most powerful states, to find peaceful solutions? A balance may be required, as was already concluded by Claude, almost 50 years ago: "[o]ne of the major tasks of twentieth-century statesmanship is to strike a balance between obsessive concern with institutional problems - which makes international organization an end in itself, and exclusive concentration upon substantive issues of current world politics - which neglects the building of an adequate institutional apparatus for international relations".[4]

It is often concluded that the demise of the League of Nations was largely or completely caused by the lack of political will of its members to use it, and to apply the rules of the League Covenant. For example, Churchill stated in 1946: "[t]he League of Nations did not fail because of its principles or conceptions. It failed because these principles were deserted by those States which had brought it into being. It failed because the Governments of those days feared to face the facts and act while time remained".[5] Goodrich and Hambro wrote in their Commentary on the UN Charter: "[t]he world-wide economic collapse of the late twenties and the early thirties, the rise in popularity of anti-democratic and nationalist doctrines, and the unwillingness of peace-loving peoples to assume necessary responsibilities for the maintenance of peace resulted in the disintegration and the collapse of the League system. Into the vacuum produced by the lack of vision and power of decision of the peace-loving peoples of the world stepped the confident and aggressive forces of Italian Fascism, German Nazism and Japanese Militarism".[6] Finally, Robert Cecil observed that in the final analysis there "has been a lack of solidarity, of *esprit*

4 I. Claude, *Swords into Plowshares – The Problems and Progress of International Organization* (4th ed. 1971), p. 84.

5 In a speech delivered at Zürich University (*A 'United States of Europe'*), 19 September 1946 (reproduced in *Never give in! Winston Churchill's speeches, selected and edited by his grandson W.S. Churchill* (2004), p. 356, quotation at p. 357).

6 L.M. Goodrich and E. Hambro, *Charter of the United Nations – Commentary and Documents* (2nd and revised ed. 1949), pp. 3–4.

de corps, in the League Powers which should have induced them jointly and almost automatically to resist an armed attack on any of their number. That is partly due to want of imagination caused by geographical remoteness or other considerations, partly to the unfamiliarity of the truth that peace is in itself the greatest of national interests, and partly to the want of vigour and precision in the League organization".[7]

According to these evaluations, with different nuances, the main reason for the demise of the League and the outbreak of the Second World War was the lack of political will of 'peace-loving' states. At the same time, if the maintenance of international peace would *only* depend on the political will of states, why at all should efforts be made to build "an adequate apparatus for international relations" (Claude)? During the Second World War, states themselves considered that there was a need to establish a world organization stronger than the League of Nations, "to save succeeding generations from the scourge of war". From the perspective of today, 75 years after its foundation, what has made the UN to live so much longer than its predecessor? Is it the political will of the member states, or the effectiveness of the "institutional apparatus" (Claude) of the world organization? Or both? We will return to this question in Chapter 5.

∴

It may be concluded already from these general observations that the relationship between an organization and its members is of fundamental importance. With a small variation on what the Scottish law professor James Lorimer wrote in the 19th century, 'international organizations belong to all members and to none'.[8] The following two paragraphs will therefore focus on developments in membership of the UN during the last 75 years (paragraph 2) and on evolutions in 'organizationship' (paragraph 3). These are mostly issues external to the Security Council.[9] If the members do not fulfil their Charter

7 Cecil, op. cit. note 2, p. 349.

8 J. Lorimer, *The Institutes of the Law of Nations*, Vol. II (1884), p. 266. Lorimer drafted a "Scheme for the Organisation of an International Government", originally published in 1877, in 'Le Problème final du Droit International', *Revue de Droit International* (Vol. ix, No. 11, p. 161), later in English in *The Institutes of the Law of Nations*, Vol. II (1884), p. 181 ff. On pp. 264–267 Lorimer discusses the "Want of an International Locality" that should serve as a "centre of international life". This is where a "government" should be based "which belonged to all nations and to none" (p. 266). Lorimer uses as synonyms for "government": "international body", "institution" and "international organisation".

9 Although its recommendations are necessary for the admission of new members (as well as for the suspension of membership, and for expulsion).

obligations, and if the other organs of the organization fail in the performance of their functions, the Security Council will be largely powerless.

2 Developments in Membership

As mentioned above, the Security Council is not a self-standing institution. In performing its functions, it acts not only on behalf of its own 15 members, but on behalf of all members of the UN.[10] In addition, it reports to the General Assembly composed of all these members.[11] Every year, the General Assembly elects non-permanent members of the Security Council. It is clear therefore that developments in UN membership have implications for the Security Council and affect its functioning.

There is no organization without members. For a general political world organization, universal membership is essential. For states, membership of the UN is vital in our globalized world, as is demonstrated whenever a new independent state comes into being: applying for UN membership is often among the first sovereign activities.

Before analyzing developments in UN membership, it is instructive to briefly compare this to membership of the League of Nations. The League never became the truly universal organization that its founders wanted it to be. The US and a number of other states never became a member. The Soviet Union became a member only in 1934, and was expelled five years later (following its invasion of Finland). At most, the League had 59 members.[12] In addition, the states that became members did not always stay. The League Covenant allowed members to withdraw,[13] and no less than 17 states used this possibility (including Germany and Japan (both in 1933), and Italy (in 1937)).[14]

---

10 UN Charter, Art. 24(1).

11 UN Charter, Art. 24(3).

12 Ph. Sands and P. Klein, *Bowett's Law of International Institutions* (6th ed. 2009), p. 12.

13 League of Nations Covenant, Art. 1, final sentence: "[a]ny Member of the League may, after two years' notice of its intention so to do, withdraw from the League, provided that all its international obligations and all its obligations under this Covenant shall have been fulfilled at the time of its withdrawal".

14 See F.P. Walters, *A History of the League of Nations* (1952), pp. 64–65. The other withdrawals were by Costa Rica (1925), Brazil (1926), Paraguay (1935), Nicaragua (1936), Guatemala (1936), Honduras (1936), Salvador (1937), Chile (1938), Venezuela (1938), Hungary (1939), Peru (1939), Spain (1939), Roumania (1940) and Haiti (1942). See further K.D. Magliveras, 'The Withdrawal From the League of Nations Revisited', 10 *Penn State International Law Review* (1991), pp. 25–71.

Compared to the League of Nations experience, the record of the UN is truly impressive. In this respect, the glass is much more than half full. When the Charter entered into force, on 24 October 1945, the UN had 51 members, the so-called original members of the UN.[15] Membership of the most powerful allied powers, the five permanent members of the Security Council, was considered essential, to ensure that the new world organization would avoid one of the adversities of the League of Nations and would have the necessary military strength and political leverage. The Charter therefore provides that it would only come into force upon the deposit of ratifications by these five permanent members.[16] Of these five, the US was the first to deposit its ratification, on 8 August 1945,[17] during the days of the atomic bombings of Hiroshima and Nagasaki, shortly before Japan surrendered and the war came to an end. It was followed by France (31 August 1945), China (28 September), the United Kingdom (20 October 1945) and the Soviet Union (24 October 1945).[18] Within 15 years, membership doubled, when on 20 September 1960 14 states were admitted. Less than two decades later, membership reached the number of 150 with the admission of Djibouti and Vietnam on 20 September 1977. Since 2011, when South Sudan was admitted, the UN counts 193 member states.[19]

The UN is therefore a truly universal organization, certainly after China became represented by the Beijing government in 1971,[20] and when gradually

---

15 As defined in Art. 3 UN Charter. See Goodrich and Hambro, op. cit. note 6, pp. 122–125.

16 UN Charter, Art. 110(3). In addition, ratification by a majority of the other signatory states was required.

17 See https://treaties.un.org/Pages/ViewDetails.aspx?src=TREATY&mtdsg_no=I-1&chapter=1&clang=_en. See further S.C. Schlesinger, *Act of Creation – The Founding of the United Nations* (2003), pp. 263–279. In fact, Nicaragua and El Salvador ratified before the US did, on 6 and 12 July respectively, but they only deposited their ratifications in September (see R.B. Russell, *A History of The United Nations Charter – The Role of the United States 1940–1945* (1958), p. 947).

18 See United Nations Treaty Collection, Multilateral Treaties Deposited with the Secretary-General, at https://treaties.un.org/Pages/ViewDetails.aspx?src=TREATY&mtdsg_no=I-1&chapter=1&clang=_en.

19 For details of the dates of accession and the growth of UN membership, see https://www.un.org/en/member-states/index.html.

20 After the 1949 revolution, a communist government led by Mao Zedong came to power in mainland China. The previous Chiang Kai-Shek government only remained in control of Taiwan. In the UN (and in other organizations) both governments claimed that they were the lawful representative of (member state) China. In the UN, from 1950 to 1971, the credentials of the Mao government were rejected; China was represented in that period by the Chiang Kai-Shek government. This changed in October 1971, when the credentials of the Mao government were accepted (GA Res. 2758 (XXVI)). See further, with references to literature: H.G. Schermers and N.M. Blokker, *International Institutional Law* (6th ed. 2018), p. 216.

almost all states joined that were not yet members (such as Switzerland in 2002[21]). The most important political development explaining the large increase in membership is decolonization. For example, in 1945 only four African states belonged to the group of 51 original members (Egypt, Ethiopia, Liberia, South Africa). At present, 54 African states are UN members. In addition, following the disintegration of the Soviet Union in the late 1980s and early 1990s, 12 former Soviet states joined the UN (the three Baltic states in 1991, the others in 1992). During the last 75 years, the newly born states did not use their young sovereignty to isolate themselves and stay out of the UN. On the contrary, they used their new capacity to apply for membership, often immediately after becoming independent. Nowadays, UN membership is almost generally seen as part of state sovereignty rather than being opposed to it. In our globalized world, the UN is a truly universal organization.

Nevertheless, the process of expanding membership has had ups and downs. Membership applications have not always been immediately accepted. Unlike in a few other international organizations, states cannot join automatically by giving unilateral notification of their wish to join.[22] The UN must admit them. In most international organizations, the power to admit new members is attributed to the organization's plenary organ, so that all members are involved in the preparation of the relevant decision. During the UN Charter negotiations, there was much support for the idea to give such a power to the General Assembly only (just as the Assembly of the League of Nations had the exclusive competence to decide about admissions to the League).[23] However, the five most powerful allied powers insisted on staying in control of membership; therefore, the Security Council was also given a role in this field. As a result, each of the permanent members may use its veto over membership applications (and also over proposals to suspend or expel members). This is precisely what one of them - the Soviet Union - often did in practice, especially during the early years of the UN.[24]

21 GA Res. 57/1.

22 Examples of organizations accepting new members by unilateral notification are the International Bureau of Weights and Measures, the International Whaling Commission and the Organization for the Prohibition of Chemical Weapons.

23 This idea was not only supported by many states other than the five most powerful allied powers at the 1945 UNCIO Conference. Originally the US was also in favour of 'admission free of veto'. See E. Luard, *A History of the United Nations* (1982), p. 64.

24 Before 1960, the Soviet Union was almost the only permanent member using its veto. It did so on 90 occasions, more than half of which (49) concerned applications for membership. See further Chapter 2 on the use of the veto.

In particular in the 1940s and 1950s, the effects of the Cold War made decision-making on membership applications difficult. A practice started to evolve according to which the permanent members, in particular the Soviet Union, did not agree to admit candidate members (belonging to 'the other bloc') if not at the same time other candidate members (belonging to 'their own bloc') were admitted. However, a large majority in the General Assembly was in favour of admitting new members without applying this political 'Cold War condition'. While this was mainly a political issue, a legal question was also involved. Article 4(1) of the UN Charter specifically lists a number of conditions for UN membership: membership "is open to all [...] peace-loving states which accept the obligations contained in the present Charter and, in the judgment of the Organization, are able and willing to carry out these obligations". It was questioned whether it was lawful for the General Assembly and the Security Council (and therefore also for the members of these two organs) to add a new condition for membership (such as, in this case, the political condition that another candidate is also admitted). The General Assembly decided in 1947 to request an advisory opinion from the International Court of Justice on this legal question. The opinion of the Court was clear. In this highly politicized context, it observed that "[t]he political character of an organ cannot release it from the observance of the treaty provisions established by the Charter when they constitute limitations on its powers or criteria for its judgment".[25] The Court concluded:[26]

> a member of the United Nations which is called upon, in virtue of Article 4 of the Charter, to pronounce itself by its vote, either in the Security Council or in the General Assembly, on the admission of a state to membership in the United Nations, is not juridically entitled to make its consent to the admission dependent on conditions not expressly provided by paragraph 1 of the said Article;
>
> [...] in particular, a member of the organization cannot, while it recognizes the conditions set forth in that provision to be fulfilled by the state concerned, subject its affirmative vote to the additional condition that other states be admitted to membership in the United Nations together with that state.

---

25 *Admission of a State to the United Nations (Charter, Art. 4)*, Advisory Opinion, ICJ Rep. 1948, p. 56 (quotation at p. 64).

26 Id., p. 65 (adopted by nine votes to six).

The General Assembly supported the Court's view. It declared that admission decisions "ought to be based exclusively on the conditions contained in Article 4 of the Charter", and it requested the permanent members of the Security Council "to confer with one another soon with a view to assist the Council to come to positive recommendations in regard to the pending applications for membership".[27] However, the permanent members did not follow the advice of the Court and the recommendation of the General Assembly. It took until 1955 before a political compromise was found, in a 'package deal', when 16 states were admitted on one day (14 December 1955).

The General Assembly has also attempted to bypass the political stalemate caused by the five permanent members of the Security Council in another way. According to Article 4(2), states are admitted to UN membership "by a decision of the General Assembly upon the recommendation of the Security Council". If "recommendation" would be interpreted as a non-binding decision, the question could be raised whether it was really *necessary* to have a recommendation at all. If this would not be the case, the General Assembly could go ahead and admit states to membership. The Assembly sought support for this approach from the International Court of Justice by requesting another advisory opinion. However, the Court rejected such an interpretation (by a vote of twelve to two):[28]

> the admission of a State to membership in the United Nations, pursuant to paragraph 2 of Article 4 of the Charter, cannot be effected by a decision of the General Assembly when the Security Council has made no recommendation for admission, by reason of the candidate failing to obtain the requisite majority or the negative vote of a permanent Member upon a resolution so to recommend.

27 GA Res. 506 A (VI). This resolution was adopted with 43 votes in favour, 8 against, and 7 abstentions (see UN Doc. A/PV.369, p. 456). Before the draft of this resolution was put to the vote, the Rapporteur of the General Assembly's First Committee stated: "[i]f there is any conclusion which can be drawn from the discussions in the Committee about the question of the admission of new Members, it is that there is a common sentiment in favour of the universality of the United Nations. The permanent members of the Security Council have been called upon to confer with one another so that the present deadlock does not become a permanent one. Most of the delegations have expressed the desire that the doors of the United Nations should be open to all States that are qualified in accordance with the Charter" (id.).

28 *Competence of Assembly regarding admission to the United Nations, Advisory Opinion*, Advisory Opinion, ICJ Rep. 1950, p. 4 (quotation at p. 10).

The Court considered that[29]

> [t]o hold that the General Assembly has power to admit a State to membership in the absence of a recommendation of the Security Council would be to deprive the Security Council of an important power which has been entrusted to it by the Charter. It would almost nullify the role of the Security Council in the exercise of one of the essential functions of the Organization.

Concluding these observations on the admission of new members, it is most important to keep in mind that UN membership has almost quadrupled since 1945. In total, 142 applications for membership have been accepted since the entry into force of the Charter. Only exceptionally, an application has not (yet) been accepted; a main example is the application by Palestine.[30] The near quadruplicating of membership is a formidable development. When the Charter was drafted, the allied powers insisted on having a veto over admission decisions. This explains the involvement of the Security Council in the admission procedure. Apart from the Security Council and the General Assembly, also a third principal organ of the UN, the International Court of Justice, has played a role by giving interpretations of the conditions for admission in Article 4(1) and of the procedure laid down in Article 4(2). Each of these three organs has used its powers in relation to the conditions and the procedure for the admission of new members: the General Assembly has in particular promoted the universality of the UN, the role of the Security Council has been to assure the support of the permanent members for the admission of new members, and the International Court of Justice has encouraged the General Assembly, the Security Council and the members of these organs not to bypass the Charter rules in taking admission decisions.

While there has been extensive practice with respect to the *admission* to membership, there is hardly any practice concerning other membership decisions: withdrawal from membership, suspension and expulsion. Each of these three membership decisions will be briefly discussed.

The Charter does not contain a provision on withdrawal from the UN. At the UNCIO Conference in San Francisco this was a hotly debated issue, partly due

29 Id., p. 9.

30 See UN Docs. A/66/371-S/2011/592 and S/2011/705.

to the experience with the League of Nations, as discussed above. The League of Nations Covenant included a provision on withdrawal, and in practice 17 members withdrew. In 1945, during the Charter negotiations, a number of states feared that a provision on withdrawal might send a wrong signal to members of an organization with the ambition of universality. However, other states were afraid that it might become difficult to obtain support for the Charter in their countries if they would never be able to withdraw, even if amendments would be adopted which they had voted against and had refused to ratify. It was also felt that the mere absence of a withdrawal provision in the Charter would in practice not prevent members from withdrawing, if they really would no longer want to participate. As a compromise, a declaration of interpretation was adopted in June 1945.[31] This declaration disapproved of withdrawal and stated:[32]

> If [...] a member because of exceptional circumstances feels constrained to withdraw, and leave the burden of maintaining international peace and security on the other members, it is not the purpose of the Organization to compel that member to continue its cooperation in the Organization. It is obvious, however, that withdrawal or some other forms of dissolution of the Organization would become inevitable if, deceiving the hopes of humanity, the Organization was revealed to be unable to maintain peace or could do so only at the expense of law and justice. Nor would it be the purpose of the Organization to compel a member to remain in the Organization if its rights and obligations as such were changed by Charter amendment in which it has not concurred and which it finds itself unable to accept, or if an amendment duly accepted by the necessary majority in the Assembly or in a general conference fails to secure the ratification necessary to bring such amendment into effect.

The last phrase illustrates the living character of the Charter. The non-entry into force of an amendment considered by the organization as necessary is given the same legal effect, as far as the right to withdraw is concerned, as a constitutional amendment. For example, in the context of discussions on Security Council reform, if a compromise solution to amend the Charter would be adopted by the necessary two-thirds majority of UN membership, according to

31 This description of the Charter negotiations on withdrawal from the UN is partly reproduced from Schermers and Blokker, op. cit. note 20, pp. 110–111 (with references to literature).

32 See UNCIO Vol. VII, p. 267 ("commentary on withdrawal from the Organization", adopted on 17 June 1945).

this declaration of interpretation a withdrawal from the UN would be acceptable in case such an amendment would not be adopted (due to, for example, the non-ratification by one of the permanent members). It would not be "the purpose of the Organization to compel a member to remain in the Organization" if, after so many years of discussions and negotiations, the necessary reform of the Security Council could not be achieved and that member would no longer take the view that the Council could carry out its primary responsibility for the maintenance of international peace and security on its behalf (Article 24(1) of the Charter).

In practice, no member state has withdrawn from the UN in its 75 years of existence.[33] This is a significant achievement, in particular against the background of the 16 withdrawals from the League of Nations during its less than twenty years of life. During the past 75 years, there have been a considerable number of situations in which, using the terms of the 1945 declaration of interpretation, "deceiving the hopes of humanity, the Organization was revealed to be unable to maintain peace or could do so only at the expense of law and justice". Nevertheless, even though such situations could justify a withdrawal from the UN, members have apparently generally considered that the advantages of membership outweighed the disadvantages of a withdrawal.

However, in the recent era of rising nationalism and populism, political leaders of UN member states have exceptionally not only criticized the UN, but also announced that their country would withdraw from the world organization. In August 2016, President Duterte of the Philippines threatened to leave the UN, because the UN High Commissioner for Human Rights (Prince Zeid) was criticizing extrajudicial killings in Duterte's war on drugs. This threat to leave the UN received worldwide attention and criticism, and one day later Duterte said that this threat was a joke.[34] President Bolsonaro of Brazil stated on 18 August 2018, a few months before he was elected President: "[i]f I'm elected president, I will leave the UN. This institution serves no purpose ... It's

---

33 In 1965, Indonesia notified the Secretary-General of the UN that it had decided to withdraw (the main reason being the election of Malaysia as a member of the Security Council). However, in 1966 it announced that it would resume full cooperation with the UN. Subsequently, this temporary absence of Indonesia was interpreted by the President of the General Assembly as "based not upon a withdrawal from the United Nations but upon a cessation of cooperation". See Schermers & Blokker, op. cit. note 20, pp. 114–115 (with references to literature).

34 See various reports in the press: https://www.reuters.com/article/us-philippines-duterte-un-idUSKCN10W05W;https://www.straitstimes.com/asia/se-asia/philippines-not-leaving-un-foreign-minister; https://cnnphilippines.com/news/2016/08/25/Duterte-on-leaving-U.N.-Can%E2%80%99t-you-take-a-joke.html.

a meeting place for communists".[35] Nevertheless, so far Brazil has not taken the initiative to withdraw.

As the Swedish sociologist Gunnar Myrdal once wrote, "facts kick".[36] Alternative facts don't. While withdrawing from international organizations may seem fashionable today (for example: the UK withdrawal from the EU (Brexit), Burundi and the Philippines from the International Criminal Court, Japan from the International Whaling Commission), in fact, such withdrawals have taken place regularly since 1945, in some 200 cases, without a significant surge in recent years.[37] In addition, in most of these cases, the states that withdrew rejoined the organization after some time. Thus they may have experienced that you can withdraw from an international organization, but not from globalization. Usually staying is more in the self-interest of states than leaving, even though it may not always be *perceived* that way.

∴

While there are no Charter provisions on withdrawal from the UN, there are rules and procedures for suspension and expulsion from the organization. According to Article 5 of the Charter, a member "may be suspended from the exercise of the rights and privileges of membership" if "preventive or enforcement action has been taken by the Security Council" against that member. The more far-reaching sanction of expulsion may be taken if a member "has persistently violated the Principles contained in the present Charter". The language of these provisions implies that there is no obligation for the organization to apply these sanctions if the conditions mentioned would be fulfilled; both suspension and expulsion are sanctions that the UN *may* take. The procedure to suspend or expel a member is similar, and is the same as the procedure for admission to membership: the General Assembly decides upon the recommendation of the Security Council.

In practice, UN member states have never been suspended or expelled from UN membership. While in numerous cases, "preventive or enforcement action has been taken by the Security Council" (Article 5), and while it could be argued that members have in certain cases "persistently violated the Principles contained in the present Charter" (Article 6), the UN has never used its discretionary power to impose these sanctions. Exceptionally, initiatives have been taken

35 See https://www.telesurenglish.net/news/Bolsonaro-Vows-to-Leave-UN-Its-Where-Communists-Meet-20181028-0007.html.

36 G. Myrdal, *Objectivity in Social Research* (1969), p. 40.

37 I. von Borzyskowski en F. Vabulas, 'Hello, goodbye: When do states withdraw from international organizations?', *The Review of International Organizations* (2019), pp. 335–366.

to apply these provisions. For example, in 1974 a draft resolution was presented in the Security Council recommending to the General Assembly "the immediate expulsion of South Africa from the United Nations", mainly in view of the apartheid policies of the South African government.[38] However, this draft resolution was not adopted (10 votes in favour, 3 votes against by permanent members (France, UK, US), 2 abstentions).[39] In addition, while no member state has been suspended or expelled from the UN, their membership of organs of the UN has occasionally been suspended. For example, in 2011 the General Assembly suspended Libya's rights of membership of the Human Rights Council.[40]

It may be concluded that UN membership has gradually become near universal during the last 75 years. Currently, the most well-known non-members are Kosovo, Palestine and Taiwan, which are not recognized as states by some of the five permanent members. Members have never withdrawn, neither have they been suspended or expelled. The power to take membership decisions is shared by the General Assembly and the Security Council. The five permanent members of the Security Council play a crucial role in the decision-making on membership issues. They may block the admission of new members, and have done so in particular in the early years of the UN, but also more recently (Palestine). They may also block a proposed suspension or expulsion, and have done so when this was – exceptionally – raised (South Africa - apartheid). After the admission difficulties of the 1940s and 1950s, the Security Council (including its five permanent members) has generally contributed to the current situation, in which almost all peoples of the world have become "peoples of the United Nations determined to save succeeding generations from the scourge of war".

3 Evolutions in 'Organizationship'

3.1 *Introduction: No Security Council without the United Nations*

The functioning of the Security Council, as a non-self-standing institution, is not only closely connected to developments in membership of the UN, but

38 UN Doc. S/11543.

39 See UN Doc. S/PV. p. 1808 (30 October 1974).

40 GA Res. 65/265. In the resolution, the Assembly expressed its "deep concern over the human rights situation" in Libya. For more examples, see R. Higgins, P. Webb, D. Akande, S. Sivakumaran and J. Sloan, *Oppenheim's International Law United Nations*, Vol. I (2017), pp. 284–285.

also to evolutions in 'organizationship', i.e. evolutions in the organization of which it forms part. It was never considered to establish the Security Council as a separate international organization. The idea has always been that it would be part of something larger, just as the League Council was part of the League of Nations. The Security Council is firmly embedded in the United Nations. Who else would be able "to provide legitimacy for the actions that the Security Council takes in addressing conflicts today?".[41] Being part of the UN, the life of the Security Council must be seen in the context of the life of the UN. The Security Council at 75 cannot be fully understood without looking at the UN at 75.

The Charter demonstrates how the Security Council is embedded in the United Nations, as a few examples may illustrate. The members of the UN confer on the Security Council primary responsibility for the maintenance of international peace and security "[i]n order to ensure prompt and effective action *by the United Nations*".[42] In discharging its duties under this responsibility, "the Security Council shall act in accordance with the Purposes and Principles *of the United Nations*".[43] The General Assembly elects the ten non-permanent members of the Security Council.[44] In addition, the Charter provides for a joint responsibility or for cooperation between the Security Council and other UN organs. For example, key membership decisions of the UN are taken by the General Assembly upon the recommendation of the Security Council.[45] The Security Council submits "annual and, where necessary, special reports to the General Assembly for its consideration".[46] The UN Secretary-General is "appointed by the General Assembly upon the recommendation of the Security Council".[47] The Secretary-General performs the functions entrusted to him by the Security Council,[48] and he may bring to the attention of the Security Council "any matter which in his opinion may threaten the maintenance of international peace and security".[49] In addition, when making recommendations for the pacific settlement of disputes between states, the Security Council "should also take into consideration that legal disputes should as a general

41 This rhetorical question was asked by former Secretary-General Ban Ki-moon when he addressed the Security Council on 21 February 2018 (see UN Doc. S/PV. 8185, p. 4).
42 UN Charter, Art. 24(1) (italics added).
43 UN Charter, Art. 24(2) (italics added).
44 UN Charter, Art. 23(1).
45 UN Charter, Arts. 4–6 (see above, para. 2).
46 UN Charter, Art. 24(3).
47 UN Charter, Art. 97.
48 UN Charter, Art. 98.
49 UN Charter, Art. 99.

rule be referred by the parties to the International Court of Justice".[50] It may make recommendations or decide upon measures to be taken to give effect to judgments of the Court.[51] Finally, it may request advisory opinions from the International Court of Justice on any legal question.[52]

These and other Charter provisions, embedding the Security Council in the United Nations, have been interpreted and applied in practice. During the past 75 years, the evolution of the UN qua organization and the Security Council within it demonstrate how the world organization and its members have pursued the purposes of the UN in a world that is no longer how it was in 1945. This section will not give a full overview of the institutional growth of the UN. Instead, it will focus on two important facets of this growth: the concept of legal personality and the notion of practice of the organization.

3.2 *Legal Personality of the United Nations*

As was mentioned in paragraph 2, there is no organization without members. At the same time, the reverse is also true: there are no member states without an organization. The organization must be sufficiently well built and robust; otherwise, the members are not really part of something larger and remain as unorganized as before.

During the Second World War, it was agreed that there was a need to establish a world organization stronger than the League of Nations. This related primarily to the teeth the new organization should have, its enforcement powers. However, it was clear that the new organization should also be stronger from an institutional perspective. The Covenant of the League of Nations was rather short, covering 26 articles, without even explicitly establishing the League as an international organization and with only limited provisions on the League's organs. In contrast, the UN Charter formally established "an international organization to be known as the United Nations",[53] having a much more detailed institutional structure, centralized in the area of the maintenance of international peace and security and decentralized in the field of international economic and social cooperation. For the latter field, the Charter's Preamble refers to the determination to employ "international machinery" (in the French version of the Charter: "institutions internationales").

This is another area in which the International Court of Justice has played an important role in the early years of the UN, by concluding in its seminal

50 UN Charter, Art. 36(3).
51 UN Charter, Art. 94(2).
52 UN Charter, Art. 96(1).
53 UN Charter, final sentence of the Preamble.

Reparation for Injuries Advisory Opinion that the world organization is an international legal person, i.e. that it has the capacity to have rights and duties of its own.[54]

This advisory opinion was triggered by the assassination in Jerusalem of the UN Mediator in Palestine, Count Folke Bernadotte from Sweden.[55] The question arose whether the UN, as an organization, had the capacity to bring a claim against Israel, in order to obtain reparation for the injuries suffered. There was no doubt that under existing international law Sweden had the capacity to do so. However, Count Bernadotte was performing his functions not for Sweden, but as a mediator for the UN. The question was therefore whether the UN could bring a claim. On 3 December 1948, the General Assembly requested an advisory opinion from the ICJ on this issue. Within a few months, on 11 April 1949, the Court delivered its opinion.

The Court found that, before answering the question whether the UN had the capacity to bring a claim, it "must first enquire whether the Charter has given the Organization such a position that it possesses, in regard to its Members, rights which it is entitled to ask them to respect. In other words, does the Organization possess international personality?".[56] As the Court noted, the UN Charter does not answer this preliminary question. In 1945, at the UNCIO Conference, the committee discussing this issue "considered it superfluous to make this the subject of a text. In effect, it will be determined implicitly from the provisions of the Charter as a whole".[57] According to the report to the US President on the results of the San Francisco Conference, by the Chairman of the US delegation to this conference, "[t]he Committee which discussed this matter was anxious to avoid any implication that the United Nations will be in any sense a 'superstate' ".[58] Less than four years later, in the absence of an explicit Charter provision about the international legal status of the world organization, the Court needed to address this delicate question.

54 *Reparation for injuries suffered in the service of the United Nations*, Advisory Opinion, ICJ Rep. 1949, p. 174.

55 In accordance with UNGA Res. 186 (14 May 1948). Bernadotte was assassinated on 17 September 1948.

56 *Reparation for injuries suffered in the service of the United Nations*, Advisory Opinion, ICJ Rep. 1949, p. 178.

57 UNCIO, Vol. XIII, at 710. See id., at 622–623 for a report of the brief discussion on this subject. See id., at 63 for the proposal by Belgium in which "international status, together with the rights this involves" is given to the UN.

58 Department of State publication 349, Conference Series 71 (quoted by C.W. Jenks, 'The Legal Personality of International Organizations', 22 *British Yearbook of International Law* 1945, pp. 269–270).

Perhaps it could be expected that the Court would try to base its answer on sources of law outside the UN Charter, since the Charter was silent on the issue. However, this was not the Court's approach. In order to answer the question, "which is not settled by the actual terms of the Charter, we must consider what characteristics it was intended thereby to give to the Organization".[59] The approach of the Court was to base its answer on the Charter, on the nature of the organization created by it. In doing so, the Court stayed close to the intentions of the members of the UN, even though these intentions had not resulted in a clear and explicit Charter provision stating that the UN is an international legal person. The Court concluded that in order to achieve the UN's purposes, as specified in the Charter, "the attribution of international personality is indispensable".[60]

This is not an example of broad teleological reasoning without any more detailed underpinning. The Court referred to a number of specific characteristics of the UN, as follows: "[t]he Charter has not been content to make the Organization created by it merely a centre 'for harmonizing the actions of nations in the attainment of these common ends' (Article 1, para. 4). It has equipped that centre with organs, and has given it special tasks. It has defined the position of the Members in relation to the Organization by requiring them to give it every assistance in any action undertaken by it (Article 2, para. 5), and to accept and carry out the decisions of the Security Council [...]".[61] Also in view of what will be discussed in paragraph 3, an additional argument mentioned by the Court deserves special attention: "[p]ractice – in particular the conclusion of conventions to which the Organization is a party – has confirmed this character of the Organization, which occupies a position in certain respects in detachment from its Members, and which is under a duty to remind them, if need be, of certain obligations".[62]

Therefore, *inter alia*, the special tasks given to the Security Council and the obligation of the members to accept and carry out the decisions of the Security Council are part of the arguments on the basis of which the Court draws its conclusion. It stated that[63]

---

59 *Reparation for injuries suffered in the service of the United Nations*, Advisory Opinion, ICJ Rep. 1949, p. 178.

60 Id.

61 Id.

62 Id., p. 179.

63 Id.

> the Organization was intended to exercise and enjoy, and is in fact exercising and enjoying, functions and rights which can only be explained on the basis of the possession of a large measure of international personality and the capacity to operate upon an international plane. It is at present the supreme type of international organization, and it could not carry out the intention of its founders if it was devoid of international personality.

These considerations and conclusions of the Court on this preliminary question, in this early advisory opinion, have had a significance far beyond the specific issue at hand.[64] However, for the purpose of the current study, it suffices to underline the importance of this advisory opinion in establishing the independent, separate status of the UN in international law and in the relations with its members. The organization, a newcomer in the international arena, received strong support in its infancy from its principal judicial organ, on an issue that was to some extent left open at San Francisco but that is essential for the performance of its functions in a globalizing world.

A remaining question that has not yet been resolved in doctrine, and to which different answers are given in practice, is the (in)divisibility of international legal personality of the UN, and of other international organizations. As a rule, international legal personality is enjoyed by international organizations, not by one or more of their organs as well – just as states are international legal persons, not also their ministries, their provinces or other governmental bodies. The six principal organs of the UN are integral part of the UN, and do not have their own legal personality.[65] However, the language of the Charter may seem to suggest otherwise. Article 63 provides that the Economic and Social Council may enter into agreements with specialized agencies. According to Article 43, agreements by which member states undertake to make armed forces, assistance and facilities available to the Security Council "shall be concluded between the Security Council and Members or between the Security Council and groups of Members". In practice, various UN organs (such as UNICEF and UNDP) have regularly concluded agreements with states and international organizations in their own name.[66]

Provided with clarity about its international legal status (leaving aside the issue of separate personality of UN organs), the UN could now not only bring

64 See further Schermers & Blokker, op. cit. note 20, pp. 1028–1036, and the literature mentioned there.

65 See A.J. Miller, 'The Privileges and Immunities of the United Nations', 6 *International Organizations Law Review* 7–115 (2009), p. 25.

66 See in more detail Schermers & Blokker, op. cit. note 20, pp. 1035–1036.

a claim against Israel, but also more generally manifest itself more easily at the international level, by concluding international agreements and establishing external relations. The contents of the annually published *United Nations Juridical Yearbook* provide many examples of the variety and richness of the instruments used by the UN in international affairs.[67] First of all, during the past 75 years, the UN has concluded many international agreements: with its members, with non-members, with other international organizations. The UN is conducting diplomatic relations: it sends and receives temporary or permanent missions. The 1975 Vienna Convention on the Representation of States in their Relations with International Organizations of a Universal Character contains rules on the establishment and functioning of permanent missions to international organizations.[68] Members of the UN have permanent missions at the headquarters of the UN in New York, and often also at other UN offices, for example in Geneva. Non-member states, the European Union, other international organizations as well as liberation movements (in particular in the era of decolonization) may also have permanent missions at the UN. The other way around, the UN also has many temporary and permanent missions. For example, Resident Coordinators of the UN Development Programme lead UN country teams in some 130 countries.[69] In addition, the UN has some 60 information centres (UNICs), services and offices in its member states.[70]

UN peace operations also demonstrate how the Security Council is intimately connected to other parts of the UN. For good reasons, however, it is 'UN peace operations' and 'UN peacekeeping', not 'UN Security Council peace operations' and 'UN Security Council peacekeeping'. Obviously, it is almost always the Security Council that is at the origin of a UN peace operation. Security Council resolutions are the first step in establishing a peace operation, determining their mandate, duration and further details.[71] However, it is normally

67 E.g. *UN Juridical Yearbook 2015*, pp. 5–69. As is indicated on p. 5: "[i]n the light of the large number of treaties concluded, only a selection of the relevant treaties is reproduced herein".

68 This Convention has not yet entered into force.

69 See https://undg.org/about/un-country-level/.

70 See unic.un.org.

71 See e.g. SC Res. 1990 (2011) establishing the UN Interim Security Force for Abyei (UNISFA), and more recently SC Res. 2476 (2019) requesting the UN Secretary-General to establish the UN Integrated Office in Haiti (BINUH). Peace operations have carried out a wide variety of mandates, from traditional peacekeeping (where UN troops are positioned between the parties in dispute, e.g. UNFICYP in Cyprus) to much more complex peacekeeping in which a UN operation is tasked, for example, to protect civilians, assist in state-building and disarmament (e.g. the UN Mission in the Republic of South Sudan).

for the UN Secretariat to take care of the implementation, and report on this to the Security Council. It must seek the necessary troops and staff from the member states, conclude an agreement with the host state, etc.[72] In addition, it is not for the Security Council but for the General Assembly to adopt the budget for peace operations.[73] While it is true that the Security Council plays a key role, the full involvement of other organs of the UN is a *conditio sine qua non* for the success of the operation. The achievements of UN peacekeeping over the years have therefore truly been achievements of the UN organization as a whole.

UN peace operations offer examples of close cooperation between the Security Council and other organs of the UN. However, the Security Council is not only part of the UN proper. Indirectly, by being part of the UN, it is also embedded in the larger UN family,[74] the interrelated system of organizations that includes the UN, the specialized agencies and a few others such as the International Atomic Energy Agency, the World Trade Organization, the Organization for the Prohibition of Chemical Weapons and the International Criminal Court. The UN has concluded relationship agreements with these organizations, many of which are rather similar. They provide for reciprocal

---

72 See e.g. SC Res. 1990 (2011), para. 4, requesting the Secretary-General and the Government of Sudan to conclude a status-of-forces agreement. In para. 13, the Security Council "[r]equests the Secretary-General to take the necessary measures to ensure full compliance of UNISFA with the United Nations zero tolerance policy on sexual exploitation and abuses and to keep the Council informed if cases of such conduct occur". See for the Model Status of Forces Agreement (Model SOFA): UN Doc. A/45/594. On the basis of this model, the UN and the host state negotiate their bilateral SOFA, containing the rights, obligations and duties of the parties. The Model SOFA is often declared to be in force at the beginning of a peace operation; often it takes time before the final SOFA is concluded.

73 UN Charter, Art. 17. See International Court of Justice, *Certain expenses of the United Nations (Article 17, paragraph 2, of the Charter)*, Advisory Opinion, ICJ Rep. 1962, p. 151. For a recent example, see GA Res. 73/323 (financing of the UN Mission in South Sudan). Since it is for the General Assembly to adopt the budgets of the UN and of peace operations, it was not within the competence of the Security Council to decide in 1993 that the costs of the UN Force in Cyprus (UNFICYP) that are not covered by voluntary contributions should be treated as expenses of the UN under Art. 17(2) of the Charter (SC Res. 831). Subsequently, the General Assembly agreed to this approach, but also expressed "concern that advice given to the Security Council by the Secretariat on the nature of the financing of the Force did not respect the role of the General Assembly as set out in Article 17 of the Charter" (GA Res. 47/236).

74 On the notion of family in this context, see S. Bastid, 'Sur quelques problèmes juridiques de coordination dans la famille des Nations Unies', in *Mélanges Reuter* 75–101 (1981), who observes that the notion of UN family "peut évoquer suivant les circonstances le noeud de vipères [- nest of vipers -] ou la chaleur confiante [the confident warmth] du foyer" (at p. 75).

representation, the proposal of items on each other's agendas and further arrangements for mutual cooperation. Under these agreements, the partner organization concerned usually agrees to render "such assistance to the Security Council as that Council may request including assistance in carrying out decisions of the Security Council for the maintenance or restoration of international peace and security".[75] The IMF and the World Bank are less closely connected to the UN than the other agencies, as is also reflected in the provisions concerning cooperation with the Security Council.[76] The 2004 Negotiated Relationship Agreement between the International Criminal Court and the United Nations has extensive provisions on cooperation between the Court and the Security Council.[77]

Two specific examples may illustrate that in practice situations have occurred, in which the UN carried out operations that were different from peacekeeping and that required cooperation with other organizations of the UN family. The Security Council was closely involved in both cases. A first example is the Joint OPCW-United Nations Mission for the Elimination of Syrian Chemical Weapons. The Security Council determined that the use of chemical weapons in Syria constituted a threat to international peace and security.[78] This mission was established to perform an almost impossible task: to remove chemical weapons from a country where a civil war was fought.[79] An agreement was concluded with Syria "to ensure the timely, safe and secure conduct of the mandate of this mission".[80] Another agreement was concluded with Syria concerning the maritime transport operation for the removal and transport of Syrian chemical agents (carried out by Denmark and Norway).[81]

75 E.g. Agreement between the United Nations and the United Nations Educational Scientific and Cultural Organizations (1946), Art. VIII (UN Doc. A/77); Agreement between the United Nations and the World Health Organization (1947), Art. VII (UN Doc. A/348).

76 See Arts. I(2) and VI of these agreements (1947) (UN Doc. A/349). The IMF and the World Bank will only have "due regard" for Security Council decisions under Articles 41 and 42 of the Charter.

77 Art. 17 of this agreement. For the text of this agreement, see Res. ICC-ASP/3/Res. 1 and UN Doc. A/ 58/874, annex.

78 SC Res. 2118, Preamble.

79 The mandate of this mission was given in decisions of the OPCW and of the Security Council: OPCW Doc. EC-M-33/DEC.1 and SC Res. 2118, both adopted on 27 September 2013.

80 Agreement between the OPCW, the UN and the Government of Syria concerning the status of the Joint OPCW-United Nations Mission for the Elimination of Syrian Chemical Weapons (5 February 2014), reproduced in *UN Juridical Yearbook 2014*, pp. 5–23 (the quoted text is in the preamble of this agreement).

81 Reproduced in *UN Juridical Yearbook 2014*, pp. 60–62.

A second example is the UN Mission for Ebola Emergency Response (UNMEER), established by the UN Secretary-General on 19 September 2014, following the adoption of UN General Assembly Resolution 69/1 and Security Council Resolution 2177. In the latter resolution, the Security Council determined "that the unprecedented extent of the Ebola outbreak in Africa constitutes a threat to international peace and security". The mission's priority was "to stop the spread of the disease, treat the infected, ensure essential services, preserve stability and prevent the spread to countries currently unaffected".[82] An agreement was concluded between the UN and Liberia concerning UNMEER's status, privileges and immunities in that country.[83] Operations such as the Joint OPCW-UN Mission and UNMEER would not be able to function if the UN (and the other organizations involved, OPCW and WHO) would not enjoy international legal personality, providing them with the necessary legal status, independence and political leverage to operate at the same level as the states involved.

∴

Apart from international agreements and the receiving and sending of missions, the UN has also used other instruments in its external relations. For example, it has issued passports, it is a depository of treaties and it has its own flag and its own emblem.[84] Originally, the use of the name and emblem of the UN for commercial purposes was strictly forbidden.[85] However, in recent years, as a result of the evolving closer relationship with the private sector, the UN has become somewhat more lenient in allowing private enterprises to use its name and emblem, even though a number of strict conditions continue to apply.[86]

∴

A question that emerged in the conduct of the external relations by the UN (and by other international organizations) is whether this conduct is similar to the way in which states operate at the international level. Often this question was dealt with in practice, but it was discussed more generally and

82 UN Doc. A/69/389-S/2014/679, p. 2.

83 Reproduced in *UN Juridical Yearbook 2015*, pp. 5–21.

84 For the text of the UN Flag Code and Flag Regulations, see UN Doc. ST/SGB/132.

85 See GA Res. 92(I) (1946).

86 See Section IV of the Guidelines on a Principled-based Approach to the Cooperation between the UN and the Business Sector, reproduced at https://www.unglobalcompact.org/docs/news_events/9.6/RevisedGuidelines_UN-BizCooperation.pdf . See for more details: Schermers & Blokker, op. cit. note 20, pp. 1249–1252.

fundamentally on the occasion of new lawmaking.[87] Examples are the Vienna Convention on the Law of Treaties between States and International Organizations or between International Organizations (1986)[88] and the Articles on the Responsibility of International Organizations (2011).[89]

In practice, there are many similarities in the way in which international organizations such as the UN conduct their external relations, compared to relations between states. However, both in the relevant rules and in practice there are always cases and situations in which the differences become clear. Some of these differences boil down to the simple fact that international organizations such as the UN, unlike states, do not have their own territory. This may affect the functioning of the UN, including the Security Council. When the Foreign Minister of Iran Mohammed Javad Zarif in January 2020 wanted to participate in a meeting of the Security Council, after a US drone killed the Iranian General Soleimani, the US refused to give him a visa. Even though this was a violation of the US-UN headquarters agreement, Foreign Minister Zarif was unable to travel to the US.[90]

3.3 *Constitutional Development through 'Practice of the Organization'*

As mentioned above, during the past 75 years, both the evolution of the UN qua organization and the development of the Security Council within it demonstrate how the world organization and its members have pursued the purposes of the UN in a world that is no longer how it was in 1945. Paragraph 3.2 was devoted to the international legal personality of the UN, and how important this has been for the UN to perform its Charter functions. As already became clear from some of the examples mentioned, the concepts and rules laid down in the Charter are not static and must be interpreted and applied in a rapidly changing international society, responding to needs unforeseen in 1945 on pain of the UN becoming obsolete and irrelevant. Having discussed legal personality, this paragraph will focus on another important facet of this growth of the UN and the Security Council: constitutional development through 'practice of the organization'.

---

87 See on this question in particular the publications of Catherine Brölmann, for example her *The Institutional Veil in Public International Law – International Organizations and the Law of Treaties* (2007).

88 Published in UN Doc. A/CONF.129/15.

89 See GA Res. 66/100, Annex.

90 See the records of the meeting of the Security Council on 9 January 2020, UN Doc. S/PV.8699.

The importance of the notion of 'practice of the organization' was already foreseen as early as 1946, by an author using the pseudonym Pollux, who observed in an article about the interpretation of the Charter that "[a] constitutional customary law will grow up and the Charter itself will merely form the framework of the Organization which will be filled in by the practice of the different organs".[91] This is indeed what has happened: in 75 years, the UN has developed a considerable amount of practice. This is the organization's own practice, to be distinguished from that of its members. The important question for the UN is, as it is for any other international organization, how much leeway there is for such practice to 'further develop' the constitution of the organization. What are the limits for such 'constitutional stretch'? Related questions are: what is the borderline between a 'further development' in the interpretation and application of the constitution, and a violation? When does it become necessary to consider a formal amendment of the constitution, because the limits of stretching its terms have been reached? These general questions may be illustrated by the example of the creation of ad hoc criminal tribunals by the Security Council.

There is little to no indication that the drafters of the Charter had in mind that the Security Council should have the power to create ad hoc criminal tribunals. Yet this is what happened in the 1990s. One of the measures taken by the Council during the war in the former Yugoslavia was the creation of an ad hoc criminal tribunal for the prosecution of persons responsible for serious violations of international humanitarian law committed in the territory of the former Yugoslavia.[92] The next year, a similar ad hoc criminal tribunal was created for the prosecution of persons responsible for genocide and other serious violations of international humanitarian law committed in the territory of Rwanda, and of Rwandan citizens responsible for such violations committed

---

91 Pollux, 'Interpretation of the Charter', 23 *British Yearbook of International Law* 54–82 (1946), p. 54. Later, the identity of Pollux was revealed. It was Edvard Hambro, a member of the Norwegian delegation to the 1945 San Francisco Conference establishing the UN.

92 SC Res. 827 (25 May 1993). The Statutes of the Tribunal are contained in a report by the UN Secretary-General (S/25704), which was approved by the Security Council in Res. 827. See P. Akhavan, 'Punishing War Crimes in the Former Yugoslavia: a Critical Juncture for the New World Order', 15 *Human Rights Quarterly* 262–289 (1993); B. Broms, 'Security Council Resolution 808 (1993)', in O. Bring and S. Mahmoudi (eds.), *Current International Law Issues, Nordic Perspectives* (*Essays in Honour of Jerzy Sztucki*, 1994), pp. 51–64; P. Weckel, 'L'institution d'un tribunal international pour la répression des crimes de droit humanitaire en yougoslavie', 39 *Annuaire Français de Droit International* (1993), pp. 232–261; D. Shraga and R. Zacklin, 'The International Criminal Tribunal for the Former Yugoslavia', 5 *European Journal of International Law* (1994), pp. 360–380.

in the territory of neighbouring states, during the year 1994.[93] For many, the preferred approach for the establishment of these tribunals was to do so by treaty. However, it was expected that it could take years to negotiate such a treaty and before it would enter into force. This was generally considered too long given the circumstances in the former Yugoslavia and in Rwanda. However, it was not without controversy whether the shortcut to establish these tribunals through Security Council resolutions was lawful, as appears from the reports of the meetings of the Security Council during which the Yugoslav and Rwanda Tribunals were created. For example, Brazil stated in the Security Council, when the Rwanda Tribunal was established:[94]

> As we stated in the case of the Tribunal for the former Yugoslavia, Brazil is not convinced that the competence to establish and/or exercise an international criminal jurisdiction is among the constitutional powers of the Security Council. The authority of the Security Council is not self-constituted. It originates from the delegation of powers conferred upon it by the whole membership of the Organization under Article 24 (1) of the Charter. For that very reason, the Council's powers and responsibilities under the Charter should be strictly construed, and cannot be created, recreated or reinterpreted by decisions of the Council itself.

While the first part of this statement is certainly correct, the last part comes down to a very restrictive view of the role of the Security Council in interpreting its own powers. In the absence of a constitutional court of the UN, it is first of all for UN organs themselves to interpret the scope of their own powers.[95] At that time, broader views than Brazil's prevailed and resulted in the Security Council exercising its powers in a way not foreseen in 1945.

This episode in the life of the Security Council illustrates that, even though the scope of the Council's powers is defined in the Charter, in practice situations may arise in which there may be sufficient support for stretching the terms of the Charter. Obviously, there may be considerable doubt in these situations whether the given interpretation of the powers of the Security Council

93 SC Res. 955 (8 November 1994). See P. Akhavan, 'The International Criminal Tribunal for Rwanda: the Politics and Pragmatics of Punishment', 90 *American Journal of International Law* (1996), pp. 501–510; L.J. van den Herik, *The Contribution of the Rwanda Tribunal to the Development of International Law* (2005).

94 UN Doc. S/PV.3453, p. 9. See further Chapter 3, para. 5.3.2.

95 As the ICJ stated in 1962, in *Certain expenses of the United Nations (Article 17, paragraph 2, of the Charter)*, Advisory Opinion, ICJ Rep. 1962, p. 151 (in particular at p. 168).

is still within, or just outside the Charter terms. Such questions about the legality or, broader, the legitimacy of such activities may result in a request for an advisory opinion from the International Court of Justice. In the case of the creation of the Yugoslav and Rwanda criminal tribunals this did not happen. Instead, they were addressed to these tribunals themselves, in their respective first cases.[96] In other cases however, the ICJ has offered some guidance, both in the specific cases at hand and more generally, as will now be examined.

Even though no judicial review power was given to the ICJ in 1945 – as was emphasized by the ICJ in *Certain Expenses* – the Court has in practice played an important role in this field: by giving concrete interpretations of the UN Charter (and of constitutions of other international organizations), by the approach it has followed in giving such interpretations, and by making some general observations that transcend specific individual advisory opinions. Moreover, additional guidance has come from the broad definition of the concept of 'rules of the organization' in some legal instruments, covering also "established practice" of the organization.

3.3.1 Guidance from the International Court of Justice

The relevance of the organization's practice has been fully recognized by the International Court of Justice.[97] A first example is the Court's above-mentioned Advisory Opinion in *Reparation for Injuries*, in which it argued that practice had confirmed the character of the organization that flowed from the Court's analysis of the Charter. In this Advisory Opinion and in most others, the Court has referred to 'practice of the organization' as an interpretative device. When doing so, the Court is using this as a supplementary argument for a particular interpretation. It has the effect of a 'reality check', by demonstrating that a particular interpretation is not out of tune with practice. Needless to say, the older the organization, the more relevant this may be, also taking into account how difficult it is to amend the Charter.

96 Yugoslav Tribunal: *Tadić* Case, Case No. IT-94-1-AR72 (decision of 2 October 1995 on the defence motion for interlocutory appeal on jurisdiction). On this case, see J.E. Alvarez, 'Nuremberg Revisited: The Tadić Case', 7 *European Journal of International Law* (1996), pp. 245–264. Rwanda Tribunal: *Kanyabashi* Case, Case No. ICTR-96-15-T. On this case, see V. Morris, 92 *American Journal of International Law* (1998), pp. 66–70 (1998).

97 What follows is mostly reproduced from Schermers & Blokker, op. cit. note 20, p. 879 ff.

Following *Reparation for Injuries* (1949), the ICJ took into account 'practice of the organization' in the following way in the *Second Admissions* Advisory Opinion: "[t]he organs to which Article 4 entrusts the judgment of the Organization in matters of admission have consistently interpreted the text in the sense that the General Assembly can decide to admit only on the basis of a recommendation of the Security Council".[98] The Court did not only follow this approach in interpreting the UN Charter. It did the same when it was requested to advise on the law of other international organization, for example when interpreting the constitution of the International Maritime Consultative Organization (the predecessor of the International Maritime Organization). In the 1960 *Maritime Safety Committee* Advisory Opinion, it considered, "[t]he practice followed by the Assembly in relation to other Articles reveals the reliance placed upon registered tonnage".[99]

The importance attached by the Court to the organization's practice is particularly clear from its 1971 *Namibia* Advisory Opinion, in which it accepted a practice that seemed to be against the explicit text of the Charter.[100] According to Article 27, paragraph 3, of the UN Charter, decisions of the Security Council on non-procedural matters "shall be made by an affirmative vote of nine members including the concurring votes of the permanent members". A textual interpretation would lead to the conclusion that it is required that the five permanent members would need to vote in favour for the relevant draft decision to be adopted lawfully. A textual analysis of this provision in the other authentic languages of the Charter would lead to the same conclusion.[101]

---

98 *Competence of Assembly regarding admission to the United Nations*, Advisory Opinion, ICJ Rep. 1950, p. 4 (quotation at 9).

99 *Constitution of the Maritime Safety Committee of the Inter-Governmental Maritime Consultative Organization*, Advisory Opinion, ICJ Rep. 1960, p. 150 (quotation at 168). See for a more recent example: *Legal Consequences of the Construction of a Wall in the Occupied Palestinian Territory*, Advisory Opinion, ICJ Rep. 2004 (at 149–150). In 2016 the President of the General Assembly referred to the latter advisory opinion in the context of the establishment of an International Mechanism Concerning Syria. In the relevant meeting of the General Assembly, Syria had claimed that Art. 12 of the Charter prohibited the General Assembly from considering issues of which the Security Council is seized. The President ruled that "[t]he accepted practice of the General Assembly to consider, in parallel with the Security Council, the same matter concerning the maintenance of international peace and security has also been noted by the International Court of Justice in its advisory opinion of 2004" (UN Doc. A/71/PV.66, at 28–29).

100 *Legal Consequences for States of the Continued Presence of South Africa in Namibia (South West Africa), notwithstanding Security Council Resolution 276 (1970)*, Advisory Opinion, ICJ Rep. 1971, at 22.

101 See e.g. the French text: "un vote affirmatif de neuf de ses membres dans lequel sont comprises les voix de *tous* les membres permanents" (emphasis added).

Nevertheless, ever since the 1940s, such a textual interpretation has not been followed in the practice of the Security Council: abstentions by permanent members were not considered as an impediment to the lawful adoption of decisions on non-procedural matters. This practice could be considered as a violation of the UN Charter. However, in its *Namibia* advisory opinion, the ICJ took the following position:[102]

> [...] the proceedings of the Security Council extending over a long period supply abundant evidence that presidential rulings and the positions taken by members of the Council, in particular its permanent members, have consistently and uniformly interpreted the practice of voluntary abstention by a permanent member as not constituting a bar to the adoption of resolutions. By abstaining, a member does not signify its objection to the approval of what is being proposed; in order to prevent the adoption of a resolution requiring unanimity of the permanent members, a permanent member has only to cast a negative vote. This procedure followed by the Security Council, which has continued unchanged after the amendment in 1965 of Article 27 of the Charter, has been generally accepted by Members of the United Nations and evidences a general practice of that Organization.

This demonstrates the far-reaching implications that the 'recourse to practice' technique may have – it may result in an interpretation that some would consider *contra legem*.[103] It also raises the question how much practice is needed

102 *Legal Consequences for States of the Continued Presence of South Africa in Namibia (South West Africa), notwithstanding Security Council Resolution 276 (1970)*, Advisory Opinion, ICJ Rep. 1971, at 16 (quotation at 22).

103 See further C.A. Stavropoulos, 'The Practice of Voluntary Abstentions by Permanent Members of the Security Council under Article 27, Paragraph 3, of the Charter of the United Nations', 61 *American Journal of International Law* (1967), pp. 737–752; B. Simma (ed.), *The Charter of the United Nations – A Commentary* (2nd ed. 2002), at 493–499 (analyzing the relevant literature, in which "two fundamentally different opinions can be found": according to one view, this practice is based on an interpretation of Art. 27.3, according to the other view, this is a "progressive modification of the Charter"- e.g. "[a]ccording to a widespread view, Art. 27(3) has been modified by customary law between the contracting States" (id., at 493, 495)). The third edition of the last mentioned UN Charter commentary prefers the first, 'interpretation view': "this accepted interpretation of Art. 27(3) has become binding upon all member States of the Organization [...]. There is therefore no need to further consider the possibility of a customary law norm having superseded Art. 27(3)" (B. Simma et al. (eds.), *The Charter of the United Nations – A Commentary* (3rd ed. 2012), at 915); see also B. Conforti and C. Focarelli, *The Law and Practice of the United Nations* (5th rev. ed. 2016), at 80–84. This case of the interpretation

before it would qualify as a supportive argument for a certain interpretation. In *Namibia*, the Court used a temporal requirement ("extending over a long period"), a frequency requirement ("abundant evidence"), an interest requirement ("members of the Council, in particular its permanent members"), a stability requirement ("consistently and uniformly") and the fact that the practice continued following the 1965 amendment (that did not codify this interpretation). In addition, the Court did not consider it sufficient to exclusively take into account the position of the members of the Security Council; it also observed that the practice concerned "has been generally accepted by Members of the United Nations". It is therefore clear that the attitude of both the organization and its members is relevant. This is in line with the *travaux préparatoires* of the Charter. Committee IV/2 of the San Francisco conference not only stated in its report that "each organ will interpret such parts of the Charter as are applicable to its particular functions", it added:[104]

> It is to be understood, of course, that if an interpretation made by any organ of the Organization or by a committee of jurists is not *generally acceptable* it will be without binding force. In such circumstances, or in cases where it is desired to establish an authoritative interpretation as a precedent for the future, it may be necessary to embody the interpretation in an amendment to the Charter.

This 'recourse to practice' technique has not only been used by the International Court of Justice, but also by other international courts and tribunals.[105] Already in 1976, E. Lauterpacht therefore rightly concluded that:[106]

> It is probably necessary to recognize that recourse to the practice of international organizations now stands on an independent legal basis; that is to say, that there exists a specific rule of the law of international

of Art. 27.3 of the Charter could also be seen as an example of "established practice" of the organization, which (in accordance with the definition of 'rules of the organization' given in the 1986 Vienna Convention and in the 2011 Articles on responsibility of international organizations) is not required to be in accordance with the constitution of the organization (i.e. the UN Charter).

104 Doc. 933, IV/2/42(2), UNCIO Vol. XIII, p. 709 (emphasis added).

105 See for examples N. Blokker, 'Beyond 'Dili': On the Powers and Practice of International Organizations', in G. Kreijen et al. (ed.), *State, Sovereignty and International Governance* (2002), pp. 299–322, in particular at p. 315.

106 E. Lauterpacht, 'The Development of the Law of International Organization by the Decisions of International Tribunals', 152 *Receuil des Cours* (1976 IV), pp. 379–478, at p. 460.

> organization to the effect that recourse to such practice is admissible and that States, on joining international organizations, impliedly accept the permissibility of constitutional development in this manner.

The 'recourse to practice' approach serves as a 'reality check': it will be more convincing to follow a particular interpretation if this interpretation finds support in practice. However, at the same time there are limits to this technique. If not used properly, it could easily amount to circular reasoning, because 'practice' is used as an argument for a particular interpretation, while it is precisely the lawfulness of this practice that is questioned. In the twilight zone between legality and illegality, between dynamic development of the law driven by practical needs and a violation of the law,[107] courts must take 'day or night' decisions: ultimately, a practice is either lawful or unlawful. Taking recourse to 'practice' as an argument certainly serves an important 'reality check' purpose, but must be handled with care. The Court has therefore almost always used this technique to supplement and seek to confirm a provisional conclusion drawn on the basis of a preceding legal analysis in which other means of interpretation are applied.

3.3.2 A Legal Basis for 'Interpretation through Practice'?

The ICJ has always considered it important to take into account the practice of the organization in giving an interpretation of constitutional provisions, but only in its 1996 *WHO Nuclear Weapons* Advisory Opinion the Court gave some legal underpinning of this approach. Having observed that "constituent instruments of international organizations are also treaties of a particular type", the ICJ stated that "[s]uch treaties can raise specific problems of interpretation owing, *inter alia,* to their character which is conventional and at the same time institutional".[108] The Court specified this as follows: "the very nature of the organization created, the objectives which have been assigned to it by its founders, the imperatives associated with the effective performance of its functions, as well as its own practice, are all elements which may deserve special attention

107 See A. Peters, 'International Organizations and International Law', in J. Katz Cogan, I. Hurd, I. Johnstone (eds.), *The Oxford Handbook of International Organizations*, pp. 33–59, in particular at p. 39: "[t]he fine line between legitimate and lawful evolution and unlawful mission creep may not be easy to draw". And even if a practice may originally be a violation of the law, it may lead to the formation of new law (R. Higgins, *Problems and Process - International Law and How we Use it* (1994), p. 19).

108 *Legality of the Use by a State of Nuclear Weapons in Armed Conflict,* Advisory Opinion, ICJ Rep. 1996, p. 66, quotation at p. 75.

when the time comes to interpret these constituent treaties".[109] In this way, the Court distinguished constitutions from other treaties (that do not establish an international organization). In the interpretation of constitutions, their institutional nature should be taken into account.

At the same time, the Court did not explicitly indicate what this means. Articles 31–33 of the 1969 and 1986 Vienna Conventions on the Law of Treaties contain rules about the interpretation of treaties. To what extent should these rules be applied differently when interpreting constitutions? For example, when compared to the interpretation of other treaties, should "the ordinary meaning" of the terms of the treaty be less important and their "object and purpose" more important? Should the *travaux préparatoires* be less important and subsequent practice more important?

In the 1996 *WHO Nuclear Weapons* Advisory Opinion, the ICJ, having mentioned the elements "which may deserve special attention when the time comes to interpret these constituent treaties", does not refer to Articles 31–33 of the 1969 and 1986 Vienna Conventions in their entirety. Instead, the Court singles out some of the means of interpretation laid down in these articles as follows:[110]

> According to the customary rule of interpretation as expressed in Article 31 of the 1969 Vienna Convention on the Law of Treaties, the terms of a treaty must be interpreted "in their context and in the light of its object and purpose" and there shall be "taken into account, together with the context:
>
> -
>
> (*b*) any subsequent practice in the application of the treaty which establishes the agreement of the parties regarding its interpretation.

It is noteworthy that the Court does not explicitly refer to textual interpretation,[111] which is laid down in the first part of Article 31(1) of the 1969 and the 1986 Vienna Conventions ("[a] treaty shall be interpreted in good faith in accordance with the ordinary meaning to be given to the terms of the treaty [...]"), but, instead, starts its reference to Article 31 by quoting the final part of paragraph 1 ("in their context and in the light of its object and purpose").

∴

109 Id.

110 Id.

111 As it has done earlier, for example in *Competence of Assembly regarding admission to the United Nations*, Advisory Opinion, ICJ Rep. 1950, p. 8.

3.3.3 Whose Practice?

In addition, the Court selects another means of interpretation mentioned in Article 31: "any subsequent practice in the application of the treaty which establishes the agreement of the parties regarding its interpretation". This is remarkable, as the Court has usually been reluctant to conclude that a specific method of interpretation should be followed *because* of the 'constitutional' character of the treaty in question.[112] In the subsequent sections of this advisory opinion, the Court pays ample attention to the practice of the WHO, sometimes referring to "practice of the Organization",[113] sometimes to "a practice establishing an agreement between the members of the Organization to interpret its Constitution as empowering it to address the question of the legality of the use of nuclear weapons".[114]

Three comments are called for. First, the ICJ has now attempted to formulate a legal basis for referring to the practice of the organization. However, secondly, it may be questioned whether this legal basis is accurate because 'subsequent practice' as a canon of interpretation laid down in the 1969 Vienna Convention refers to the practice of the *states* that are party to a particular treaty ("the application of the treaty which establishes the agreement of the parties regarding its interpretation"), and not to the practice of the *organization* itself. In this sense, Article 31(3)(b) of the Vienna Convention seems to be incorrect as a foundation on which the 'practice of the organization' may rest.[115] This also has a very practical implication: whereas it is required that *all parties* to the constitution must agree to a certain interpretation if it were to be considered as "subsequent practice", such unanimous support is not required for the "practice of the organization". Thirdly, the Court does not refer

112 Lauterpacht, op. cit. note 106, pp. 414–416.

113 *Legality of the use by a state of nuclear weapons in armed conflict*, Advisory Opinion, ICJ Rep. 1996, p. 66; see paras. 21 and 27.

114 Id., p. 66, para. 27.

115 A few authors have, briefly or in more detail, paid attention to the distinction between subsequent practice (Art. 31.3(b) of the Vienna Convention) and 'practice of the organization'. See S. Rosenne, 'Is the constituent instrument of an international organization an international treaty?', in S. Rosenne, *Developments in the Law of Treaties 1945–1986* (1989), p. 241; Brölmann, op. cit. note 87, pp. 120–121; L. Boisson de Chazournes, 'Subsequent Practice, Practices, and 'Family-Resemblance': Towards Embedding Subsequent Practice in its Operative Milieu', in G. Nolte (ed.), *Treaties and Subsequent Practice* (2013), pp. 53–68. Nolte, in the context of his work for the ILC on the topic 'Treaties over Time', has briefly observed that "the distinction between the practice of the organization itself and that of its member states must be taken into account". See his Introductory Report for the ILC Study Group on Treaties over Time. This report has not been published as a UN Document, but is reproduced in G. Nolte (ed.), *Treaties and Subsequent Practice*

to the notion of "established practice", which is another notion that will now be examined.

As mentioned above, the notion of "established practice" has been developed, as part of the concept of 'rules of the organization'.[116] This 'catch-all' term 'rules of the organization' is used in a number of legal instruments, most recently in the Articles on Responsibility of International Organizations (ARIO), adopted by the International Law Commission of the UN in 2011.[117] In the ARIO, 'rules of the organization' "means, in particular, the constituent instruments, decisions, resolutions and other acts of the international organization adopted in accordance with those instruments, and established practice of the organization".[118]

This definition is not exhaustive ("in particular") and may seem rather broad, since it also covers the notion of "established practice". While it is clear that this notion does not cover *any* 'practice' (indeed, it would be difficult to see how a simple *practice* could be regarded as a *rule* (of the organization)), the qualifier "established" is somewhat vague. Its purpose is to add a legal dimension to a practice of an organization, as a requirement for this practice to qualify as a rule of the organization. In this way, it resembles *opinio iuris* as a requirement for rules of customary international law. "Established practice" has therefore also been referred to by some as the "quasi-customary law" of the particular organization.[119] But why "quasi"? Is it not 'simply' customary law of the organization? The Statute of the International Court of Justice refers to customary law as "international custom, as evidence of a general practice

(2013), pp. 169–209, quotation at p. 204. The only more extensive studies are C. Peters, 'Subsequent Practice and Established Practice of International Organizations: Two Sides of the Same Coin?', 3 *Goettingen Journal of International Law* (2011), pp. 617–642; C. Peters, *Praxis Internationaler Organisationen – Vertragswandel und völkerrechtlicher Ordnungsrahmen* (2016).

116 What follows is mostly reproduced from Schermers & Blokker, op. cit. note 20, pp. 754–755.

117 UN Doc. A/66/10, at 52. In Res. 66/100 the UN General Assembly "takes note" of the ARIO.

118 ARIO, Art. 2(b). An almost similar definition of 'rules of the organization' is given in the 1975 Vienna Convention on the Representation of States in Their Relations with International Organizations of a Universal Character (Art. 1.1(34)) and (in particular) in the 1986 Vienna Convention on the Law of Treaties between States and International Organizations or between International Organizations (Art. 2.1(j)). These two Vienna conventions have not yet entered into force. On the genesis and development of the notion of 'established practice' in these Vienna Conventions, see E. Roucounas, 'Practice as a Relevant Factor for the Responsibility of International Organizations', in M. Ragazzi (ed.), *Responsibility of International Organizations* (2013), pp. 159–171.

119 See C. Peters, *Praxis Internationaler Organisationen – Vertragswandel und völkerrechtlicher Ordnungsrahmen* (2016), at pp. 176–178, 241.

accepted as law".[120] "Established practice of the organization" could indeed be seen as "customary law of the organization".[121] As more often is the case, in the context of international organizations law, a term is used that is different from the term used in inter-state relations, even though the two essentially have the same legal meaning.[122]

A disadvantage of the rather common use of the term "established" (as a requirement for practice of the organization to be accepted as a rule of the organization) is therefore that it does not clearly express the *opinio iuris* or "accepted as law" purpose that it serves. In addition to this lack of 'legal appearance' of the term "established" there is another notable feature of the definition of established practice as a rule of the organization. Due to its positioning in the definition, "established practice" is not required to be in accordance with the constitution of the organization, unlike other elements of the legal order mentioned (decisions, resolutions, and other acts of the international organization). This may seem at odds with the principle of attributed powers and may lead to criticism of mission creep.[123] However, the condition that the practice concerned must be "established" is an important safeguard that there is at least broad support for constitutional development in this way. In this way,

120 ICJ Statute, Art. 38.1(b).

121 Also: ILC Special Rapporteur P. Reuter in the ILC, *Yearbook ILC 1974*, Vol. I, at 163 ("[...] established practice, which was to say customary rules [...]"); P. Gautier, in O. Corten and P. Klein (eds.), *The Vienna Conventions on the Law of Treaties – A Commentary*, Vol I, at 64–65 ("This expression [- established practice -] may be understood as referring to a form of customary law"). See for an early reference Pollux, op. cit. note 91, p. 54. It should be noted that the ILC in its commentary to the 1986 Vienna II Convention stated that "by referring to 'established' practice, the Commission seeks only to rule out uncertain or disputed practice; it is not its wish to freeze practice at a particular moment in an organization's history" (*Yearbook ILC 1981*, Vol. II, Part Two, at 124 (para. (24)).

122 Other examples are the use of the term "juridical personality" (international organizations) rather than "international personality" (states) during the *travaux préparatoires* of the UN Charter (see UNCIO Vol. XIII, Doc. 622–623 (1945)) and the use of the term "act of formal confirmation" (international organizations) rather than "ratification" (states) in the 1986 Vienna Convention on the Law of Treaties between States and International Organizations or between International Organizations (Art. 2.1(b)).

123 According to the principle of attributed powers, international organizations may only exercise those powers that have been given (attributed) to them. On this principle, see Schermers & Blokker, op. cit. note 20, pp. 163–171. The ICJ referred to this principle in the following way: "international organizations are subjects of international law which do not, unlike states, possess a general competence. International organizations are governed by the 'principle of speciality', that is to say, they are invested by the states which create them with powers, the limits of which are a function of the common interests whose promotion those states entrust to them" (*Legality of the Use by a State of Nuclear Weapons in Armed Conflict*, Advisory Opinion, ICJ Rep. 1996, p. 66, quotation at p. 78).

"established practice" gives the organization the necessary flexibility to perform its functions in a rapidly changing world, in particular when it is difficult to amend its constitution.

Obviously, all these general considerations do not provide concrete answers to practical questions such as the following. When precisely is a practice "established"? How much support from the members does this require? How long should a certain practice exist before it can be regarded as "established"? Nevertheless, emphasizing the *opinio iuris* purpose that the qualifier "established" serves as well as the similarity to customary international law could assist in finding answers to such practical questions. One example is the "established practice" that abstentions by permanent members of the UN Security Council are not considered to mean that a draft decision is not adopted, even though the UN Charter requires "the concurring votes" of the permanent members, as discussed above.[124]

∴

As the United Nations grows older, its practice becomes more important in interpreting the Charter. The Charter remains the anchor of the UN legal order, but the sea in which the UN is now located is much, much deeper than in its early days. Those were the days when Pollux wrote that "[a] constitutional customary law will grow up and the Charter itself will merely form the framework of the Organization which will be filled in by the practice of the different organs".[125] This is indeed what has happened: in 75 years, the UN has developed a considerable amount of practice, to be distinguished from that of its members. As discussed above, this practice has important normative dimensions. In a rapidly changing world, there should be considerable leeway for constitutional development by a flexible interpretation of the Charter; otherwise, the organization runs the risk of becoming irrelevant. However, at the same time the Charter should continue to offer, also after 75 years, sufficient constitutional rigour to preserve the key purposes and principles of the UN. The need "to save succeeding generations from the scourge of war" is as strong and undisputed as it was in 1945.

The organization and its member states sail in daily practice between the Scylla of the Charter and the Charybdis of contemporary global needs. In doing so the world court is a judicial lighthouse that offers guidance. It has demonstrated, in particular in its 1971 *Namibia* Advisory Opinion, that there is much room for constitutional development by giving a flexible and dynamic

124 See for more examples: Peters, op. cit. note 115 (Praxis book), pp. 245–391.

125 Pollux, op. cit. note 91, p. 54.

interpretation of the Charter. Additional room for constitutional development is provided by the broad definition of the concept of 'rules of the organization' in some legal instruments, covering also "established practice" of the organization. It is crucial that this "established practice" is not required to be in accordance with the constitution of the organization.

4 Concluding Observations

Since the Security Council is not a self-standing institution, but part of the United Nations, this first chapter has discussed this larger institutional structure in which it is embedded. When comparing the UN with its predecessor the League of Nations, a first experiment in world organization, two immediate conclusions may be drawn. First of all, the League was widely seen as a failure, for a mix of reasons. As mentioned in paragraph 1, in evaluating the League, a distinction must be made between the League itself and its member states. Most evaluations conclude that for the most part the members failed, rather than the League. At the same time, it is generally not concluded that the organization, the institutional structures created to prevent war are irrelevant. Following the demise of the League, states were therefore determined to create a stronger 'world organization 2.0', in order to prevent another world war for "succeeding generations" – much longer therefore than the lifetime of the League.

This brings us to another conclusion: the UN has been much more successful. While the League hardly existed for 20 years, the UN is now at the respectable age of 75. Former Secretary-General Ban Ki-moon was invited to address the Security Council in February 2018 and stated: "without the United Nations, the international community could have never succeeded in preventing another world war in the past 70-plus years".[126] Obviously, this second conclusion lacks important nuances. There may not have been another world war, but there have been and there are a number of devastating armed conflicts that the UN, in particular the Security Council, has not been able to prevent or stop.[127] In addition, while we can say that there has not been another World War during the last 75 years, we cannot say that this is exclusively *because of*

126 UN Doc. S/PV.8185, p. 4.

127 As was recognized by United Kingdom in the Security Council on 21 February 2018: "[o]ur predecessors drafted the Charter of the United Nations in the name of the peoples of the world to help save succeeding generations from the scourge of war. In some places, we are succeeding; elsewhere, we are falling woefully short" (UN Doc. S/PV.8185, p. 15).

the United Nations. Nevertheless, if the UN is compared with the League of Nations, the glass is at least half full, rather than half empty.

Being embedded in a larger institutional context, being a principal organ of the UN, the functioning of the Security Council is closely connected to developments in membership of the UN and to evolutions in 'organizationship', i.e. evolutions of the organization of which it forms part. Paragraph 2 concluded that UN membership has gradually become near-universal during the last 75 years. Members have never withdrawn. Compared to the League of Nations (17 withdrawals), this is a significant improvement. In addition, members have neither been suspended nor expelled. The power to take membership decisions is shared by the General Assembly and the Security Council. The five permanent members of the Security Council play a crucial role in the decision-making on membership issues. They may block the admission of new members, and have done so in particular in the early years of the UN, but also more recently (Palestine). They may also block a proposed suspension or expulsion, and have done so when this was – exceptionally – raised (South Africa - apartheid). After the admission difficulties of the 1940s and 1950s, the Security Council (including its five permanent members) has generally contributed to the current situation, in which almost all peoples of the world have become "peoples of the United Nations determined to save succeeding generations from the scourge of war".

Paragraph 3 has analyzed evolutions in 'organizationship'. The nature of the UN as an organization is fundamental for the functioning of the Security Council. The Charter lays down the characteristics of the UN on which the negotiators could agree in 1945. Determined "to save succeeding generations from the scourge of war, which twice in our lifetime has brought untold sorrow to mankind", a robust new institutional structure was built. The Security Council was to play a key role; the intention was to make it much more powerful than the Council of the League of Nations. It was given the primary responsibility for the maintenance of international peace and security. At the same time, the Security Council is not hierarchically superior to the other principal organs of the UN and is firmly embedded in the larger UN organization.

While the drafters of the Charter could agree on many of the characteristics of the new world organization, they decided not to be explicit about the precise international legal status of the UN, and concluded that this "will be determined implicitly from the provisions of the Charter as a whole".[128] It did not take long before this happened. Within four years after the end of the Charter

128 UNCIO, Vol. XIII, at 710. See id., at 622–623 for a report of the brief discussion on this subject. See id., at 63 for the proposal by Belgium in which "international status, together

negotiations, the International Court of Justice found that the attribution of international personality is indispensable for the UN. It concluded that the UN is an international legal person, as the organization "was intended to exercise and enjoy, and is in fact exercising and enjoying functions and rights which can only be explained on the basis of the possession of a large measure of international personality and the capacity to operate upon an international plane".[129]

International legal personality is an essential building block when constituting new international organizations. The 1949 *Reparation for Injuries* Advisory Opinion has been of fundamental importance for international organizations generally, through its reasoning that international legal personality could not only explicitly, but also implicitly be attributed in the constituent instrument of an organization. As was demonstrated not only in 1945 during the UN Charter negotiations, but also decades later in the context of the European Union and the Organization on Security and Cooperation in Europe,[130] the notion of international legal personality can be politically sensitive as it is sometimes associated, in particular by politicians with a more nationalist or (nowadays) populist orientation, with the building of a 'superstate', a Leviathan, a threat to sovereignty. The ICJ was aware of this sensitivity and addressed it. In its level-headed, down-to-earth approach it simply reasoned that international legal personality is the implication of establishing the United Nations with its purposes, principles and characteristics as laid down in the Charter.

For the United Nations, being an international legal person has enabled it to fully manifest itself at the international level during the past 75 years, as is illustrated by the examples given in paragraph 3.2. What also becomes clear from these examples, is that the Security Council – as a principal organ of the UN – is fully partaking in the UN's legal personality. Without its independent, separate status in international law and in the relations with its members, the UN (including the Security Council) would not be able to perform its functions.

However, although international legal personality has been and will remain an essential building block for international organizations including the UN, it is certainly not the only one. Apart from key elements such as the political will of the members to actually use the institution in practice, from an institutional legal perspective another important building block is the integration of the practice of the organization in the constitutional development of the

---

with the rights this involves" is given to the UN.

129 *Reparation for injuries suffered in the service of the United Nations*, Advisory Opinion, ICJ Rep. 1949, p. 174 (quotation at p. 179).

130 See in more detail, with references to literature, Schermers & Blokker, op. cit. note 20, pp. 1031–1034.

organization. As was demonstrated in paragraph 3.3, 'practice of the organization' is used by the International Court of Justice as an interpretative device, assisting in the interpretation of the constitution in accordance with present-day conditions. The *Namibia* Advisory Opinion has illustrated the far-reaching stretch of this technique, applied to the use of abstentions by the permanent members in the decision-making of the Security Council. Additional guidance has come from the broad definition of the concept of 'rules of the organization' in some legal instruments, covering also "established practice" of the organization. It is somewhat paradoxical but crucial that, even though this is another normative device for *constitutional* development, "established practice" is *not* required to be in accordance with the constitution of the organization. This may seem at odds with the principle of attributed powers and may lead to criticism of mission creep. However, the condition that the practice concerned must be "established" is an important safeguard that there is at least broad support for constitutional development in this way.

As this chapter has shown, the Charter has firmly embedded the Security Council in the United Nations. To "save succeeding generations from the scourge of war" is a central aim of the UN. In order to pursue this aim, primary responsibility for international peace and security was given to the Security Council. However, the Security Council cannot fulfil this responsibility in isolation. Without other UN organs, it would not be able to fully implement its primary responsibility. In practice, a 'united UN' is therefore needed to respond effectively to threats to and breaches of the peace.

Having analyzed the larger UN framework, the three following chapters will focus on the specific role of the Security Council in the maintenance of international peace and security. Chapter 2 will analyze the right of veto, which is decisive for the way in which the Council can perform its functions. In Chapter 3 a rule of law perspective will be given on the Council's role and functioning. Chapter 4 will focus on the issue that has dominated the Security Council reform discussions already during the time-span of one generation: the need to enlarge membership of the Council.

CHAPTER 2

The Security Council and the Right of Veto

1 Introduction

The previous chapter has demonstrated that there would be no Security Council without the United Nations. This chapter and chapters 3 and 4 will show that the reverse is also true: there would be no United Nations without the Security Council. Without the Security Council, the United Nations would not be able to save succeeding generations from the scourge of war. Following the League of Nations experience, the drafters of the Charter agreed to give the primary responsibility for the maintenance of international peace and security to a non-plenary organ that differed from its League predecessor, both in powers and in decision-making.

This chapter will discuss a predominant and most well-known characteristic of decision-making of the Security Council: the right of veto. In a way, in this respect the Security Council is similar to the League of Nations Council: in the League Council, the major powers had the right of veto as well. However, the main difference is that all members of the League Council had the right of veto (decisions were taken unanimously), whereas in the Security Council this right is enjoyed by each of the five permanent members only. During the 1945 UNCIO Conference at San Francisco, the five most powerful allied powers attempted to relativize their future right of veto by arguing that they were about to obtain nothing new compared to their position in the League Council: "[a]s regards the permanent members, there is no question under the Yalta formula of investing them with a new right, namely the right of veto, a right which the permanent members of the League Council always had".[1] This is true. However, the other side of this truth is that whereas the permanent members of the Security Council kept the right of veto, the other members lost it.

As a result, the Charter has formalized the inequality between the permanent members and the non-permanent members. The position of the former

1 UNCIO Vol. XI, p. 713 (Statement by the delegations of the four sponsoring governments on voting procedure in the Security Council, para. 7; as indicated on p. 710, "the Delegation of France associates itself completely with this statement"). In addition, para. 7 of this Statement argued: "[t]he formula proposed for the taking of action in the Security Council by a majority of seven would make the operation of the Council less subject to obstruction than was the case under the League of Nations rule of complete unanimity" (id.).

 | DOI:10.1163/9789004443921_004

would not only be stronger because of their permanent membership, but also and in particular because of their prerogative to prevent, each individually, the Security Council from taking decisions. Formalizing the inequality between permanent and non-permanent members by keeping the veto only for the five permanent members was far from obvious. It was at odds with the principle of sovereign equality of states, reflected in the Charter as the principle of sovereign equality of all members of the UN.[2] It has been qualified as "a form of legalized hegemony".[3] The right of veto for the permanent members of the Security Council was the most difficult issue during the 1945 Charter negotiations. However, the future permanent members made clear that for them, this prerogative was a *conditio sine qua non* for joining the UN. In effect, the veto was therefore non-negotiable, since, without the most powerful allied powers, the UN would have been a failure from the start. Below, paragraph 2 will discuss this *conditio sine qua non*. Paragraph 3 will analyze how the veto has been used in practice. Following a brief overview of proposals for veto reform (paragraph 4), paragraph 5 will offer some concluding observations.

2 A Problematic Beginning: without the Veto No United Nations

It is unlikely that the United Nations would have existed without the veto.[4] Nevertheless, even though the most powerful allied powers insisted on having this prerogative, and even though the other states did not want a UN without the teeth of the most powerful, the brief overview below will demonstrate how and why the veto became the most difficult hurdle to take during the Charter negotiations. First of all, it was difficult for the most powerful allied powers to define its scope: to what Security Council decisions should it apply? Next, once they agreed, this agreement was difficult to swallow for the other 45 states in the Charter negotiations.

Unlike the League of Nations Covenant, negotiated after the end of the First World War, the UN Charter was intensively prepared and negotiated long before the Second World War was over. Preparations took place in particular by 'the Big Three' (Soviet Union, United Kingdom, United States), mostly by the US. President Roosevelt was determined to avoid a repetition of post-World

2 UN Charter, Art. 2(1).

3 G. Simpson, *Great Powers and Outlaw States – Unequal Sovereigns in the International Legal Order* (2004), p. 170.

4 See also D.E. Lee, 'The Genesis of the Veto', 1 *International Organization* (1947), pp. 33–42, at p. 41.

War One events and wanted to secure US participation in a future world organization. As he stated in a radio address on 9 December 1941, following the attacks on Pearl Harbor: "[w]e are going to win the war, and we are going to win the peace that follows".[5] Early in the Second World War, the US administration started preparing for a new world organization that should bring a more lasting peace than the League of Nations had done.[6] Extensive discussions took place within the US, accompanied by consultations at the highest levels amongst the 'Big Four' (the 'Big Three' and China), between Roosevelt, Churchill, Stalin and Chiang Kai-shek. This wartime planning for the postwar order culminated in the 1944 'Dumbarton Oaks Conversations', in which China, the Soviet Union, the UK and the US prepared a draft of the future UN Charter.[7]

The Dumbarton Oaks Conversations took place in two stages because the Soviet Union did not recognize the then ruling Chiang Kai-shek government of China.[8] During the first stage (21 August – 28 September), the UK and the US met with the Soviet Union, during the second stage (29 September – 7 October) with China.[9] The veto was discussed but could not be agreed. It was mostly the Soviet Union (Stalin) that took a rather absolute view on the veto and was opposed to any limitation of the veto on substantive matters. Stalin indicated that among the Big Four, "there is no room for mutual suspicion", but the existence of "certain absurd prejudices" against the Soviet Union by some states made an absolute veto necessary for self-protection.[10] The text of the Dumbarton Oaks Proposals mentioned the issue of voting in the Security Council but only contained the following text: "(Note: The question of voting procedure in the Security Council is still under consideration)".[11] The key

5 Reproduced in US Department of State, Publication 1983, *Peace and War: United States Foreign Policy, 1931–1941* (Washington DC, US Government Printing Office 1943), pp. 841–847.

6 See in particular R.B. Russell, *A History of The United Nations Charter – The Role of the United States 1940–1945* (1958).

7 Dumbarton Oaks is an estate in Georgetown, Washington DC. On the reasons why this location was selected, see T. Hoopes and D. Brinkley, *FDR and the Creation of the U.N.* (1997), pp. 130–132.

8 See Simma et al. (eds.), *The Charter of the United Nations – A Commentary* (3rd ed. 2012), pp. 14–16.

9 The results of the Dumbarton Oaks Conversations were laid down in the Dumbarton Oaks Proposals, the text of which is reproduced in *Yearbook of the United Nations 1946–47* (1947), pp. 4–9.

10 Quoted in S.C. Schlesinger, *Act of Creation – The Founding of the United Nations* (2003), p. 151. See also the correspondence between Roosevelt and Stalin, September 1944, obtained from the Marxists Internet Archive (2010), available at https://www.marxists.org/reference/archive/stalin/works/correspondence/02/44.htm (Nos. 226–227).

11 Schlesinger, op. cit. note 10, p. 6.

question in Dumbarton Oaks was whether or not the veto holders should also be allowed to use the veto in cases in which they were party to the dispute.[12] The question was whether the old maxim *nemo iudex in sua causa* should apply (no one is judge in his own cause). If a veto holder would have the right to use its veto in a case in which it was involved, the Security Council would not be able to act, however unacceptable the position or the conduct of that veto power would be. At the same time, it was beyond reality to see how peace could be maintained if the Security Council could take enforcement action against one of the superpowers. Agreement on the veto was to be found on a later occasion, at the Yalta Summit.

At Yalta in February 1945,[13] Churchill and Stalin agreed to a proposal by Roosevelt that the veto would apply to all non-procedural Security Council decisions, with the exception of decisions on the basis of provisions for peaceful settlement and for the pacific settlement of local disputes by regional arrangements or agencies.[14] This is what later became Article 27(3) of the Charter. The text of this provision was almost completely determined and agreed in Yalta. At Yalta, it was also agreed to establish "a general international organization to maintain peace and security", to start the negotiations on the future UN in San Francisco on 25 April 1945, and to consult China and France, inviting them to sponsor invitations to the San Francisco conference. China agreed. France agreed to participate in the conference but did not want to act as a sponsoring state.[15]

12 See in more detail Lee, op. cit. note 4, pp. 36–37, pp. 149–158, and the correspondence between Roosevelt and Stalin, op. cit. note 10.

13 The Yalta Summit was held in palaces near Yalta, on the south coast of Crimea. In February 2020, commemorative events took place in one of these palaces, the Livadia Palace (see https://www.mbs.news/a/2020/02/us-and-uk-experts-will-travel-to-crimea-to-commemorate-the-yalta-conference.html). In addition, an exhibition ('Yalta 1945. Truth about Victory. Lessons of history.') was organized in the State Duma (the lower house of the Parliament of the Russian Federation). See http://duma.gov.ru/en/news/47677/ (quoting the Chairman of the Duma's Committee on Education and Science, Viacheslav Nikonov, who stated: "Yalta is still the pinnacle of cooperation between Russia and Western powers. Not only in the 20th century, not only during the war, but in the history in general. We managed to create a framework for the world that has been existing since 1945 and prevented the possibility of major conflicts".

14 See Lee, op. cit. note 4, at 37; Hoopes and Brinkley, op. cit. note 7, pp. 174–175; Schlesinger, op. cit. note 10, pp. 58–59.

15 See the report of the Yalta conference, reproduced in *Yearbook of the United Nations 1946–47* (1947), pp. 9–10, and Schlesinger, op. cit. note 10, mentioning that General Charles de Gaulle was "angered by his exclusion from Yalta" (at 64) and therefore did not want to become a sponsoring state of the San Francisco conference.

A few months later, at the United Nations Conference on International Organization (UNCIO) in San Francisco, it became more than clear that almost all other participating states were unwilling to immediately accept the veto as proposed in the Yalta agreement as a *fait accompli*. New Zealand stated: "The veto which can be exercised by one of the great powers, both in regard to itself and other nations, is unfair and indefensible and may, if retained and exercised, be destructive not only to the main purposes of the International Organization but to the Organization itself".[16] The criticism by 'the others' is understandable. The UN Charter would prohibit them to use force, even to threaten to use force. Instead, the Security Council was given the primary responsibility to maintain international peace and security. However, how reliable was this 'supranationalization' of the use of force, if it could be blocked by any of the big five, for whatever reason?

However, for the five future permanent members of the Security Council, their veto privilege was a *conditio sine qua non* for membership of the UN, and during the San Francisco negotiations it was clear to everyone that without their membership the world organization would be a 'Non-United Nations', ineffective and powerless. It was clear in particular to the 45 delegations other than those of the five most powerful allied powers, that they had no alternative but to accept the prerogative of the veto power for the future permanent members of the Security Council. This was also underlined by a US delegate, who "asked if delegates could face public opinion at home if they reported that they had killed the veto but had also killed the Charter".[17]

The veto became the most difficult issue during the two months of UNCIO negotiations.[18] A "questionnaire", a list of 23 questions to the future permanent members was prepared.[19] These questions concerned, for example, the meaning of an abstention by a permanent member, whether the veto would apply to the recommendation to appoint the Secretary-General, to the recommendation to refer a legal dispute to the International Court of Justice, and to the preliminary decision as to whether a certain issue is a procedural matter or not (the question of the 'double veto'). It took a pause in the negotiations, a flight by US Foreign Minister Stettinius to Washington to have private consultations with President Truman, a visit by special adviser Harry Hopkins to Marshall Stalin in Moscow, and a lot of arm-twisting in San Francisco to come to a final

16 UNCIO, Vol. I, pp. 510–511.

17 UNCIO, Vol. XI, p. 493 (12 June 1945).

18 See *Yearbook of the United Nations 1946–47* (1947), pp. 23–25.

19 UNCIO, Vol. XI, pp. 699–709 (Doc. 852; III/1/37(1)). The questions were filed by noon May 21 and submitted to the four sponsoring governments (China, UK, US, USSR).

agreement. On 7 June, the future permanent members presented their reply to the list of 23 questions.[20] They did not answer each of the 23 questions individually, but put forward a "statement of their general attitude toward the whole question of unanimity of permanent members in the decisions of the Security Council".[21] They justified the veto by mentioning a number of considerations, in particular the following one:

> [i]n view of the primary responsibilities of the permanent members, they could not be expected, *in the present condition of the world*, to assume the obligation to act in so serious a matter as the maintenance of international peace and security in consequence of a decision in which they had not concurred.[22]

On the veto issue, as finally resolved in Article 27(3) of the Charter, the glass may seem half empty, or less than half empty. Nevertheless, it is also half full. It should not be forgotten that, in the Council of the League of Nations, all members had the right of veto. Now, the UN Security Council not only had many more enforcement powers than the League Council, the right of veto was also limited to the most powerful members. It secured their participation in the new world organization.

3 A Problematic Practice

If we now look back after 75 years, how has the veto been used in practice? At the San Francisco Conference, the future permanent members attempted to play down the importance of the veto and tried to assuage the fears of smaller powers. For example, the US delegation "contended that, far from frequently used, the veto would seldom, if ever, be exercised. Far from being used perniciously, it would be used by the great powers, he was convinced, not for their own selfish interests but in the interests of the world Organization".[23] A few

20 UNCIO, Vol. XI, pp. 710–714. The answers were published in a document of the Technical Committee III/I on the structure and procedures of the Security Council, dated 8 June 1945. In its chapeau, the document states: "[i]n view of the great interest which has been shown in the question of the voting procedure in the Security Council, and on the recommendation of Subcommittee III/1/B, I am releasing this statement to the full membership of Committee III/1, and simultaneously to the press". The delegation of France associated itself completely with the statement of the four sponsoring governments (id. p. 710).

21 Id., at 711.

22 UNCIO, Vol. XI, p. 713, para. 9 (italics added).

23 UNCIO, Vol. XI, p. 493 (12 June 1945).

days later, the delegate from China stated: "[h]is own view was that the veto might prove much less important than expected and might, in fact, never be used; he felt that it was not unreasonable to suppose that after a time the great powers would be willing to consider elimination of the veto".[24]

Things turned out differently, as is illustrated by the figures given in this section.[25] The first meeting of the Security Council was on 17 January 1946 in London. Within a month, the veto was used for the first time, by the Soviet Union.[26] Subsequently, the Soviet Union used its veto regularly: on 80 occasions during the next ten years. Of the other permanent members, only France (twice) and China (represented by the Taiwan government, once) cast their vetoes in this first decade.

The regular use of the veto by the Soviet Union prevented the Security Council from acting on many occasions in this first decade. Due to the Cold War, a precondition for the adoption of resolutions of the Security Council – agreement amongst the permanent members – often did not exist. This was one of the fears expressed during the Charter negotiations in San Francisco.

Following these frequent deadlocks in the Security Council, the General Assembly – dominated by Western countries at the time – took a number of initiatives. In 1950, it adopted the *Uniting for Peace* resolution (called *Disuniting for War* by the Soviet Union), in which it gave a very broad interpretation of its own powers in the field of the maintenance of international peace and

24 UNCIO, Vol. VII, p. 244 (16 June 1945).

25 The figures in this section have been taken from the overview of the use of the veto prepared by Security Council Report, available at https://www.securitycouncilreport.org/un-security-council-working-methods/the-veto.php, reproduced in the Appendix. Another overview of the meetings in which the veto was used has been prepared by the Dag Hammarsköld Library, see https://research.un.org/en/docs/sc/quick. For the latter overview, data from 1946–2004 were taken from the official list of vetoes in UN Doc. A/58/47, Annex III. For the period before 1986, there are small differences between these two overviews, depending on how the use of the veto is counted (e.g. only when used for draft resolutions, or also for amendments to drafts). A good overview of the use of the veto until 1 May 2014 is given in L. Sievers and S. Daws, *The Procedure of the UN Security Council* (4th ed. 2014), pp. 296–316; an update website of this book is available at www.scprocedure.org.

26 UN Doc. S/PV.23 (16 February 1946), pp. 367–368. On this occasion of the first use of the veto, there was a misunderstanding in the Security Council room. After the vote was taken (seven votes in favour), the President concluded: "[i]t is therefore carried". The representative of the Soviet Union protested, referring to Art. 27(3) of the Charter and stating that he had voted against the proposal. Following some discussion, the President concluded the meeting by stating: "I understand that it is the consensus of the opinion of the Council that Article 27, paragraph 3, [...] would mean that in respect of the last vote taken, the motion was not carried" (id., p. 368).

security.[27] It requested advisory opinions from the International Court of Justice when legal questions were involved. Furthermore, it adopted Resolution 267 ("The problem of voting in the Security Council"),[28] in which it recommended to the permanent members of the Security Council:

> in order to avoid impairment of the usefulness and prestige of the Council through excessive use of the veto:
> (a) To consult together wherever feasible upon important decisions to be taken by the Security Council;
> (b) To consult together wherever feasible before a vote is taken if their unanimity is essential to effective action by the Security Council;
> (c) If there is not unanimity, to exercise the veto only when they consider the question of vital importance, taking into account the interest of the United Nations as a whole, and to state upon what ground they consider this condition to be present.

Specifically, the General Assembly recommended to the members of the Security Council that they would consider the decisions set forth in an annex to this resolution as procedural decisions (and therefore, the veto would not apply). In addition, the General Assembly recommended to the permanent members of the Security Council "that they seek agreement among themselves upon what possible decisions by the Security Council they might forbear to exercise their veto, when seven affirmative votes have already been cast in the Council, giving favourable consideration to the list of such decisions" included in a report of the General Assembly's Interim Committee.

These recommendations did not break the deadlock in the Security Council. The Soviet Union continued to use its veto regularly until 1970, 107 times in total. The other permanent members hardly used their vetoes in the period 1945–1970 (France on four occasions, the UK three times, China once (represented by the Taiwan government)). The US did not cast its veto at all in the UN's first 25 years. In this period, in which China was not yet represented by the Beijing government and in which the Soviet Union must have lacked trust in the UN (mostly dominated by Western states) and in the Security Council, the emergency brake that is the veto has been *de facto* the almost exclusive prerogative of the Soviet Union.

---

27 GA Res. 377 (V), adopted 3 November 1950.

28 GA Res. 267(III), adopted 14 April 1949 by 43 votes in favour, 6 against, with two abstentions (see UN Doc. A/PV.195, p. 129).

This monotonous state of veto affairs changed in the 1970s, when all permanent members invoked their right of veto. The US did so most frequently (on 21 occasions, using its veto for the first time in 1970), in sharp contrast to its prediction in 1945 ("the veto would seldom, if ever, be exercised").[29] The number of vetoes used by the other permanent members in this decade are as follows: the UK (14), France (7), the Soviet Union (7) and China (2, now represented by the Beijing government). During the 1970s, the veto was used much more often (51 times) than in the previous decade (18 vetoes in the 1960s) and slightly more than in the 1950s.[30] At the same time, it is useful to see how often the veto was *not* used in this decade, and compare the veto data to the number of resolutions adopted: 186 in the 1970s (compared to 143 in the 1960s and 54 in the 1950s).

These patterns continued in the 1980s. The use of the veto increased to 72, while the number of resolutions adopted was almost the same as in the 1970s (185). The US was again the most frequent user (46 times, more than twice as often as in the 1970s), followed by the UK (15), France (7) and the Soviet Union (4). China did not use its veto during the 1980s.

In the first decade after the end of the Cold War (1990–1999), it seemed that for the first time in the history of the UN the main precondition for the effective functioning of the Security Council - agreement amongst the permanent members – was fulfilled. The Security Council became much more active, as can be seen not only in the numbers of decisions taken but also in the types of measures adopted: economic sanctions, more robust UN peacekeeping, frequent authorizations of the use of force, etc. A certain euphoria seemed to prevail. "[A] new Security Council emerged since the end of the Cold War".[31] As the Security Council itself concluded in 1995, on the occasion of the UN's 50th anniversary "[t]he past few years in particular have been ones of momentous change, bringing fresh hope and new challenges".[32]

While a number of international and in particular internal armed conflicts took place in this decade as well, including genocides in Rwanda and in the former Yugoslavia (Srebrenica), it seemed that the Security Council was no longer almost by definition sidelined and could now play a more active role.

29 UNCIO, Vol. XI, p. 493 (12 June 1945).

30 From 1950 to 1959, the veto was cast on 49 occasions (18 of these relate to the large number of membership applications discussed in the Security Council from 13–15 December 1955).

31 P. Wallensteen and P. Johansson, 'Security Council Decisions in Perspective', in D.M. Malone, *The UN Security Council – From the Cold War to the 21st Century* (2004), pp. 17–33, quotation at p. 21.

32 Presidential Statement adopted on 26 September 1995 (S/PRST/1995/48).

These major political climate changes are reflected in the number of resolutions adopted by the Security Council during the 1990s (638, more than tripling the number of resolutions adopted during each of the previous two decades); many of these resolutions were based on Chapter VII of the Charter.[33] In all these cases, the veto has not been used; it was only cast on 9 occasions during this first post-Cold war decade. The US was the most frequent user (5), followed by China (2) and the Russian Federation (2).[34] After half a century, the Security Council finally seemed to act in the spirit of San Francisco.

The patterns of the 1990s continued to some extent in the new millennium, although the veto was gradually cast more often and by different permanent members. In the period 2000 – 2009, 623 resolutions were adopted; the veto was invoked on 16 occasions. Most frequent user was the US (10), followed by the Russian Federation (4) and China (2). France and the UK did not use their vetoes. In the most recent decade (2010 – 2019), 596 resolutions were adopted and the use of the veto almost doubled (31 vetoes). There was a shift in the exercise of the veto power. Following Chinese and in particular Russian criticism of the intervention in Libya, these two permanent members regularly blocked proposed draft resolutions in the context of the war in Syria. The Russian Federation used its veto 19 times in this decade, China 9. The US did so on 3 occasions only. Again, France and the UK did not use their veto. These first two decades of the 21st century have demonstrated a decreasing consensus in the Security Council, although, taking the above mentioned figures as a criterion, the Security Council did not return to the level of inactivity of the Cold War.

Following these developments in figures over the decades, some overall statistics will now be given to conclude this section. From 1945 until 1 January 2020, the UN Security Council has adopted 2503 resolutions. During the Cold War (1945 – 1989), it passed 646 resolutions, which is on average some 14 each

33 Of all Chapter VII resolutions passed from 1946 to 2002, 93% have been adopted since the end of the Cold War (Wallensteen and Johansson, op. cit. note 31, p. 19).

34 Following the disintegration of the Soviet Union, the Russian Federation continued the membership of the Soviet Union in the UN. In December 1991, Boris Yeltsin, the President of the Russian Federation, informed the UN Secretary-General that “the membership of the Union of Soviet Socialist Republics in the United Nations, including the Security Council and all other organs and organizations of the United Nations system, is being continued by the Russian Federation (RSFSR) with the support of the countries of the Commonwealth of Independent States”. See 31 ILM 138, 151 (1992). See also Y.Z. Blum, ‘Russia Takes Over the Soviet Union’s Seat at the United Nations’, 3 *European Journal of International Law* 354–361 (1992); M.P. Scharf, ‘Musical Chairs: The Dissolution of States and Membership in the United Nations’, 28 *Cornell International Law Journal* 29–70 (1995); K.G. Bühler, *State Succession and Membership in International Organization – Legal Theories versus Political Pragmatism* (2001), pp. 151–170.

year (the all-time low was 1959, when the Security Council only adopted one resolution, a one sentence resolution in which it appointed a subcommittee[35]). After the end of the Cold War (1990 – 1 January 2020), the Security Council adopted 1857 resolutions, which is on average some 62 per year. One way to approach these figures is that since the establishment of the UN, vetoes have not been used on 2503 occasions. The glass is certainly not empty.

In total, the veto has been used on 294 occasions. Many draft resolutions have not been adopted during the last 75 years for this reason. In addition: it is likely that in many cases draft resolutions have not been put to the vote because it was assumed they would be vetoed.

If we now look at the individual permanent members, the figures for casting the veto are as follows: (the USSR/) the Russian Federation (143, so almost half of all vetoes), the United States (85), the UK (32), France (18), and China (16). The Soviet Union was almost the only user of the veto until 1970. The US started to use the veto regularly from the 1970s, but less frequently during the 2010–2020 decade. China hardly used its veto in the 20th century, but more often from 2000. France and the UK have not used their vetoes in the post-Cold War period, now for more than 30 years (the last time was on 23 December 1989).

The figures presented in this section should be taken *cum grano salis*. The mere existence of the veto may work preventively to a considerable extent. If it is more or less clear beforehand that a permanent member would block the adoption a particular resolution, a draft resolution may not be put to a vote. In other words, behind the veil of the vetoes used in reality, many more unused vetoes are hidden.[36] In addition, the situations in which the veto is used may differ, and the criticism of its use by UN members varies. Furthermore, in some cases the veto may have been used to protect directly the interests of the permanent member concerned (as was criticized during the UN Charter negotiations, against the background of the maxim *nemo iudex in sua causa*), in other cases those interests might have been more remote. Nevertheless, to some extent these figures concerning the use of the veto paint a picture that is useful when assessing the way in which the decision-making rules, so difficult to agree upon in 1944–1945, have worked out in practice. The picture is certainly

35 SC Res. 132.

36 A former permanent representative to the UN, representing Singapore in the Security Council in 2001 and 2002, even wrote: "while the formal veto is rarely used, the informal veto is used almost every day, especially in the frequent and more important informal consultations among Council members" (K. Mahbubani, 'Council Reform and the Emerging Powers', in S. von Einsiedel, D.M. Malone, B. Stagno Ugarte (eds.), *The UN Security Council in the Twenty-First Century* (2016), pp. 157–173, quotation at p. 158).

different from what two permanent members envisaged in 1945 (the US,[37] "the veto would seldom, if ever, be exercised" and China,[38] "the veto might, in fact, never be used").

4 Problematic Reform Discussions: *l'histoire se répète*

As discussed in the previous paragraph, practice has demonstrated that the fears and doubts expressed by many of the smaller states at the 1945 San Francisco Conference were not unwarranted. The main precondition for the successful functioning of the Security Council, agreement amongst the permanent members, more or less ceased to exist after the Second World War was over. During the Cold War, such an agreement only surfaced exceptionally and the Security Council was mostly paralyzed, notwithstanding pressure from member states and from the General Assembly. After the end of the Cold War, it seemed for some years that this precondition was at last fulfilled. However, the armed conflict in Syria and other events of the last decade have again illustrated how uncertain the response of the Security Council is if there are threats to the peace, breaches of the peace and acts of aggression. The San Francisco fears and doubts have materialized, again.

Therefore, the arduous discussions on the veto in San Francisco only temporarily ended when the Charter was signed. The arguments against the introduction of the veto expressed during the UNCIO Conference were often repeated when the use of the veto in practice prevented the Council from performing its functions. However, they were voiced in particular when proposals were discussed to limit the use of the veto and to reform the Security Council. This paragraph will give a brief overview of such proposals. Two types of proposals may be distinguished. Firstly, rather than abolishing the veto, it would be more realistic to attempt to moderate its use, which does not necessarily require a Charter amendment. Secondly, if however in the future such an amendment were to be considered, the veto as it exists today could be changed in a variety of ways.

4.1 *Moderating the Use of the Veto without Charter Amendment*

First, a number of proposals have been developed over the years to guide the use of the veto, without amending the Charter. In a way, the history of such

37 UNCIO, Vol. XI, p. 493 (12 June (1945).

38 UNCIO, Vol. VII, p. 244 (16 June 1945).

proposals is almost as old as the Charter itself. As discussed above, already in 1949 the General Assembly issued a number of recommendations to the permanent members, "in order to avoid impairment of the usefulness and prestige of the Council through excessive use of the veto".[39] One of those recommendations was "to exercise the veto only when they consider the question of vital importance, taking into account the interest of the United Nations as a whole, and to state upon what ground they consider this condition to be present".[40] Another one was that the permanent members should "seek agreement among themselves upon what possible decisions by the Security Council they might forbear to exercise their veto, when seven affirmative votes have already been cast in the Council, giving favourable consideration to the list of such decisions contained in conclusion 2 of part IV of the report of the Interim Committee".[41] The first of these two amounts to an appeal to individual permanent members to limit the use of the veto to essential questions, taking into account the common interest, and being transparent about how it would apply these two conditions. The second recommendation was addressed to the five permanent members collectively, urging them to prepare a list of decisions (e.g. decisions on the admission of a new member state) and not to use the veto in a case covered by this list, if there were already seven (now: nine) votes in favour.

In more recent years similar recommendations have been made, in particular after the failed attempt to reform the Security Council in 2005. The so-called S5 group was created, consisting of Costa Rica, Jordan, Liechtenstein, Singapore and Switzerland.[42] This group prepared a number of proposals to improve the working methods of the Security Council. Two draft resolutions of the General Assembly were proposed, the first in 2006,[43] the second in 2011.[44]

39 GA Res. 267 (III), para. 3 (adopted 14 April 1949).

40 Id., para. 3(c).

41 Id., para. 2. For the report of the Interim Committee to which this recommendation refers, see UN Doc. A/578. Conclusion 2 of part IV of this report lists 21 items on the agenda of the Security Council; decisions on these items should be considered as procedural, therefore the right of veto should not apply.

42 See C. Wenaweser, 'Working from the Outside to Change the Working Methods of the Security Council: Elected Members as a Bridge between the Permanent Members and the Rest of the UN Membership', in N. Schrijver and N. Blokker (eds.), *Elected Members of the Security Council* (2020), pp. 279–283. The S5 group was created in 2005. Wenaweser explains that the acronym S5 "stands for 'small five' and is a self-ironic play on the acronym 'P5'" (p. 280).

43 UN Doc. A/60/L.49 17 March 2006).

44 Reproduced in https://www.globalpolicy.org/images/pdfs/S5_April_2011_Tabled_Resolution.pdf.

As far as the use of the veto is concerned, the latter suggested the following measures "for consideration by the permanent members of the Security Council:

> 18. Explaining the reasons when resorting to a veto or declaring its intention to do so, in particular its consistency with the Charter of the United Nations and international law. A copy of the explanation should be circulated as a Security Council document to all Members of the Organisation.
>
> 19. Refraining from using a veto to block Council action in situations involving serious allegations of genocide, crimes against humanity and grave breaches of international humanitarian law.
>
> 20. Establishing a practice, in appropriate cases, of declaring, when casting a negative vote on a draft resolution before the Council that such a negative vote shall not constitute a veto in the sense of Article 27, paragraph 3 of the Charter.

The permanent members rejected these suggestions.[45] In 2012, the S5 group withdrew its draft resolution, when it appeared that it lacked the necessary support from UN membership.[46] Other (earlier) proposals of the S5 group were more successful. In particular, their work brought the Security Council to adopting "under its own authority, a set of measures on working methods which were strongly inspired by the work of the S5, while avoiding the most political provisions, in particular those dealing with the use of the veto".[47] Indeed, the relevant Security Council document does not mention the veto at all.[48]

In 2012, following the withdrawal of its draft resolution, the S5 group was dissolved and was replaced by the Accountability, Coherence, Transparency group (ACT group), composed of 28 small and mid-sized UN member states.[49] The ACT group concentrated on two issues: the election of the Secretary-General of the UN and the use of the veto. As to the latter issue, the group continued earlier work by France and Mexico on voluntary restraint of the

---

45 See M. Hansen, 'The S5 Presents Draft Resolution', 10 April 2012 (published by the Global Policy Forum), available at https://www.globalpolicy.org/component/content/article/200-reform/51541-the-s5-presents-draft-resolution-on-the-improvement-of-the-working-methods-of-the-security-council.html.

46 See in detail C. Wenaweser, 'Working Methods: The Ugly Duckling of Security Council Reform', in Von Einsiedel, Malone, Stagno Ugarte (eds.), op. cit. note 36, pp. 175–194.

47 Wenaweser, op. cit. note 42, p. 280.

48 UN Doc. S/2017/507.

49 Wenaweser, op. cit. note 42, p. 281.

veto by the permanent members in situations of mass atrocities, as well as the above-quoted paragraph 19 of the proposals of the S5 group, and drafted a 'Code of conduct regarding Security Council action against genocide, crimes against humanity or war crimes'.[50] This Code of Conduct was launched in October 2015, on the occasion of the 70th anniversary of the UN.[51]

Under the Code of Conduct, the member states that committed themselves to the Code pledged "to support timely and decisive action by the Security Council aimed at preventing or ending the commission of genocide, crimes against humanity or war crimes".[52] In particular, they pledged, "to not vote against a credible draft resolution before the Security Council on timely and decisive action to end the commission of genocide, crimes against humanity or war crimes, or to prevent such crimes".[53] In addition, they invited the Secretary-General "to continue to bring to the attention of the Council situations that, in her or his assessment, involve or are likely to lead to genocide, crimes against humanity or war crimes".[54] On 1 January 2020, 119 member states as well as two non-UN members, the Holy See and Palestine, supported the Code of Conduct. Amongst these supporters are two of the five permanent members, France and the United Kingdom.[55]

All these recommendations and proposals under this first scenario are creative attempts to bypass as much as possible the negative effects of the veto. So far, the Code of Conduct drafted by the ACT group in 2015 has been most successful since it received considerable support including from two permanent members. However, the scope of the Code is limited to certain Security Council decisions only, and critical observers could say that France and the UK have not used their vetoes during the last three decades anyway. Neither the Code nor other recommendations and proposals under this first scenario provide a solution for cases in which the Security Council is widely expected to perform its functions but is unable to do so due to the exercise of the veto at the full discretion of a single permanent member. The only way to overcome this hurdle is to amend the Charter.

---

50 Id.

51 For the text of the Code, see UN Doc. A/70/621 – S/2015/978.

52 Id., para. 1.

53 Id., para. 2.

54 Id., para. 3.

55 The list of supporters of the Code of Conduct is published on the website of the Permanent Mission of Liechtenstein to the United Nations; see https://www.regierung.li/media/medienarchiv/2020-6-9_CoC_List_of_supporters.pdf.

4.2 *Changing the Veto, Amending the Charter*

A number of Charter amendments on Security Council reform (including the veto) have been suggested over the years, by UN member states, institutions, academics, critics and others.[56] Most well-known are:[57]

- the 'Razali Reform Paper': the proposal informally submitted in 1997 by Razali Ismael (Malaysia), the President of the General Assembly during its 51st session.[58] According to this proposal, the number of members of the Security Council would increase to 24 (five permanent (without the veto) and four non-permanent additional members). It recognized that "an overwhelming number of Member States consider the use of veto in the Security Council anachronistic and undemocratic, and have called for its elimination", and urged the permanent members to limit the use of the veto to actions under Chapter VII of the Charter.
- the G4 proposal, presented by Brazil, Germany, India and Japan, according to which the Council should have six additional permanent members (without the veto) and four new non-permanent members. The co-authors of the proposal would be among the new permanent members.
- the proposal by the 'Uniting for Consensus Group' (originally named 'Coffee Club'). This group, led by Italy, is opposed to the G4 ideas. It suggests to have ten more non-permanent members of the Security Council.
- the proposal by the African Group, often referred to as the 'Ezulwini consensus' (named after the valley in Swaziland where agreement was reached in 2005). The African Group wants at least two more permanent members, from Africa, with the right of veto, as well as five new

56 For an extensive chronologic overview of proposals for UN reform in general, see J. Müller, *Reforming the United Nations* (1997, 2001, 2006, 2010). For a collection of documents on Security Council reform, see B. Fassbender (ed.), *Key documents on the Reform of the UN Security Council 1991–2019* (2020).

57 See the very brief overview by Security Council Report, *In Hindsight: Security Council Reform* (30 August 2019). More extensive overviews are: B. Fassbender, 'All Illusions Shattered? Looking Back on a Decade of Failed Attempts to Reform the UN Security Council', 7 *Max Planck Yearbook of United Nations Law* (2003), pp. 183–218; Simma et al (eds.), op. cit. note 8, pp. 54–55, 63–64, 928–931; E.C. Luck, 'The Security Council at Seventy: Ever Changing or Never Changing?', in Von Einsiedel, Malone, Stagno Ugarte (eds.), op. cit. note 36, pp. 195–214 (with his own proposal: five more non-permanent members, elected for three years, re-electable for one additional term).

58 For the text of the proposal, see https://www.globalpolicy.org/component/content/article/200/41310.html.

non-permanent members. While the African Group is in principle opposed to the veto, it takes the view that so long as it exists, all permanent members should have it.[59]

- The proposal by the 'Group L69' (named after the number of a draft resolution tabled in 2007 (A/61/L.69/Rev.1)), according to which there should be six new permanent members, and one non-permanent seat for a small island developing state.

However, so far, these proposals for veto reform have not resulted in concrete successful steps to amend the Charter.[60] UN membership is united about the need for Security Council reform, but is deeply divided over how this should be done. The most recent rounds of high-level discussions or negotiations involving – inter alia – Security Council reform did not even mention the veto, or touched upon it only superficially. The first of those rounds resulted in the Millennium Declaration, adopted in 2000 by the General Assembly. The second and most important round took place following the 2003 Iraq crisis, when two permanent members (the US and the UK) and others initiated a war against Iraq that was widely seen as unlawful, or at least not legitimate, and when the relevance of the Security Council and the UN's collective security system was questioned.

The Millennium Declaration was adopted in September 2000.[61] Meeting at the level of heads of state and government, the General Assembly adopted this Declaration "to reaffirm our faith in the Organization and its Charter as indispensable foundations of a more peaceful, prosperous and just world".[62] The Declaration expresses the determination "to establish a just and lasting peace all over the world in accordance with the purposes and principles of the Charter".[63] Today's "central challenge [...] is to ensure that globalization becomes a positive force for all the world's people. For while globalization offers great opportunities, at present its benefits are very unevenly shared, while its costs are unevenly distributed. [...] only through broad and sustained efforts to create a shared future, based upon our common humanity in all its diversity, can globalization be made fully inclusive and equitable".[64] One of the key objectives

59 UN Doc. A/74/PV.33, p. 3.

60 Since 2008 (GA Decision 62/557), Security Council reform is discussed in the context of an "informal plenary" of the General Assembly. See for the records of the most recent (2019) meetings: UN Docs. A/74/PV.33–35. These records demonstrate that there is hardly any progress; the positions of most of the above-mentioned reform groups are repeated.

61 GA Res. 55/2 (adopted without a vote).

62 Id. para. 1.

63 Id., para. 4.

64 Id., para. 5.

mentioned in the Millennium Declaration is "to free our peoples from the scourge of war, whether within or between States".[65] In order to strengthen the UN, the Declaration resolved, "to intensify our efforts to achieve a comprehensive reform of the Security Council in all its aspects".[66]

However, only one year later, before efforts to reform the Security Council could bear fruit, international relations and the commitments made in the Millennium Declaration were put to a first test, when the 9/11 terrorist attacks marked the beginning of a new era.[67] Another test came when the US started to put pressure on Iraq in 2002 and finally decided to use force against the Saddam Hussein regime in 2003, without a specific Security Council authorization. Less than three years earlier, world leaders had agreed in the Millennium Declaration that "[r]esponsibility for managing worldwide economic and social development, as well as threats to international peace and security, must be shared among the nations of the world and should be exercised multilaterally. As the most universal and most representative organization in the world, the United Nations must play the central role".[68] However, the unilateral use of force against Iraq by the US and other states undermined the commitments made in 2000 and the necessary trust in a multilateral system based on the rule of law in which all states including the most powerful would respect the central role and the primary responsibility of the Security Council.

At the same time, the absence of a specific authorization to use force against Iraq and the bypassing of the Security Council by the US, the UK and others triggered the most recent high-level round of negotiations on Security Council reform, in the years 2004–2005. UN Secretary-General Kofi Annan saw the need to seek a recommitment of member states to the Charter's collective security system. In his address to the General Assembly on 23 September 2003, he stated, "we have come to a fork in the road. This may be a moment no less decisive than 1945 itself, when the United Nations was founded".[69] Secretary-General Annan announced his intention to create a high-level panel to examine threats to international peace and security and to suggest institutional reform (inter alia on an enlargement of the Security Council), and ended his address as follows:[70]

---

65 Id., para. 8.

66 Id. para. 30.

67 See E.C. Luck, 'Tackling Terrorism', in Malone (ed.), op. cit. note 31, pp. 85–100.

68 Id., para. 6.

69 See https://www.un.org/webcast/ga/58/statements/sg2eng030923.htm.

70 Id.

> institutional reforms alone will not suffice. Even the most perfect instrument will fail, unless people put it to good use.
>
> The United Nations is by no means a perfect instrument, but it is a precious one. I urge you to seek agreement on ways of improving it, but above all of using it as its founders intended – to save succeeding generations from the scourge of war, to reaffirm faith in fundamental human rights, to reestablish the basic conditions for justice and the rule of law, and to promote social progress and better standards of life in larger freedom.
>
> The world may have changed, excellencies, but those aims are as valid and urgent as ever. We must keep them firmly in our sights.

"Saving succeeding generations from the scourge of war": Annan reminded the member states of that first sentence of the UN Charter, and took the initiative to request a high-level advisory panel to make recommendations in this spirit, following the challenges of the UN's collective security system during the first years of the new millennium.

Secretary-General Annan established the 'High-level Panel on Threats, Challenges and Change' in November 2003. It was composed of 16 members.[71] The Panel's report came in December 2004.[72] Partly on this basis, Secretary-General Annan prepared his own report, 'In Larger Freedom', published in March 2005.[73] These two reports set the stage for a few months of intense diplomatic efforts that resulted in an agreement on a broad variety of issues, including for example 'Responsibility to Protect', but excluding Security Council reform. Although this round of negotiations did not result in the adoption of amendments to the Charter, in particular on Security Council reform, it is revealing to analyze these two reports and the final outcome (the General Assembly's 'World Summit Outcome' Resolution) in some more detail, focusing on the right of veto.

---

71 The Panel's members came from all parts of the world and brought a variety of experiences and expertise. The Panel's Chair was Anand Panyarachun, former Prime Minister of Thailand. The other members were Robert Badinter (France), João Baena Soares (Brazil), Gro Harlem Brundtland (Norway), Mary Chinery Hesse (Ghana), Gareth Evans (Australia), David Hannay (United Kingdom of Great Britain and Northern Ireland), Enrique Iglesias (Uruguay), Amre Moussa (Egypt), Satish Nambiar (India), Sadako Ogata (Japan), Yevgeny Primakov (Russian Federation), Qian Qiqian (China), Salim Salim (United Republic of Tanzania), Nafis Sadik (Pakistan) and Brent Scowcroft (United States of America). See UN Doc. A/59/565, p. 1.

72 UN Doc. A/59/565.

73 UN Doc. A/59/2005. This report was also based on other input, as explained on p. 3.

Of these three documents, the two reports and the 'World Summit Outcome Resolution', only the report of the High-level Panel paid attention to the veto. The relevant paragraphs of this report will be quoted here in full. They demonstrate that not much had changed since the days of San Francisco. Having presented two models for enlarging the Security Council, the Panel stated the following:

> 256. Neither model involves any expansion of the veto or any Charter modification of the Security Council's existing powers. We recognize that the veto had an important function in reassuring the United Nations most powerful members that their interests would be safeguarded. We see no practical way of changing the existing members' veto powers. Yet, as a whole the institution of the veto has an anachronistic character that is unsuitable for the institution in an increasingly democratic age and we would urge that its use be limited to matters where vital interests are genuinely at stake. We also ask the permanent members, in their individual capacities, to pledge themselves to refrain from the use of the veto in cases of genocide and large-scale human rights abuses. We recommend that under any reform proposal, there should be no expansion of the veto.
>
> 257. We propose the introduction of a system of "indicative voting", whereby members of the Security Council could call for a public indication of positions on a proposed action. Under this indicative vote, "no" votes would not have a veto effect, nor would the final tally of the vote have any legal force. The second formal vote on any resolution would take place under the current procedures of the Council. This would, we believe, increase the accountability of the veto function.

The Panel was as critical of the right of veto as the vast majority of states in 1945. However, just as this vast majority had no choice but to accept the veto ('no United Nations without the veto'), the Panel saw "no practical way of changing the existing members' veto powers". Realism prevailed.

At the same time, the Panel did not want to stop here and merely present its realistic recommendation not to start a discussion on the veto. It also expressed its view that the veto is outdated, by referring to its "anachronistic character" and by stating that it "had" (past tense) "an important function in reassuring the United Nations most powerful members that their interests would be safeguarded".

The dilemma that the veto is outdated but cannot be abolished brought the Panel to a number of recommendations. Two recommendations were addressed to the permanent members. The Panel urged them to limit the use of the veto to "matters where vital interests are genuinely at stake". Secondly, it asked them "in their individual capacities, to pledge themselves to refrain from the use of the veto in cases of genocide and large-scale human rights abuses". A third recommendation related to the future enlargement of the Security Council: the right of veto should not be given to any possible additional permanent members of the Council. In short, the Panel recommended not to have more veto powers and to contain the exercise of the right of veto by the current veto holders. The fourth and final recommendation of the Panel was to introduce a system of "indicative voting", as mentioned above, "to increase the accountability of the veto function". This recommendation would use the 'mobilization of shame' technique, by creating the possibility of making public that a resolution is not adopted because of the lack of the majority of nine votes, but because of the use of the veto.

This condense summary of the reflections of the Panel in two paragraphs of its report is the latest occasion that high-level consideration was given to the right of veto. It demonstrated that it is beyond reality to propose to do away with it, but also that the 1945 criticism of the veto has remained, or has even become stronger.

The next step in this 2004–2005 round of discussions and negotiations was the report 'In Larger Freedom', presented a few months later by Secretary-General Annan.[74] This report did not pay specific attention to the veto, but only considered that "the Security Council has increasingly asserted its authority and, especially since the end of the cold war, has enjoyed greater unity of purpose among its permanent members but has seen that authority questioned on the grounds that its composition is anachronistic or insufficiently representative".[75] The report fully focused on other reforms of the Security Council, in particular its enlargement, to be discussed in Chapter 4.

The report by the High-level Panel, carrying the authority of its members, and the report by Secretary-General Annan set the stage for intense months of negotiations on a variety of issues including Security Council reform. At the end of the day, these extensive preparations did not succeed in mobilizing the necessary political will to reach agreement on such a reform. The relevant paragraphs of the Assembly's 'World Summit Outcome' Resolution demonstrate that the General Assembly did no more than – again – expressing its support for a reform:[76]

74 UN Doc. A/59/2005 (21 March 2005).

75 Id., para. 165.

76 GA Res. 60/1.

> 152. We reaffirm that Member States have conferred on the Security Council primary responsibility for the maintenance of international peace and security, acting on their behalf, as provided for by the Charter.
>
> 153. We support early reform of the Security Council - an essential element of our overall effort to reform the United Nations - in order to make it more broadly representative, efficient and transparent and thus to further enhance its effectiveness and the legitimacy and implementation of its decisions. We commit ourselves to continuing our efforts to achieve a decision to this end and request the General Assembly to review progress on the reform set out above by the end of 2005.
>
> 154. We recommend that the Security Council continue to adapt its working methods so as to increase the involvement of States not members of the Council in its work, as appropriate, enhance its accountability to the membership and increase the transparency of its work.

The expression 'never waste a good crisis' (attributed to Churchill) may sometimes hold true, but not in this case, either because it simply *was* wasted or because it was not 'a good crisis'. The 2004–2005 round of negotiations, triggered by the Iraq crisis and initiated by Secretary-General Annan in September 2003, was a missed opportunity. Since then, no further high-level negotiations have taken place to amend the Charter in order to reform the Security Council. This unsuccessful round of negotiations also demonstrated that it is more realistic that such a future reform will entail the enlargement of the Council, and is unlikely to also touch upon the right of veto of the current permanent members.

4.3 *The Gordian Knot of Vetoes on Veto Reform*

Leaving aside the two above mentioned scenarios for dealing with the veto, without and with Charter amendment, there is another and even more fundamental problem. This is not so much the veto as such, but the near impossibility to change it when there are fundamental power changes in the world. The Charter rules freeze the power structures as they existed in 1945. During the last 75 years however, these power structures have changed significantly. The Charter veto arrangement has often been referred to as realistic, but it is *not* realistic in the sense that it is not open to changes in power structures. This built-in rigidity of the Charter may threaten the future of the UN.

As long as the Security Council, in order to perform its functions, needs the right of veto for the most powerful states in the world, it is essential that the list of veto holders can be updated with substantial power changes in the world. The most fundamental problem is therefore the Charter provision making it next to impossible to change the list of five who enjoy the right of veto, when one or more of the current permanent members are no longer amongst the most powerful states in the world. Changing this list requires an amendment of the Charter, in particular of Article 23(1) that explicitly mentions the current five permanent members.

According to Article 108 of the Charter, amendments to it

> come into force for all Members of the United Nations when they have been adopted by a vote of two thirds of the members of the General Assembly and ratified in accordance with their respective constitutional processes by two thirds of the Members of the United Nations, including all the permanent members of the Security Council.

Without ratification by the permanent members, the list of five cannot be changed. They can therefore 'veto' a proposed Charter amendment (technically this is not a veto, defined as the right to say 'no' to decisions on substantive matters in the Security Council). Each of the five permanent members needs to voluntarily agree to a 'demotion', a removal from the list of five. However, it is not realistic to assume that a permanent member is willing to concur in removing its right of veto when it is no longer amongst the most powerful states in the world. This is also demonstrated whenever Security Council reform is discussed in the UN: some permanent members indicate that they would agree neither to changes in the current veto rules nor to giving a right of veto to possible new permanent members.[77] Therefore, whenever Charter amendments are discussed in relation to the veto, even more important than changing the list of current permanent members in Article 23 is an amendment of Article 108, to remove the power of veto holders to block a removal of their veto. *Nemo iudex in causa sua.*

It is not surprising that there was considerable opposition in 1945 at UNCIO to the proposal that amendments to the Charter should require ratification by each of the five permanent members of the Security Council. For example, the delegate of New Zealand "reiterated the arguments against the principle of the veto in general, and insisted that it was particularly objectionable that the principle should be given permanent status by incorporating it in the

77 See eg. UN Docs. A/74/PV.33, at 17 (Russian Federation), A/74/PV.34, at 12 (US).

amending process".[78] Nevertheless, at the end of the day this opposition was unsuccessful.

In the context of Charter amendment, it is useful to discuss not only the text of Article 108 but also how this provision was applied in the 1960s, when the Charter was amended to increase the number of non-permanent members of the Security Council. As mentioned above, proposed Charter amendments enter into force in two steps. First, they must be adopted by two-thirds majority in the General Assembly, next they must be ratified by two thirds of the members of the UN, including the five permanent members. In 1963, the proposal to increase membership of the Security Council from 11 to 15, by adding four non-permanent members, was adopted in the General Assembly by 97 votes in favour, 11 against and four abstentions.[79] It is remarkable that two of the five permanent members of the Security Council, France and the Soviet Union, voted against. Two other permanent members, the UK and the US, abstained. However, the veto does not apply at this first step of amending the Charter, and the resolution was therefore adopted. Nevertheless, the prospect for entry into force of this amendment was far from positive, given that only one of the permanent members (China) voted in favour of the amendment. However, within two years the other four permanent members changed their minds and deposited their ratifications. The amendment entered into force on 31 August 1965.[80] Therefore, even during the Cold War, in a political climate not conducive to receiving the support of all five permanent members, it was proved possible to amend the Charter. The need for an enlargement of the Security Council, supported by an overwhelming majority of the members of the UN, overcame resistance by permanent members. It remains to be seen how this could be accomplished again. Very broad support amongst UN membership is a first requirement. In the current negotiations about Security Council reform, such a requirement is far from being fulfilled, as will be discussed in Chapter 4.

---

78 UNCIO, Vol. VII, p. 243.

79 GA Res. 1991(A), adopted 17 December 1963. For the voting records, see UN Doc. A/PV.1285, p.15.

80 For a discussion of the history of this first amendment of the Charter, see R. Zacklin, *The Amendment of the Constitutive Instruments of the United Nations and Specialized Agencies* (1968), pp. 121–129. The Soviet Union voted against because it insisted that China should be represented in the UN by the Beijing government before the Charter should be amended. France voted against because it wanted to postpone the amendment.

5 The Veto: Indispensable or Obsolete? Concluding Observations

Against this background of the origins and the practice of the veto, and the discussions on reform, how to evaluate the right of veto of the permanent members of the Security Council?

Not much has changed since the heated negotiations about the veto in 1945 in San Francisco. At the time, by far most states excluding the most powerful rejected it for a number of reasons. At present, this is still the case. Perhaps the only difference is that two of the five veto holders, France and the United Kingdom, have shown much restraint in using it. They did not cast their vetoes for more than 30 years, and also pledged not to use it in cases of Security Council action against genocide, crimes against humanity or war crimes (by supporting the 2015 Code of Conduct drafted by the ACT group). However, some observers could relativize this by commenting that France and the United Kingdom are now the least powerful among the five permanent members.

In 1945 as much as now, the many critics and opponents did not have much choice but to accept the veto, for different reasons. Not accepting the veto in 1945 would in effect mean 'no United Nations'. At present, it is not a question of not accepting the veto, but of the near impossibility to abolish it since each of the current veto holders must accept changes to the veto. As the High-level Panel concluded in 2004, there is "no practical way of changing the existing members' veto powers".[81]

There are good reasons to argue that, in an ideal world, there should be no veto. This was the prevailing sentiment in 1945 in San Francisco, leaving aside the views of the most powerful, perhaps excluding China. As was mentioned above,[82] China stated "that it was not unreasonable to suppose that after a time the great powers would be willing to consider elimination of the veto".[83] This time has not yet come.

In an ideal world, there should be no veto. This was also the prevailing sentiment - not counting the permanent members - during the life of the UN, particularly in many of the discussions for reform. No single Security Council member should have the possibility to prevent the Council from performing its key functions. If a state is under serious security threat and there is near universal support for the Security Council to intervene, a single permanent member should not be able to stop this. The veto is widely seen as undemocratic and unfair. It is against the fundamental rule of state equality. If one of

81 UN Doc. A/59/565, p. 68.

82 Para. 2.3.

83 UNCIO, Vol. VII, p. 244 (16 June 1945).

the permanent members, or one of its allies, would conduct policies comparable to those of Germany in the 1930s, the Security Council would not be able to act, and would not be able to protect member states against such aggressive policies peoples against the scourge of war.

However, we do not live in an ideal world, neither in 1945 nor now. In 1945, in San Francisco, the future permanent members stated that "they could not be expected, *in the present condition of the world*, to assume the obligation to act in so serious a matter as the maintenance of international peace and security in consequence of a decision in which they had not concurred".[84] Is this still true today, after 75 years, in the *current* condition of the world? In reality today, we still live in a world of sovereign and *de facto* highly unequal states, some of which are superpowers. While it is reasonable to assume that the Security Council could have acted much more often if the right of veto did not exist, it is also reasonable to assume that world peace could be endangered if the Council had acted in these cases against what one or more permanent members would perceive as their essential interests. Unity among the permanent members is key. Any reform should strengthen this, not make it weaker.[85] Abolishing the veto now seems almost as unrealistic as not accepting it in 1945. It would alienate the most powerful from the Security Council, they could use their power to bypass the Council, and the Council would risk to become powerless, a bystander rather than a key player. This is undesirable. It would preclude the Security Council from taking "effective collective measures for the prevention and removal of threats to the peace, and for the suppression of acts of aggression or other breaches of the peace".[86] Also, it would not bring about justice and a world governed by the rule of law. To recall Blaise Pascal's famous words: "la justice sans la force est impuissante" ('justice without might is powerless').[87]

As soon as the abovementioned *condition of the world* would permit, the challenge is to find a compromise solution that would, on the one hand, remove the right of veto from the decision-making of the Security Council, but that would also, on the other hand, still fully commit the most powerful to the purposes of the UN and the functions of the Security Council. In preparing

84 UNCIO, Vol. XI, p. 713, para. 9 (italics added).

85 See also Luck, op. cit. note 57, and D.L. Bosco, *Five to Rule them all* (2009).

86 UN Charter, Art. 1(1).

87 B. Pascal, *Pensées* (2008), p. 124 (original edition published posthumously in 1669 (Pascal died in 1662). This is only the first half of Pascal's proposition. The other half is: 'la force sans la justice est tyrannique' ('might without justice is tyrannical'). This second part will be discussed in Chapter 3.

such a compromise solution, the decision-making rules and practice of other international organizations may provide some inspiration. Examples are the 'consensus minus one' rule (OSCE), weighted voting (financial organizations) and qualified majority voting (European Union).[88] The most powerful should continue to have a dominant, very strong position in the decision-making of the Security Council, but no longer an individual veto, enabling them to hold the Council hostage. In principle, the most powerful should not be opposed to Security Council decisions, but this should no longer be an absolute principle. The challenge is to find a formula, according to which the Security Council would still be able to take decisions, even after it does not seem possible to secure the support of all permanent members. The mere existence of a possibility to bypass opposition of a permanent member will encourage this member to accept a compromise decision, knowing that otherwise an alternative decision might be taken that it would find less preferable.

Until the time is ripe for such a compromise solution, the veto will apply. Leaving aside fundamental criticism of the veto and accepting that it was a price to be paid for the creation of the UN, there are two in-built deficiencies in how the veto has been implemented in the Charter. As long as the veto exists, remedies may be sought for such deficiencies, no matter how difficult this is and how unlikely it may seem that an agreement can be reached. First of all, as discussed above, it is almost impossible to change the composition of group of veto holders. This is a deficiency because it must be assumed that power relations in the world are subject to change. Even though it is difficult to measure such changes in detail, it is obvious that there have been significant shifts in power during the past 75 years. However, the very *raison d'être* of the veto is the need that decisions and action by the UN to maintain or restore international peace and security are backed by (super)power. What if such (super)power is no longer fully represented in the Security Council? The rules on amendment of the Charter, effectively freezing the 1945 global power structures, are at odds with the *raison d'être* of the veto.

A second deficiency of the current veto rules is that they do not offer a 'fall back scenario' when the five permanent members fail to agree in cases in which it is beyond any doubt that the Security Council should act. It is true that the General Assembly may step in and act as a substitute. This is what has happened at times, in particular during the Cold War (the Uniting for Peace Resolution; peacekeeping) but also in recent years.[89] However, there are clear

88 These and other examples are discussed in H.G. Schermers & N.M. Blokker, *International Institutional Law* (6th ed. 2018), Chapter Six.

89 See further Chapter 5.

political and legal limitations to an extensive subsidiary role of the General Assembly. In addition, organizations outside the UN may step in, such as the Organization on the Prohibition of Chemical Weapons when it declared its Secretariat competent to identify "those who were the perpetrators, organizers, sponsors or otherwise involved" in the use of chemical weapons.[90] The only remaining alternative is unilateral action, by states individually or in smaller groupings or organizations such as NATO. However, such unilateral action undermines the UN collective security system and the very reason why the UN was created in the first place. Therefore, for good reasons Secretary-General Annan took his 'fork in the road' initiative in September 2003. He could not be blamed for 'wasting a good crisis'. This is what a good Secretary-General could and should do under the circumstances. But there is also not much more that he can do. Subsequently it is for the member states to forge an agreement on how to deal with unilateralism and threats to the UN, and the member states largely failed to do so in 2005.

The above mentioned two deficiencies can only be remedied by Charter amendments that would remove the 'veto' of the permanent members in Article 108 and that would provide better 'fall back options' in cases of Security Council inaction than currently exist.

As analyzed in this Chapter, the veto of the permanent members was a *conditio sine qua non* for having the United Nations, a world organization that should have the teeth that its predecessor lacked. The Security Council was created as a political organ with strong enforcement powers. However, is the exercise of such powers completely governed by (super) power politics, or also by law (and if so, by what rules of law)? In particular during the last three decades, the Security Council has faced fundamental rule of law questions. For example, is it within the discretion of the Security Council to introduce individual sanctions without any remedial mechanism? Is it within its full discretion to refer the situations in Darfur and in Libya to the International Criminal Court, but not the situation in Syria? The next chapter will show how rule of law issues concerning the Security Council were debated in the 1945 San Francisco conference, how they are reflected in the Charter, and how they were addressed during the last few decades.

90 OPCW Conference Decision C-SS-4/Dec.3, par. 19, adopted by 82 in favour, 24 against (27 June 2018).

CHAPTER 3

The Security Council, the Rule of Power and the Rule of Law

1 Introduction

The previous chapter has discussed the veto of the permanent members. This chapter will focus on another topic that is essential when evaluating the Security Council at 75: the rule of power and the rule of law. Much of the criticism of the Security Council concerns the substance of its decisions or the absence of any decisions. Why did it introduce individual sanctions without any remedies? Why did it refer the situations in Darfur and in Libya to the International Criminal Court, but not the situations in Syria or in Myanmar (Rohingya crisis)? Why did it authorize an armed intervention in Libya in 2011 but not in Syria? These and many other examples boil down to the question: what prompts the Security Council (not) to act? The answer to this question can usually be found in the arena of power politics. To a large extent this is for good reasons. After all, the Security Council *is* a political organ. It was deliberately created as such. The founders of the United Nations wanted a new world organization backed by power, epitomized in permanent Security Council membership of the principal allied powers and their right of veto. However, is this a conclusive answer? At the national level, it is long required that governments operate within the law and cannot simply take all their decisions randomly, arbitrarily. If this is required at the national level, why not at the international level? Long ago, the international order was often characterized as an anarchical society, governed by the law of the jungle. However, globalization and interdependence called for international cooperation and the creation of international organizations. When powers are attributed to international organizations, why should such powers no longer be subjected to the rule of law checks and balances required at the national level? If large discretionary powers are given to the Security Council, to save succeeding generations from the scourge of war, should 'the rule of power' or the rule of law govern the exercise of those powers?

These are fundamental questions, and the present chapter will not provide any definite answers. Within the confines of this book it aims to examine how 'rule of power versus rule of law' questions were addressed in the 1945 negotiations for the UN Charter and subsequently in practice.

 | DOI:10.1163/9789004443921_005

Chapter 2 discussed the right of veto and demonstrated how this was instrumental in empowering the Security Council and the United Nations, based on the experience of the League of Nations lacking the necessary teeth. It ended by quoting Pascal: "la justice sans la force est impuissante" ('justice without might is powerless'). But this is only the first half of Pascal's proposition. The other half is: "la force sans la justice est tyrannique" ('might without justice is tyrannical').[1] The drafters of the Charter, including the future permanent members of the Security Council, fully subscribed to this view. Paul-Boncour, the head of the French delegation to the UNCIO conference, quoted this proposition by Pascal in his statement during the closing plenary session of UNCIO, 26 June 1945.[2] On the same occasion, US President Truman stated, "[b]y their own example the strong nations of the world should lead the way to international justice. That principle of justice is the foundation stone of this Charter".[3] However, do these words really apply to the Security Council as well? Is the Council not first and foremost an instrument of pure power? Is it not essentially *legibus solutus*, unbound by law? Or is Security Council power an instrument to bring about justice? Is the Security Council ultimately governed by the rule of power, or by the rule of law?

Below, paragraph 2 will start by briefly discussing the notion of the rule of law. Following, paragraph 3 will demonstrate that the five most powerful states in 1945, although they were given a very special position in the Security Council, do not have unbridled powers. Their *marge de manoeuvre* in the Security Council is contained by the UN Charter in five ways. In order to fully understand the constitutional Charter framework for such containment, paragraph 4 will highlight the most relevant parts of the 1945 UNCIO negotiations. It will show that the wish to create the UN as a much more powerful organization than its predecessor prevailed, even though the negotiators were also convinced that the exercise by the UN of its powers should serve the interests of justice, not merely the pure political self-interest of the most powerful (as is also illustrated by the statements of Paul-Boncour and Truman quoted above). Paragraph 5 will look back at relevant Security Council practice during its 75 years of existence, analyzing both thematic debates devoted to the rule of law and specific measures in the field of international criminal justice and individual sanctions. Paragraph 6 will offer some concluding observations.

---

1 B. Pascal, *Pensées* (2008), p. 124 (original edition published posthumously in 1669 (Pascal died in 1662). This second part of Pascal's famous proposition may also be recognized in what was written by Locke some years later, in 1690: "wherever law ends, tyranny begins".

2 UNCIO, Vol. I, p. 668.

3 UNCIO, Vol. I, p. 682.

2 The Notion Rule of Law

'The rule of law' is a somewhat paradoxical notion. In international relations, it is sometimes used as a catch-all expression for a wide variety of ideas, values, principles and rules.[4] At the national level, it will be difficult to find a government claiming that it does not observe or promote the rule of law. The concept suffers from a certain indeterminacy.[5] At the same time, it is universally perceived as something good, helped by the fact that it has a certain indeterminacy.[6] Even more, it is generally seen as something fundamental, in particular relating to the way in which governmental authority is exercised. This explains why key elements of the concept of the rule of law trace back to ancient writings (Aristotle's "it is better for the law to rule than one of the citizens") and constitutional documents (Magna Carta), long before the arrival of the sovereign state. The English term 'rule of law' is therefore better than many of its equivalents in other languages, which are limited to the exercise of authority by the state: *Rechtsstaatlichkeit* in German, *l'État de droit* in French, etc.[7]

Against this background, it is hardly surprising that there is no single definition of the rule of law. The standardization that has resulted in a worldwide similar definition of weights, measures and many other indicators, in order to facilitate comparison, trading and globalization, has not yet been developed to the same degree for the concept of the rule of law. While there are definitions of the state and of an international organization in international law on which there is a fair amount of consensus, this is lacking for the notion of the rule of law. Existing definitions vary widely, ranging from very simple to utterly complex. An example of a rather simple definition is the following: "[i]n essence, the rule of law means that citizens and those who govern them should obey the law".[8] While this is clear and simple, a disadvantage is that it would be difficult

---

4 See also R. Higgins, 'The Rule of Law: Some Skeptical Thoughts', in R. Higgins, *Themes and Theories: Selected Essays, Speeches and Writings in International Law* (2009), pp. 1330–1339 (in particular at pp. 1334–1335).

5 See e.g. B. Tamanaha, *On the Rule of Law. History, Politics, Theory* (2004), p. 4: the rule of law "stands in the peculiar state of being *the* preeminent legitimating political ideal in the world today, without agreement upon precisely what it means".

6 See also the Final Report and Recommendations from the Austrian Initiative, *The UN Security Council and the Rule of Law*, prepared by S. Chesterman (2008), p. 3: "Such a high degree of consensus on the virtues of the rule of law is possible in part because of relative vagueness as to its meaning".

7 Other examples: *Estado de Derecho* (Spanish), *Stato di diritto* (Italian), *rechtsstaat* (Dutch), *Estado de direito* (Portugese), *rätstaten* (Swedish).

8 Hiil/Raoul Wallenberg Institute, *Rule of Law – A Guide for Politicians* (2012), p. 7.

to conclude that, solely on this basis, a regime such as that of the Nazis did not respect the rule of law. A more complex and substantive definition was given by UN Secretary-General Annan:[9]

> The 'rule of law' [...] refers to a principle of governance in which all persons, institutions and entities, public and private, including the State itself, are accountable to laws that are publicly promulgated, equally enforced and independently adjudicated, and which are consistent with international human rights norms and standards. It requires, as well, measures to ensure adherence to the principles of supremacy of law, equality before the law, accountability to the law, fairness in the application of the law, separation of powers, participation in decision-making, legal certainty, avoidance of arbitrariness and procedural and legal transparency.

These two examples also illustrate the difference between what is often referred to as 'thin' and 'thick' definitions of the rule of law. The former are narrower and cover formal and procedural rules, while the latter also include substantive rules, in particular fundamental human rights.[10]

Furthermore, the rule of law can be defined in either a negative or a positive way. It may be defined in a negative way by saying what it is not or, more precisely, by referring to its opposite: the rule of power.[11] The meaning of 'the rule of power' is more or less clear. It refers to reign by the whims of those in power, based on the arbitrary, and robust control by force. The supremacy of power rather than the supremacy of the law.

Defining the rule of law in a positive way is more difficult. The expression 'rule of law' is usually attributed to A.V. Dicey, an English law professor at Oxford who wrote about it in 1885.[12] According to Dicey, the rule of law has three

---

9 UN Doc. S/2004/616 (23 August 2004), p. 4.

10 WJP Rule of Law Index 2020, p. 9 (available at https://worldjusticeproject.org/sites/default/files/documents/WJP-ROLI-2020-Online_0.pdf). See also Council of Europe, European Commission for Democracy through Law (Venice Commission), Report on the Rule of Law (2011).

11 As Watts wrote: "[t]he rule of law is the counterweight to political power" (A. Watts, 'The International Rule of Law', 36 *German Yearbook of International Law* (1993), pp. 15–45, at p. 23).

12 In his book *An Introduction to the Study of the Law of the Constitution* (first published in 1885, the latest (8th) edition published in 1915). It is therefore fitting that a British permanent representative to the UN, Sir Mark Lyall Grant, referred to him in one of the rule of law debates in the Security Council. He did so in the following way: "[t]he rule of law is a term that was coined by the great British constitutionalist A.V. Dicey in the nineteenth century. It is a concept that lies at the heart of the unwritten Constitution of the United

meanings.[13] Firstly, it refers essentially to the *nullum crimen sine lege* principle (the principle of legality): someone cannot be punished for an act not prohibited by law before it was committed. Secondly, no one is above the law, and everyone is subject to the jurisdiction of the ordinary tribunals. The third meaning specifically relates to English law: the general principles of the constitution are the result of judicial decisions. For the purpose of this book, the second meaning is most relevant, much more than the other two. The first meaning is limited to criminal law; the third applies only to English law. However, the substance covered by this notion of the rule of law has much deeper roots and can be found in well-known charters and other fundamental constitutional texts. Most famous are Magna Carta (1215), the Constitution of the United States (1787) and the American Bill of Rights (the first ten amendments to the US Constitution, 1791), and the French *Déclaration des Droits de l'Homme et du Citoyen* (1789).

Dicey published the book in which he introduced the notion of the rule of law in 1885. Whereas the three key meanings were already well-known long before, in the course of time this general notion has been elaborated in more detailed rules of national and international law. The substance of such more detailed rules may to some extent vary from country to country, and opinions may diverge about what detailed rules should and should not be part of the rule of law. Whereas there is universal adherence to the idea of rule of law as such, there is no universally accepted list of more specific standards to make it more operational.

Nevertheless, efforts have been made to make the concept of the rule of law more concrete, to define its distinguishing features, in order to be able to compare and evaluate countries. For example, there is a 'Rule of Law Index', prepared by the World Justice Project, an NGO that is "working to advance the rule of law worldwide".[14] This Index is an annual publication measuring the rule of law situation in individual countries. For the purpose of this Index, the rule of law includes four universal principles: accountability, just laws, open government and accessible and impartial dispute resolution.[15] Rankings are based on eight factors: constraints on government powers, absence of corruption, open government, fundamental rights, order and security, regulatory enforcement,

---

Kingdom. Our reforming ancestors recognized that the fairness inherent in the rule of law was preferable to the rule of man" (UN Doc. S/PV.6705 (19 January 2012), p.10).

13 The following references to Dicey are taken from T. Bingham, *The Rule of Law* (2010), pp. 3–4.

14 See https://worldjusticeproject.org/about-us.

15 WJP Rule of Law Index 2020, p. 9 ff. (available at https://worldjusticeproject.org/sites/default/files/documents/WJP-ROLI-2020-Online_0.pdf).

civil justice and criminal justice.[16] On the basis of these factors, the 2020 Index lists 128 countries.[17]

Furthermore, in order to be able to better grasp the meaning of the rule of law, Bingham suggested and explained a list of eight principles in his 2010 authoritative book:[18]

1. The law must be accessible and so far as possible intelligible, clear and predictable.
2. Questions of legal right and liability should ordinarily be resolved by application of the law and not the exercise of discretion.
3. The laws of the land should apply equally to all, save to the extent that objective differences justify differentiation.
4. Ministers and public officers at all levels must exercise the powers conferred on them in good faith, fairly, for the purpose for which the powers were conferred, without exceeding the limits of such powers and not unreasonably.
5. The law must afford adequate protection of fundamental human rights.
6. Means must be provided for resolving, without prohibitive cost or inordinate delay, bona fide civil disputes which the parties themselves are unable to resolve.
7. Adjudicative procedures provided by the state should be fair.
8. The rule of law requires compliance by the state with its obligations in international law as in national law.

This list is neither fully endorsed by other writers nor by states, and Bingham himself does not claim this.[19] However, the eight principles at least provide more clarity about the specific meaning of the notion of the rule of law. They essentially guide the state in what it should do to comply with the rule of law. Bingham does not specifically apply his principles to international organizations such as the United Nations or the European Union. Where international law is mentioned, he focuses on what states should do with regard to their international obligations. Principle 8 declares what may be obvious in theory but

16 Id, p. 5. In addition to these eight factors, there are 44 sub-factors. It is admitted in this report that the rule of law is "notoriously difficult to define and measure" (id., at p. 9).

17 The first four on the list are Scandinavian countries (Denmark, Norway, Finland, Sweden), the last four are Egypt, the Democratic Republic of Congo, Cambodia and Venezuela. The five permanent members of the Security Council are ranked as follows: China (88), France (20), Russian Federation (94), United Kingdom (13), United States (21) (see id., pp. 6–7).

18 Bingham, op. cit. note 13, pp. 37–129. Mainly drawing on Bingham's definition, the Venice Commission listed six "necessary elements of the rule of law" (op. cit. note 10, pp. 10–13).

19 Id., at p. 37: "[t]here is no magic about these. Others would come up with different principles, or would express these principles differently".

less so in practice: states must comply with their international law obligations just as they must do with their obligations under domestic law.

This list of eight principles also makes it easier to see why the notion of the rule of law is not applicable at the international level in entirely the same way as at the national level.[20] This is particularly true for principles 6 and 7. If states are unable to resolve a dispute, they do not have access to a court that automatically has jurisdiction to resolve this. Bingham also notes this. In his view, compulsory jurisdiction of the International Court of Justice is necessary "if the rule of law is to become truly effective in this area".[21] Therefore, where these eight principles are not fully *lex lata* in the international legal order, they may be *lex ferenda*, signposts for its progressive development.

∴

At the international level, the notion of the rule of law as such did not appear in the League of Nations Covenant. It is not mentioned in the UN Charter either, although a number of Charter provisions cover some of the substance of what is often understood to be part of the rule of law.[22] For example, most generally, the second and third paragraph of the Charter's Preamble:

> We the peoples of the United Nations determined
>
> [...]
>
> to reaffirm faith in fundamental human rights, in the dignity and worth of the human person, in the equal rights of men and women and of nations large and small, and
>
> to establish conditions under which justice and respect for the obligations arising from treaties and other sources of international law can be maintained.

The representative of Ireland referred in 2018 in the Security Council to the latter paragraph of the Preamble of the Charter and subsequently stated:[23]

20 As Higgins wrote: "It is clear that the domestic rule of law model does not easily transpose to international relations in the world we live in. That seems to be an unavoidable reality" (op. cit. note 4, p. 1334).

21 Bingham, op. cit. note 13, p. 128.

22 See further B. Fassbender, 'What's in a Name? The International Rule of Law and the United Nations Charter', 17 *Chinese Journal of International Law* (2018), pp. 761–797, in particular pp. 763–772.

23 S/PV.8262 (17 May 2018), p. 45. Fundamental human rights are mentioned in the second paragraph of the Preamble of the Charter. The distinction between rule of law and rule by law is also made in the WJP Rule of Law Index 2020, op. cit. note 15, at p. 9: "a system of

> The Charter, the foundation stone of the Organization, recognizes that the rule of law must be at the heart of our shared efforts to create a peaceful world. It is important that as we strive collectively to abide by the Charter of the United Nations, we remain vigilant in differentiating between the rule of law and rule by law. The difference is human rights, the universal freedoms and rights of individuals. Rule by law can negate those rights, whereas the rule of law operationalizes them, thereby ensuring their promotion and protection in peace or war.

Although the Charter does not mention the rule of law as such, occasional references to it can be found in the reports of the 1945 UN Conference on International Organization, which resulted in the signing of the UN Charter. The Minister of Foreign Affairs of the Republic of China, T.V. Soong, referred to the notion during the first plenary session of the conference, on 26 April 1945:[24]

> Let us face hard facts. A long effort is required of all of us before an effective rule of law is established in world affairs. We in China know it by bitter experience. The rule of law was to have been defended by the old League of Nations; but it was disregarded, as we learned to our cost, despite the most solemn covenants entered into by would-be defaulters.
>
> [...]
>
> If there is any message that my country, which has been one of the principal victims of aggression and the earliest victim, wishes to give to this Conference, it is that we must not hesitate to delegate a part of our sovereignty to the new international organization in the interests of collective security. We must all be ready to make some sacrifices in order to achieve our common purpose. Among nations, no less than among individuals, we must forthwith accept the concept of liberty under law.

One day later, Deputy Prime Minister of Australia Francis Forde in his opening statement proposed that the UN Charter could "declare that the organization should exert its powers for the promotion of justice and the rule of law".[25] Later

---

law that fails to respect core human rights guaranteed under international law is at best "rule by law" and does not deserve to be called a rule of law system".

24 UNCIO, Vol. I, pp. 129–130. Later in the conference, China referred to its "absorbing interest in the promotion of the rule of law in international relations" (UNCIO, Vol. VIII, pp. 204–205).

25 Id., p. 174. Later in the conference, Australia proposed to refer to the rule of law in the context of one of the purposes of the UN, to develop friendly relations (Art. 1(2) of the Charter), see UNCIO, Vol. VI, p. 535.

in the conference, Chile proposed to include a principle in the Charter, according to which "[o]nly the International Community, by means of its various organizations, may employ force in order to prevent or repel aggression and maintain the rule of law".[26] The Dominican Republic stated, "to nations sincerely and profoundly interested, as is the Dominican Republic, in the maintenance of the rule of law in relations among States, it is evident that the general organization in question must have at its disposal armed forces to defend the existence of the international juridical order".[27] A final example is the statement by the alternate chairman of the delegation of Uruguay, as acting chair of the UNCIO committee negotiating the draft articles on the pacific settlement of disputes (Chapter VI of the Charter), who "called for faith in the spirit of conciliation among large and small powers, and for faith in the progress of the rule of law and justice in the years to come".[28]

Despite these numerous references to the rule of law during the San Francisco conference, this notion does not appear in the text of the Charter of the United Nations. In the context of the UN, it was first introduced in the 1948 Universal Declaration of Human Rights, in the third paragraph of the preamble: "[w]hereas it is essential, if man is not to be compelled to have recourse, as a last resort, to rebellion against tyranny and oppression, that human rights should be protected by the rule of law".[29] It is clear that the rule of law has a specific meaning in this context: human rights need a protective legal context. Without this, they cannot perform their function and man may be "compelled to have recourse, as a last resort, to rebellion against tyranny and oppression". The word 'tyranny' (in French: 'la tyrannie') reminds us of the second part of Pascal's proposition quoted in the beginning of this chapter: "la force sans la justice est tyrannique" ('might without justice is tyrannical').

The notion of the rule of law has not been defined by the General Assembly, neither in the Universal Declaration nor later when, for example, it adopted its Declaration on the Rule of Law in 2012.[30] The Security Council has not defined

26 UNCIO, Vol. III, p. 293.

27 Id., p. 568.

28 UNCIO, Vol. XII, p. 156.

29 GA Res. 217(III), Part A. In the General Assembly, a separate vote took place on each of the paragraphs of the preamble and on each of the articles of the Declaration. The third paragraph of the preamble (with the reference to the rule of law) was adopted unanimously (UN Doc. A/PV.183, p. 932). The Declaration as a whole was adopted by 48 votes in favour, with 8 abstentions (Byelorussian Soviet Socialist Republic, Czechoslovakia, Poland, Saudi Arabia, Ukrainian Soviet Socialist Republic, Union of South Africa, Union of Soviet Socialist Republics, Yugoslavia), see UN Doc. A/PV.183, p. 933.

30 GA Res. 67/1. Drafts of this Declaration included the definition of rule of law provided by Secretary-General Annan in 2004 (UN Doc. S/2004/616, p. 4), but "after considerable

it either, even though it devoted a number of thematic debates to the rule of law, as will be discussed in paragraph 5. It was Secretary-General Annan who in 2004 provided the definition quoted above.[31] In this definition, the rule of law is perceived as a principle of governance, applying to anyone involved in governance, both at the national and at the international level. It is therefore relevant for the United Nations. It is highly relevant for the Security Council, particularly in times when the Council is able to act, as was often the case in the 1990s.

For the purpose of this book the focus will be on the rule of law as a principle of governance for the Security Council. Above all, it is about more formal ('thin') questions such as whether the Security Council operates within a legal framework and whether it is subject to international law. If this is accepted, more detailed, substantive ('thick') questions arise: to what extent the Security Council is bound by certain specific rules of international law, for example those deriving from the fields of human rights or international humanitarian law.

These 'thin' and 'thick' questions about the rule of law are not unique for the Security Council. To a certain extent, they are relevant for all organs of international organizations that perform governance functions. This was recognized by the UN General Assembly when it stated in 2012 that the rule of law applies to international organizations and that "respect for and promotion of the rule of law and justice should guide all of their activities and accord predictability and legitimacy to their actions".[32] Some constitutions of international organizations explicitly refer to the rule of law: NATO and the Council of Europe are examples.[33] These references essentially concern the rule of law at the national level, within the member states. However, if it is required that governmental authority should be exercised in accordance with the rule of law at the national level, why should this requirement lapse when some governance powers are attributed to international organizations, resulting in a 'rule of law deficit'?

---

negotiations, the Secretary-General's definition was pared down, with core elements remaining" (see Fassbender, op. cit. note 22, p. 779 (footnote 50), quoting E. Selous).

31 In a report entitled 'The rule of law and transitional justice in conflict and post-conflict societies' (UN Doc. S/2004/616 (23 August 2004), p. 4).

32 GA Res. 67/1, para. 2.

33 North Atlantic Treaty, Preamble ("The Parties to this Treaty [...] are determined to safeguard the freedom, common heritage and civilisation of their peoples, founded on the principles of democracy, individual liberty and the rule of law"); Statute of the Council of Europe, Preamble and Art. 3 ("Every member of the Council of Europe must accept the principles of the rule of law and of the enjoyment by all persons within its jurisdiction of human rights and fundamental freedoms [...]").

So far, this question has mostly emerged in the context of international organizations upon which substantial powers have been conferred, in particular the European Union and the United Nations.[34] Not much has been written on this question more in general. While the notions *Rechtsstaat* and *État de droit* are well established, they do not yet have a sister notion called *Internationale Rechtsorganisation* or *organisation internationale de droit*. The advantage of the English expression 'rule of law' is that it transcends the level of the state; it applies to any exercise of governmental (or governance) powers.

Nevertheless, even though the above-mentioned 'thin' and 'thick' questions about the rule of law are relevant for all organs of international organizations that perform governance functions, their relevance for the Security Council is unique because it is an organ with unique powers. Trenchant questions about how these powers are exercised therefore pose themselves particularly in relation to this UN organ. Pascal's proposition is relevant here.

3 Five Ways of Containing the Power of the Permanent Members

While the right of veto clearly puts the five permanent members in a dominant, very powerful position, this should not be overstated. The Security Council is not simply an instrument of permanent member power politics. If we compare the position of the permanent members in the United Nations to that of the most powerful members of a primitive, anarchical society (in an '*Ur* situation'), we may use Thucydides' most well-known observation as an analytical starting point: "the strong do what they can and the weak suffer what they must".[35] In such a comparison, the differences are clear. It may help to relativize the dominant position of the permanent members in the Security

34 The notion rule of law was not mentioned in the three original European Community treaties (concluded in the same postwar years in which NATO and the Council of Europe were established, whose constitutions do refer to the rule of law). The European Court of Justice mentioned it first in 1986, when it stated in *Les Verts* (Case 294/83, ECR 1986, p. 1365, para. 23) that "the European Economic Community is a Community based on the rule of law, inasmuch as neither its Member States nor its institutions can avoid a review of the question whether the measures adopted by them are in conformity with the basic constitutional charter, the Treaty". The 2007 Treaty on European Union refers to the rule of law as a "value" and as a "principle", in the Preamble and in Arts. 2 and 21.

35 Thucydides, *The History of the Peloponnesian War* (431 BC), The Fifth Book, Chapter XVII (English translation by R. Crawley, available at http://classics.mit.edu/Thucydides/pelopwar.5.fifth.html).

Council, because it demonstrates that they cannot just "do what they can". The UN Charter contains their power in five ways, as will now be analyzed.

3.1 *Right of Veto ('I Forbid'), No Right of Iubeo ('I Order')*

Firstly, the right of veto only enables permanent members to do what veto means in Latin: 'I forbid' or 'I reject'. It is of a *negative* nature, allowing the permanent members to block decision-making in the Council. The permanent members do not have the opposite: the right of iubeo ('I order'), the individual, *positive* power to order something, to make the Security Council act. If a permanent member wants the Security Council to do something, it needs the support of at least eight other Council members (and no veto from another permanent member). This is no sinecure. An individual permanent member may put pressure on the other members of the Council, but if it does not receive the necessary support, it cannot impose its will on the Security Council.

3.2 *Bound by Charter Obligations*

Secondly, also *outside* the Security Council the permanent members cannot just "do what they can". They are bound by the same rules of the Charter as all other members of the UN. In this respect, the principle of sovereign equality, mentioned as first principle in Article 2 of the UN Charter, is fully applicable. The prohibition to refrain from the threat or use of force, just like other Charter obligations, applies equally to all UN member states. Therefore: while the permanent members have a privileged position in the decision-making process of the Council and are certainly strong, they cannot just "do what they can".

3.3 *Wartime Superpower Cooperation, Modified not Merely Codified by the Charter*

Putting the five principal allied powers in a privileged position in the Security Council was a reflection of political life in 1945. These were the most powerful states at the time. Being 'united nations' against Germany, Italy and Japan was essential to end the Second World War. The dominant position of these five states was frozen in the composition and decision-making rules of the Security Council. Their presence gave this body the political leverage necessary for the maintenance of international peace and security: just as the united allied powers could beat the aggressors of the Second World War, they should also beat future aggressors. Their institutionalized position in the Security Council should provide an essential guarantee that the new world organization would have the necessary teeth and could withstand any future threats to the peace, breaches of the peace and acts of aggression (except when such threats, breaches or acts would come from one or more of the permanent members themselves).

At the same time, the Charter has not simply *codified* (or 'institutionalized') wartime cooperation amongst the Allied Powers. 'P5' is not a principal organ of the UN; the Security Council is not composed of these five states only. The Charter has also *modified* this wartime cooperation in the structure of the Security Council by adding six other members of the UN.[36] The idea of composing the Security Council exclusively of the five most powerful states has not been seriously considered during the UN Charter negotiations. Nevertheless, the fact that this is not merely a theoretical possibility was demonstrated 25 years earlier. The main draft of the League of Nations Covenant (the Hurst-Miller Draft) proposed to compose the League Council only of the five main powers at the time (the US, the British Empire, France, Italy and Japan). However, this proposal was strongly criticized and rejected by the smaller and neutral states; in their view, this would be "no more than a repetition of the Holy Alliance of 1815".[37] It was finally agreed that the League Council would have four non-permanent members.

The position of the non-permanent members is certainly less prominent than that of the permanent five: they lack the right of veto and are members for two years only (and may not be immediately re-elected). However, without some of their support the Security Council cannot act. Decisions originally required seven affirmative votes, therefore at least two non-permanent members needed to support a draft decision that also had the support of the permanent members. This is how wartime cooperation was to be continued, *modified* not merely *codified*, embedded in the Security Council, in the United Nations. This in itself was a first step on the path from pure rule of power to rule of law.

36 The distinction between codification and modification is taken from T. Koopmans, 'De rol van de wetgever' ('The role of the legislator'), published in H.C.F. Schoordijk e.a. (eds.), *Honderd jaar rechtsleven – De Nederlandse Juristen-Vereniging 1870–1970* (1970), pp. 221–235 (in particular pp. 222–223). In this influential contribution, Koopmans analyzes how the role of the legislator during the past 100 years had developed from adapting the law to changes in society (*codificatie*) to actively contributing to reforms in society by changing the law (*modificatie*). This article is available online at https://openaccess.leidenuniv.nl/bitstream/handle/1887/22745/T_Koopmans-De_rol_van_de_wetgever.pdf?sequence=1.

37 F.P. Walters, *A History of the League of Nations* (1952), pp. 45–46. For further details, see D. Hunter Miller, *The Drafting of the Covenant* (1928), Vol. One, pp. 137–163, and Vol. Two, pp. 229–232, pp. 257–262, pp. 301–304, pp. 327–328, pp. 336–338.

3.4 *The Security Council Does Not Have Unlimited Powers*

Focusing now on the Security Council as an organ, it is obvious that it is not a body outside the framework of international law. It is part and parcel of the United Nations, established by a treaty ratified by all members of the UN. It does not have unlimited powers, but only those attributed to it in the Charter. As the Australian Minister of Navy Makin, the first President of the Security Council, stated in his opening words when the Council met for the first time, on 17 January 1946 in London: "[o]ur work must be based on the Charter. We are not permitted to go beyond it, but we shall not fail to exercise to the full the very great powers which have been given to this Council".[38]

Being an organ of an international organization, the Security Council is subject to the principle of speciality. As the International Court of Justice stated in 1996, "international organizations are subjects of international law which do not, unlike States, possess a general competence. International organizations are governed by the 'principle of speciality', that is to say, they are invested by the States which create them with powers, the limits of which are a function of the common interests whose promotion those States entrust to them".[39]

While this is all true, it must be admitted that the powers attributed to the Security Council are very broad. For example, it is for the Security Council itself to determine whether there is a threat to the peace, breach of the peace or act of aggression. If such a determination is made, it is for the Council to decide what measures should be taken, involving or not involving the use of armed force. Moreover, if there is any doubt about whether any proposed measures are within the scope of the Council's powers, it is "in the first place at least" for the Council itself to decide about the scope of its powers.[40] Practice has illustrated that, on this basis, the Council has considerable leeway to perform its functions. Examples are the creation of UN peacekeeping forces and of ad hoc criminal tribunals.[41]

---

38 SCOR No. 1, at 5. These words to some extent echo what the Permanent Court of International Justice stated in its 1927 Advisory Opinion on the jurisdiction of the European Commission of the Danube: "As the European Commission is not a State, but an international institution with a special purpose, it only has the functions bestowed upon it by the Definitive Statute with a view to the fulfilment of that purpose, but it has power to exercise these functions to their full extent, in so far as the Statute does not impose restrictions upon it" (PCIJ, Series B.-No. 14 (8 December 1927), p. 64).

39 *Legality of the Use by a State of Nuclear Weapons in Armed Conflict*, Advisory Opinion, ICJ Rep. 1996, p. 66 (quotation at p. 78).

40 See *Certain Expenses of the United Nations (Article 17, paragraph 2 of the Charter)*, Advisory Opinion, ICJ Rep. 1962, p. 151 (quotation at p. 168).

41 With respect to the creation of peacekeeping forces, see *Certain Expenses of the United Nations (Article 17, paragraph 2 of the Charter)*, Advisory Opinion, ICJ Rep. 1962, p. 151,

However, notwithstanding the broad scope of these powers and the Council's prerogative to interpret them, they are not unlimited. As paragraph 3.5 will show, whenever it is questioned whether the Security Council has acted within the confines of its attributed powers, a lack of support for the measures it has taken, or adaptations, is often the result. This compels the Council to respect the principle of speciality. This practice is yet another illustration of how the power of the permanent members is contained.

3.5 *The Security Council is Embedded in the United Nations Organization*

Finally, the power of the permanent members, exercised within the Security Council, is also contained because the Council is part of the UN. As discussed in Chapter 1, the Security Council is not self-standing. It is not a treaty body or treaty organ, such as the ICC's Assembly of States Parties or the Conference of the Parties of the Climate Change Convention. It is embedded in the United Nations organization.

While the Charter does not establish something like a balance of power, it attributes powers to other UN organs that are relevant for the role of the Security Council and that to some extent control the exercise of its powers.

3.5.1 The General Assembly

First of all, the General Assembly shares with the Security Council the responsibility for the maintenance of peace and security. Even though there is a clear hierarchy because the Security Council's responsibility in this field is "primary",[42] the General Assembly "may discuss any questions relating to the maintenance of international peace and security".[43] However, "[a]ny such question on which action is necessary shall be referred to the Security Council by the General Assembly either before or after discussion".[44] The International Court of Justice has stated that – in this context – "action"

p. 167: "Moreover, an argument which insists that all measures taken for the maintenance of international peace and security must be financed through agreements concluded under Article 43, would seem to exclude the possibility that the Security Council might act under some other Article of the Charter. The Court cannot accept so limited a view of the powers of the Security Council under the Charter. It cannot be said that the Charter has left the Security Council impotent in the face of an emergency situation when agreements under Article 43 have not been concluded".

42 UN Charter, Art. 24(1).

43 UN Charter, Art. 11(2).

44 Id.

means "coercive or enforcement action", taken under Chapter VII of the Charter:[45]

> The word "action" must mean such action as is solely within the province of the Security Council. It cannot refer to recommendations which the Security Council might make, as for instance under Article 38, because the General Assembly under Article 11 has a comparable power. The 'action' which is solely within the province of the Security Council is that which is indicated by the title of Chapter VII of the Charter, namely "Action with respect to threats to the peace, breaches of the peace, and acts of aggression".

This division of responsibilities between the Security Council and the General Assembly is one of the important differences between the United Nations and the League of Nations. Under the League Covenant, the powers of the Council and those of the Assembly were literally the same: each of these organs "may deal at its meetings with any matter within the sphere of action of the League or affecting the peace of the world".[46] The UN Charter makes it abundantly clear that the founders of the new world organization wanted to create a successor to the League with more teeth, and that these teeth were given to the Security Council. From a comparative institutional perspective this is remarkable. In many international organizations, the supreme powers of an organization are given to the plenary organ of the organization, since all members should have a say in the most important decisions of the organization. However, when the UN was created, a different consideration prevailed: the conviction that the organization should be able to take swift enforcement action backed by the most powerful.

Even though within the UN the Security Council has supreme powers in matters of peace and security, these powers are not exclusive.[47] The General Assembly also has a role to play, which could affect the functioning of the Council. The General Assembly has been assertive in performing this role, in

45 *Certain Expenses of the United Nations (Article 17, paragraph 2 of the Charter)*, Advisory Opinion, ICJ Rep. 1962, p. 151 (quotations at pp. 164–165). To support this interpretation, the Court observes that "[t]he practice of the Organization throughout its history bears out the foregoing elucidation of the term 'action' in the last sentence of Article 11, paragraph 2" (id.).

46 League of Nations Covenant, Arts. 3 and 4.

47 As the ICJ stated, referring to Art. 24 of the Charter: "[t]he responsibility conferred is "primary", not exclusive" (*Certain Expenses of the United Nations (Article 17, paragraph 2 of the Charter)*, Advisory Opinion, ICJ Rep. 1962, at p. 163).

particular during the Cold War. In addition, there is another dimension to the Council's relationship with the Assembly, one where a light hierarchy exists the other way around. There is some accountability of the Security Council towards the General Assembly because it must submit annual – and, when necessary, special – reports to the GA.[48] This is a minimal but fair *quid pro quo*, in an arrangement whereby sovereign states give a fundamental power to a supranational body in which most of them are not represented. The Charter explicitly states that the Security Council acts on behalf of the member states.[49] A minimum that these members could expect in return is reporting on how the arrangement is implemented, allowing them to give some form of 'feedback'.

3.5.2 The Secretariat

Another UN principal organ is also essential for the functioning of the Security Council: the Secretariat. The Charter not only gives a technical and administrative role to the Secretariat, essential for the smooth functioning of the Council.[50] The Secretary-General also has a political role, epitomized in Article 99 of the Charter. Exercising this role, the Secretary-General can trigger Security Council action and, as was set out in Chapter 2, fundamental discussions by UN membership about reform of the Security Council.[51]

It is essential that the Secretariat is independent in performing its role. The founders of the UN did not leave any doubt in this respect, by including the following closely connected obligations in Article 100 of the Charter:

1. In the performance of their duties the Secretary-General and the staff shall not seek or receive instructions from any government or from any other authority external to the Organization. They shall refrain from any action which might reflect on their position as international officials responsible only to the Organization.
2. Each Member of the United Nations undertakes to respect the exclusively international character of the responsibilities of the Secretary-General and the staff and not to seek to influence them in the discharge of their responsibilities.

By creating an independent secretariat, as another principal organ, the founders of the UN, including the superpowers, not only accepted but deliberately

48 UN Charter, Art. 24(3).
49 UN Charter, Art. 24(1).
50 See in particular UN Charter, Art. 98.
51 See Chapter 2, paragraph 2.4 (the September 2003 'fork in the road' address to the General Assembly by Secretary-General Annan).

chose that it would not simply follow whatever orders were given by the Security Council, but that it should do so in full respect of the Charter. The superpowers do not have an absolute power, acting through the Security Council or individually, to order the Secretariat what it should do.

3.5.3 The International Court of Justice

Thirdly, the International Court of Justice may in its functioning to some extent contain the powers of the Security Council. The Court is more distant from the Security Council than the General Assembly and the Secretariat, not only geographically but also in its daily functioning. There is no hierarchy in the relationship between the Council and the Court. The two operate in different fields. The Court is the UN's principal judicial organ, while the Security Council is a political organ. Nevertheless, the work of the Court is connected to that of the Council, and they are part of the larger UN organization and serve the latter's purposes. As Judge Lachs observed in 1992,[52]

> it is important for the purposes and the principles of the United Nations that the two main organs with specific powers of binding decision act in harmony - though not, of course, in concert - and that each should perform its functions with respect to a situation or dispute, different aspects of which appear on the agenda of each, without prejudicing the exercise of the other's powers.

In particular, the following specific links may be mentioned between the work of these two principal UN organs. First, in its interpretations of the Charter, either through advisory opinions or in interstate disputes, the work of the Court may be relevant for the Security Council. However, this does not include a review of Security Council decisions. The possibility of such a review was discussed in 1945 during the UN Charter negotiations, but did not obtain the necessary support. This does not mean that it was decided that the Council's decisions would not have to remain within the boundaries of international law. It only implies that it was left to the Council itself to decide where those boundaries are, without the possibility of subsequent recourse to the Court.

---

52 Questions of Interpretation and Application of the 1971 Montreal Convention arising from the Aerial Incident at Lockerbie (Libyan Arab Jamahiriya v. United States of America), Provisional Measures, Order of 14 April 1992, ICJ Rep. 1992, p. 114, separate opinion, quotation at pp. 138–139 (the same separate opinion was attached to the Order in the parallel case brought by Libya against the United Kingdom).

Another link between the Council and the Court is laid down in Article 36(3) of the Charter, according to which the Security Council, when making recommendations to parties to a dispute, "should take into consideration that legal disputes should as a general rule be referred by the parties to the International Court of Justice".

Finally, the Security Council is involved, together with the General Assembly, in the election of the members of the Court. In such elections, the veto does not apply.[53] In this respect, the permanent members are not in a privileged position compared to the other members of the Security Council and of the UN. However, they do have a special position which derives, not from the rules of the Charter or the Statute of the Court, but from practice. Until recently, there have always been nationals of each of the five permanent members on the bench of the Court. For the first time, this practice was not followed in 2017, when judge Greenwood from the United Kingdom was not reelected. In the Security Council, a majority supported Greenwood. However, his opponent (judge Bhandari from India) received more votes in the General Assembly. The latter's preference prevailed, reportedly partly because the United Kingdom was "the victim of residual resentment in the UN General Assembly of the dominance and privileges of the permanent five members of the Security Council".[54] Since February 2018 there is no national from the United Kingdom on the bench.

∴

The five above-mentioned ways in which the UN Charter has contained the power of the permanent members show how their dominant position in the Security Council should be relativized. Returning to the famous words by Thucydides, they cannot just "do what they can". Those words might be true for the position of the Athenians in the Peloponnesian war more than 24 centuries ago; in the context of the Security Council it is a cynical overstatement, not an accurate description of the position of the permanent members.

The next paragraph will analyze in some detail relevant parts of the UN Charter negotiations in San Francisco. It will demonstrate that 75 years ago fundamental debates took place on the relationship between power and law, in the context of the definition of the purpose of the future world organization.

53 Statute of the ICJ, Art. 10(2).

54 *The Guardian*, 20 November 2017.

4 The 1945 Negotiations: Peace at Any Price? the 'Rule of Power' vs. the 'Rule of Law'

Key issues analyzed in this Chapter were also discussed in the 1945 UN Charter negotiations in San Francisco, in the context of UNCIO Commission I ('General provisions'), chaired by the Belgian lawyer Henri Rolin (later judge and President of the European Court of Human Rights). The fundamental question during these negotiations was whether the Security Council should have *carte blanche*, i.e. unbound by any legal obligation, to be able to take any necessary measures to maintain or restore peace, or whether it should be subject to certain legal obligations when taking such measures. In other words: should the Security Council be *outwith* the law, because it was to perform this key function, or should it be *within* the law, because it was to perform this key function?

The final outcome of these San Francisco discussions can be found in Articles 24 and 1 of the Charter. Article 24 is placed, with Articles 25 and 26, in the Section entitled "Functions and Powers", within Chapter V ("Security Council") of the Charter. Article 24(1) defines the key role of the Security Council: "In order to ensure prompt and effective action by the United Nations, its members confer on the Security Council primary responsibility for the maintenance of international peace and security, and agree that in carrying out its duties under this responsibility the Security Council acts on their behalf".[55] The first sentence of Article 24(2) gives an answer to the above-mentioned question: in discharging its duties, "the Security Council shall act in accordance with the Purposes and Principles of the United Nations". Therefore, the Security Council does not have *carte blanche*. The UN's purposes and principles are mentioned in Article 1 ("Purposes") and Article 2 ("Principles"). This was additionally discussed in San Francisco during the negotiations on what was to become Article 1(1) of the Charter. This provision mentions the following purpose of the UN:

> To maintain international peace and security, and to that end: to take effective collective measures for the prevention and removal of threats to the peace, and for the suppression of acts of aggression or other breaches

55 Kelsen later commented that "[i]t is doubtful whether there is a difference between 'peace and security'. International security is guaranteed if international peace is maintained. It seems that the addition of the words 'and security' is rather superfluous" (H. Kelsen, *The Law of the United Nations – A Critical Analysis of Its Fundamental Problems* (1950), p. 13). In other parts, the Charter only refers to "peace" (without the addition of "and security"), for example in Art. 39 ("threats to the peace", "breaches of the peace"). But then in Arts. 42 and 43 it uses again "international peace and security".

> of the peace, and to bring about by peaceful means, and in conformity with the principles of justice and international law, adjustment or settlement of international disputes or situations which might lead to a breach of the peace;

The maintenance of international peace and security is mentioned first in the list of four purposes of the new world organization. Article 1(1) does not merely state this purpose. It also identifies, as means to that end, two ways in which the UN should pursue this goal.

The first way is, "to take effective collective measures for the prevention and removal of threats to the peace, and for the suppression of acts of aggression or other breaches of the peace".

The second way is, "to bring about by peaceful means, and in conformity with the principles of justice and international law, adjustment or settlement of international disputes or situations which might lead to a breach of the peace".

The first way covers enforcement action by the Security Council, elaborated in Chapter VII of the Charter. The second way deals with the pacific settlement of disputes, on which more detailed provisions are given in Chapter VI of the Charter. It may be surprising that the order in which these two means are mentioned in paragraph 1(1) is different from the order in which they are elaborated later in the Charter. Is it in order to show the resolve to use force if this would be necessary for the maintenance of international peace and security? As Kelsen analyzed, mentioning enforcement action first is "highly significant. The 'effective collective measures' form the centre of the political system which is at the basis of the Charter".[56]

∵

The story behind this first paragraph of the opening article of the Charter reveals that the founders of the UN had fundamentally different views on the overarching purpose of the UN and on the two ways of pursuing this.

The negotiations in San Francisco did not start from scratch but on the basis of a draft text prepared during the Dumbarton Oaks conference (21 August to 7 October 1944). This draft text ("Dumbarton Oaks Proposals for a general International Organization") mentions as a first purpose of the organization:[57]

---

56 Id., p. 14.

57 The text of the Dumbarton Oaks Proposals is reproduced in *Yearbook of the United Nations 1946–47* (1947), p. 4 ff.

> To maintain international peace and security; and to that end to take effective collective measures for the prevention and removal of threats to the peace and the suppression of acts of aggression or other breaches of the peace, and to bring about by peaceful means adjustment or settlement of international disputes which may lead to a breach of the peace;

This draft already contains the essence and most of the current text of Article 1(1) of the Charter. The focus will now be on the words that were added some eight months later in San Francisco.

In 1945 at the UNCIO Conference, the main bone of contention regarding this first purpose of the UN was whether this provision should also include a reference to justice, law, rule of justice, rule of law, or closely related notions.[58] The outcome of these negotiations is reflected in Article 1(1) of the Charter. If the current provision is compared to the Dumbarton Oaks draft, quoted above, the main addition are the words "in conformity with the principles of justice and international law". The addition of these words, and in particular their position within Article 1(1) was the subject of intense negotiations in San Francisco. This fundamental debate will now be analyzed in more detail, in order to obtain a better understanding of the different views of the founding fathers of the UN regarding the relationship between peace and justice, and between the Security Council and the rule of law.

UNCIO Commission I dealt with the Preamble and Articles 1 and 2 of the Charter. Its work was prepared in two committees (I/1 and I/2). No minutes were kept of the meetings of the two committees. As agreed in the preparatory meeting of Commission I held on 3 May 1945, discussing procedural matters, "the summary records of proceedings should be limited to a statement of subjects discussed, conclusions reached, votes taken, and any action with regard to appointing subcommittees, in order that delegates might develop discussion freely in the meetings".[59] Following the preparatory work of Committees I/1 and I/2, the first session of Commission I was held on 14 June. The Commission only had limited time, less than two weeks before the end of the San Francisco Conference, when the Charter was signed on 26 June 1945. The report of this session shows that fundamental disagreements existed amongst the delegates. The Chairman of Committee I/1 reported that the two main problems were "the problem of peace and the problem of the improvement of conditions of mankind by international cooperation".[60] The "problem of peace" involved the

58 See UNCIO, Vol. VI, p. 27 for a list of ten proposals.

59 UNCIO, Vol. VI, p. 6.

60 Id., p. 13.

relationship between peace and justice. The Chairman of Committee I/1 summarized it in the following way:[61]

> With regard to peace, we felt the need to emphasize that our first object was to be strong to maintain peace, to maintain peace by our common effort and at all costs, at all costs with one exception – not at the cost of justice. There the difficulty lay. Many of our delegates have repeatedly in our debates warned of the dangers of a repetition of the so-called "appeasement policy". Too often in the last years governments had hoped to maintain peace by sacrificing the interests of weaker countries to the greed of stronger ones, and all this on the altar of peace, with the rather deceiving result that they succeeded only in feeding what Prime Minister Churchill called "the crocodile who grow stronger and stronger every year". An organization which includes the four sponsoring governments and France and which is based on the unity of their efforts should and will be able to assume such high purpose and the protection of the fundamental rights of all members. How far we succeeded in expressing satisfactorily such an essential fundamental idea in clear terms in the document remains to be seen. An amendment on the subject will be discussed at a later hour today.

The result of the work of Committee I/1, with regard to what was to become Article 1(1) of the UN Charter became the basis for the discussion in Commission I on 14 June. The text reads as follows:[62]

> The Purposes of the United Nations are: (1) To maintain international peace and security; and to that end to take effective collective measures for the prevention and removal of threats to the peace, and the suppression of acts of aggression or other breaches of the peace, and to bring about by peaceful means, and in conformity with the principles of justice and international law, adjustment or settlement of international disputes or situations which may lead to a breach of the peace.

The Rapporteur of Committee I/1 in his summary of the discussions explained in more detail the substance of the fundamental disagreement in the committee. He reported that two motions were put forward in this committee, both

61 Id., pp. 13–14.

62 Id., p. 21.

relating to the first few words of paragraph (1) quoted above. A first motion proposed to add "justice" after "security", so that the first words would become "To maintain international peace, security, and justice". The second motion was to add after "security": "in accordance with the principles of justice and international law".[63] In the committee, both motions received a majority of votes, but not the required two-thirds majority. The Rapporteur summarized the discussions in Committee I/1 as follows:[64]

> It may seem, at first sight, that some members of the Committee who took the move to oppose the first two motions were trying to oppose justice itself. On the contrary, all those who took the floor to oppose the two motions were agreed that the concept of justice is a norm of fundamental importance; and all affirmed that peace, real and endurable, cannot be based on anything other than on justice. They held, however, that adding "justice" after "peace and security", as in the present motion, brings in at that juncture of the text a notion which lacks in clarity and welds it together with the more clear and almost tangible notion of peace and security. The resultant concept in this case does not remain sufficiently clear to be realizable. It tends, then, to provide a loophole for questioning any specific action of the Organization, and a possibility for delaying measures and procedure while discussing abstract definitions.
>
> The situations that may arise may be conceived this way. Peace is threatened by disputes, or by situations that may lead to a breach of the peace. A breach of the peace may ensue. At the first stage, the Organization should insist and take measures that states do not threaten, or cause a breach of the peace. If they do, the Organization should, at the second stage, promptly stop any breach of the peace, or remove it. After that, it can proceed to find an adjustment or settlement of that dispute or situation. When the Organization has used the power given to it, and the force at its disposal to stop war, then it can find the latitude to apply the principles of justice and international law, or can assist the contending parties to find a peaceful solution.
>
> The concept of justice and international law can thus find a more appropriate place in context with the last part of the paragraph dealing with disputes and situations. There it can find a more real scope to operate, and a more precise expression, and a more practical field of application.

63 Id.

64 Id., at 22.

> There was no intention, and this was made clear, to let this notion of justice and international law lose any of its weight and strength as an over-ruling arm of the whole Charter.
>
> The Committee had before it the amendment of the four sponsoring governments which ran this way: "To deal with international disputes, with due regard to the fundamental principles of justice and international law". The Committee decided unanimously to change the words "with due regard to the fundamental principles of justice and international law" into "in conformity with the principles of justice and international law". And the Committee, by its final vote, gave that place to this notion which you find in the text before you.

After this summary of the discussions in Committee I/1 by its Rapporteur, Egypt was given the floor to introduce its amendment. In the above quoted text of Article 1(1), Egypt proposed to move up the words "in conformity with the principles of justice and international law", so that they would come immediately after the opening words of paragraph 1 ("To maintain international peace and security").[65] Behind this proposed re-allocation of the quoted text lies something very substantive: the idea that the maintenance of international peace and security, in particular the use of enforcement measures to that end, must not be pursued by the new world organization at any price, but only if this would take place within the limits of the principles of justice and international law. Essentially, the question was therefore whether the maintenance of international peace and security by the UN was to be explicitly governed by the rule of law. In the proposed text quoted above, the words "in conformity with the principles of justice and international law" appear only later in paragraph 1, in such a way that they only relate to the peaceful settlement of disputes.

It is useful to examine in some more detail the arguments put forward by the different participants in the final discussion in Commission I on 14 June 1945.

In its intervention, Egypt stated that the question of placement (of the words "in conformity with the principles of justice and international law") "is extremely important".[66] According to Egypt, an important objection raised against its proposed amendment was "that the principle and the only aim to be indicated in the Charter should be the maintenance of peace and security and that justice was only one of the means by which such aim might be attained".[67] In addition, Egypt mentioned, "[w]e were also told later that the adoption of

65 UNCIO, Vol. VI, p. 10.
66 UNCIO, Vol. VI, p. 23.
67 Id.

our proposal might result in delaying or even preventing action by the Security Council".[68] The Egyptian delegate, Mamdouh Bey Riaz, went even so far as to say: "[i]f we want to keep peace and security only, we would not differ much from Hitler, who was also trying to do that and who, as a matter of fact, partly succeeded. But where the difference lies is that we want to maintain peace and security in conformity with the principles of international law and justice".[69]

The next speaker, Lord Halifax from the United Kingdom, spoke against the adoption of the Egyptian amendment. He observed that the placement of the relevant words ("in conformity with the principles of justice and international law") in the proposed text of paragraph (1) "insures in the first place that the actual business of maintaining peace and of preventing the guns beginning to go off, should not, in any circumstances, be delayed. That is the vital duty of the Security Council to prevent that thing beginning".[70] To illustrate this duty, the UK referred to "the policemen or the gendarme who is concerned with dealing with a wrong that he sees arising. He does not stop at the outset of what he does to inquire where exactly lies the precise balance of justice in their quarrel. He stops it, and then, in order to make adjustment and settlement, justice comes into its own".[71]

Subsequently, a second speaker in favour of the amendment was invited to take the floor, Professor Alfaro representing Panama. Alfaro referred to remarks made by the President Rolin of Commission I as follows: "[h]e [Rolin] said that we intend to maintain peace and security at all costs, save one – at the costs of justice. We will not maintain peace and security at the costs of justice; that is to say, sacrificing the rights of any nation".[72] "[W]e all want [...] a peace founded upon justice and nothing but justice, a peace that will be on no occasion a peace of expediency, a peace of force, a peace of appeasement. It must be a peace of justice".[73] In addition, Panama observed that "in this Article 1, we say 'to maintain international peace and security'. That is the object of the government of the world, to maintain peace and order, because justice and obedience to the law are the fundamental elements of any organized society".[74]

Following this intervention, a second speaker against the proposed Egyptian amendment was given the floor, the US delegate Commander Stassen. He

68 Id., p. 24.
69 Id.
70 Id., p. 25.
71 Id.
72 Id., p. 27.
73 Id.
74 Id., p. 28.

played down the fundamental nature of the issue at stake: "what we are really concerned with involves almost entirely a question of interpretation of the language that is before us".[75] He distinguished between two functions of the Security Council:

> on this matter of the future peace of the world, there will be two very important functions. These might be characterized somewhat as being the functions of a policeman and the functions of a jury. [...] It is our view that the people of the world wish to establish a Security Council, that is, a policeman who will say, when anyone starts to fight, "stop fighting". Period. And then it will say, when anyone is already to begin to fight, "You must not fight". Period. That is the function of a policeman, and it must be just that short and that abrupt; that is, unless at that place we add more, then we would say "Stop fighting unless you claim international law is on your side". That would lead to a weakening and a confusion in our interpretation.
>
> The distinguished Delegate of Egypt made a reference to Hitler. We must not forget that every time that Hitler smashed across the border to trample upon millions of innocent people, he said that he was acting in accordance with international law as he saw it, and justice as he saw it. History tells us that. So we say we shall establish this policeman who shall, in the days ahead, anytime that anyone breaks the peace and begins to fight, say, "Stop fighting"; anytime that anyone is poised and ready to fight, say "You must not fight" ".[76] [Next, Commander Stassen described the other important function of the Security Council that he distinguished, the function of a jury.] "At that point we also say, when you begin to function as a jury you must do so in conformity with justice and international law.[77]

The next and last speaker, speaking for the amendment, was Professor Payssé from Uruguay:

> [t]he draft sponsored by the great powers makes reference to justice and to international law only for purposes of adjustment and regulation, but it excludes them with respect to security measures and the immediate maintenance of the peace. Mr. Stassen [...] has defined the purposes of

75 Id., p. 29.
76 Id., pp. 29–30.
77 Id., p. 30.

> the Organization as those of security, with necessary police measures, which cannot suffer the delays which the process of defining justice would entail. He states correctly that the world is sick of wars, that it cannot stand new wars, that the threat of all war must be cut short immediately. But, honorable Delegates, at any price? [...]
>
> We firmly support a drastic system of effective security measures, but we conceive it only on the basis of justice and in conformity with the rules of international law. [...] The day when there occurs anew the illusion that by sacrificing the rights of the weak in the face of threats by the strong the peace would be saved, on that day the fuse will have been lighted which sooner or later would set off the explosion of war. Injustice is not a propitious atmosphere for peace.[78]

Subsequently the President of the Commission brought the Egyptian amendment to a vote. There were 21 votes in favour, 21 votes against. Since a two-thirds majority was required for the adoption of amendments, it lacked the necessary support. Finally, the text proposed by the sponsoring powers was put to the vote, and it was carried unanimously.[79]

It is clear from the above overview of the UNCIO negotiations relating to the future Article 1(1) of the Charter that there were two opposing views about how the Charter should refer to the first mentioned purpose of the new world organization. These two views could be summarized as the *rule of power* view ("to maintain international peace and security") and the *rule of law* view ("to maintain international peace and security, in conformity with the principles of justice and international law"). Is the UN above the law, or is it within the law? While it is clear that these are fundamentally different perspectives on what is mentioned as the first purpose of the UN, the question could be raised whether a different outcome of the UNCIO negotiations on Article 1(1) would have had serious practical implications. Would the Security Council have operated differently all these years, if the UN could maintain international peace and security only as long as this would be done in conformity with the principles of justice and international law?

The first mentioned purpose of the UN is not merely connected to the operation of the Security Council because Article 1, as an umbrella provision, covers all the activities of all organs of the UN. In addition, Article 24(2) of the Charter specifically provides that "[i]n discharging these duties [- mentioned

78 Id., p. 33.

79 Id., p. 34.

in Article 24(1) -] the Security Council shall act in accordance with the Purposes and Principles of the United Nations". Using the metaphor of the above-mentioned discussion in San Francisco, this means that the Security Council, when it is acting as a policeman, i.e. taking enforcement action under Chapter VII of the Charter, is not explicitly bound by the principles of justice and international law. On the other hand, when it is acting as a jury, in the pacific settlement of disputes, it is explicitly bound by these principles. In practice, if the Egyptian amendment had adopted in San Francisco, this would have had implications not only for the Security Council, but also for the International Court of Justice. In this scenario, if the Court would need to scrutinize Chapter VII measures taken by the Security Council, its framework of reference would have included "the principles of justice and international law".

Having reviewed these fundamental discussions, the next paragraph will provide an overview of relevant practice of the Security Council.

5 Security Council Practice and the Rule of Law

5.1 *Introduction*

First of all, if the Egyptian amendment had been adopted in San Francisco in 1945, it seems unlikely that this would have had major implications for the functioning of the Security Council during the Cold War. In these first 45 years, the question was not so much whether the Security Council acted in conformity with the principles of justice and international law, but rather why it did not act at all. To the extent that it did, not much enforcement action was taken on the basis of Chapter VII of the Charter.

This situation changed after the end of the Cold War. The Security Council became much more active than before. Many enforcement decisions were based on Chapter VII of the Charter.[80] The legitimacy or the legality of some of these decisions was questioned, for example when the Council created ad hoc criminal tribunals and when it started to impose individual sanctions. If Article 1(1) would require such measures to be in accordance with the principles of justice and international law, it is likely that this would have affected the rhetoric of the statements in the Security Council, and perhaps even the outcome. However, it can be observed with more certainty that the absence of

80 As mentioned in Chapter 2 (paragraph 3), of all Chapter VII resolutions passed from 1946 to 2002, 93% have been adopted since the end of the Cold War (P. Wallensteen and P. Johansson, 'Security Council Decisions in Perspective', in D.M. Malone, *The UN Security Council – From the Cold War to the 21st Century* (2004), pp. 17–33, at p. 19).

an explicit requirement of conformity with the principles of justice and international law did not mean that questions of legitimacy and legality were not raised. Thus, what was used in the title of a recently defended PhD is certainly true here: 'water always finds its way'.[81] If there are fundamental legitimacy or legality questions concerning enforcement measures taken by the Security Council, these questions will be addressed in some way or another, even though strictly seen, in 1945, it was decided that such measures do not need to be in conformity with the principles of justice and international law.

The end of the Cold War reinvigorated the Security Council. This is not only reflected in the number of resolutions adopted and the type of measures taken, but also in the resurgence of old questions about the legality and legitimacy of its activities, double standards and the rule of law.[82] These questions emerged in the context of specific resolutions adopted by the Council, and when it held a number of thematic debates on the rule of law. Obviously, such questions do not only concern the Security Council, but also UN membership at large and therefore the General Assembly. Over the years, the Assembly has referred to the rule of law in a number of important declarations.[83] Most recently, in 2012, the General Assembly adopted the Declaration of the high-level meeting of the General Assembly on the rule of law at the national and international levels.[84] The first two paragraphs of this Declaration provide the following:

> 1. We reaffirm our solemn commitment to the purposes and principles of the Charter of the United Nations, international law and justice, and to an international order based on the rule of law, which are indispensable foundations for a more peaceful, prosperous and just world.
> 2. We recognize that the rule of law applies to all States equally, and to international organizations, including the United Nations and its principal organs, and that respect for and promotion of the rule of law and justice should guide all of their activities and accord predictability and legitimacy to their actions. We also recognize that all persons, institutions and entities, public and private, including the

81 E.M. van Schaack, *Imagining Justice for Syria: Water Always Finds Its Way*, PhD defended at Leiden University on 29 April 2020.

82 See also I. Brownlie, *The Rule of Law in International Affairs* (1998), in particular pp. 211–228.

83 In particular: the 1948 Universal Declaration of Human Rights (GA Res. 217A (III)), the 1970 Declaration on Principles of International Law (GA Res. 2625 (XXV)), the 2000 United Nations Millennium Declaration (GA Res. 55/2) and the 2005 World Summit Outcome (GA Res. 60/1).

84 GA Res. 67/1.

> State itself, are accountable to just, fair and equitable laws and are entitled without any discrimination to equal protection of the law.

While the emphasis of this Declaration is on the rule of law at the national level, it also recognizes that the rule of law applies to international organizations, including the UN and its principal organs such as the Security Council: "respect for and promotion of the rule of law and justice should guide all of their activities and accord predictability and legitimacy to their actions". This is somewhat different from the outcome of the deliberations in San Francisco in 1945, when Chapter VII measures were excluded from the reach of the "in conformity with the principles of justice and international law" phrase in Article 1(1).

This paragraph will examine how the Security Council has used the notion of the rule of law both in general and in relation to specific topics. Paragraph 5.2 will focus on a number of thematic debates of the Security Council devoted to the rule of law. Paragraph 5.3 will briefly examine how the Council is applying its general rule of law position in practice, how it has dealt with two specific topics often mentioned in the thematic rule of law debates: international criminal justice and individual sanctions.

5.2 *General: Thematic Debates, Presidential Statements*

The Security Council has never adopted a general resolution or presidential statement on the rule of law as such, offering its general views as the General Assembly did in its 2012 Declaration. It has mostly referred to the rule of law in the national context. This is also how the concept of the rule of law has entered Security Council parlance. Nevertheless, after a while the international dimensions of the rule of law were mentioned as well in statements in the Security Council, and thematic debates were organized to discuss the rule of law in international relations, including more specifically the question of whether the Security Council is bound by international law. Themes discussed in 1945 in San Francisco re-emerged, triggered by specific issues on the agenda of the Security Council.

The Security Council referred for the first time to the rule of law in 1996, in a resolution concerning the situation in Burundi.[85] In this resolution, the Council "[e]xpresses its fullest support for the efforts of the Secretary-General and others, in support of the Convention of Government, to facilitate a comprehensive political dialogue with the objective of promoting national reconciliation, democracy, security and the rule of law in Burundi".[86] It is likely that

85 Fassbender, op. cit. note 22, p. 779.

86 SC Res. 1040, para. 2.

this reference to the rule of law originated in underlying documents for the meeting of the Security Council in which this resolution was adopted. The so-called Convention of Government of Burundi (to which the resolution refers) mentions in Article 2 that it "seeks to build a State based on the rule of law".[87] Subsequently, the Security Council has referred to the rule of law in other national contexts, often in situations of an internal armed conflict and transitional justice. After some time, when the notion of the rule of law became a recurrent topic in the work of the Security Council, it was decided to devote a general debate to it.

5.2.1 The 2003 and 2004 Thematic Debates: the Rule of Law at the National Level

Since the mid-1990s, the Security Council has organized meetings not with the purpose of addressing a specific dispute or situation, possibly resulting in the adoption of a resolution, but to hold a general debate on a particular cross-cutting theme. In this way, the Security Council and its members aim to obtain a fuller understanding of the theme, which may lead to a more consistent approach by the Council, and to its action in specific cases to become more effective. In most cases, such 'thematic debates' result in the adoption of a presidential statement. Examples include the meetings devoted to peacekeeping operations,[88] the security of United Nations operations,[89] the protection of humanitarian assistance to refugees and others in conflict situations,[90] and the protection of civilians in armed conflict.[91]

The first thematic debate devoted to the rule of law was organized in 2003, at the initiative of the United Kingdom. The agenda item was entitled 'Justice and the Rule of Law: the United Nations role'.[92] Against the background of the involvement of the UN in a number of domestic conflicts since the end of the Cold War, there was significant support for this initiative to not only focus on these specific individual conflicts, but also benefit from an exchange of views on general issues of transitional justice that are key in post-conflict assistance by the UN. As New Zealand mentioned in the debate, since much

87 UN Doc. A/50/94 – S/1995/190 (Annex) (8 March 1995), p. 4 (Art. 2); further references to the rule of law are in the Preamble of this Convention (p. 2) and in Art. 4 (p. 4).

88 E.g. the 3408th meeting on 27 July 1994, at the end of which Presidential Statement S/PRST/1994/36 was adopted.

89 3750th meeting, 12 March 1997 (S/PRST/1997/13).

90 3790th meeting, 19 June 1997 (S/PRST/1997/34) and 3933rd meeting, 29 September 1998 (S/PRST/1998/30).

91 3978th meeting, 12 February 1999 (S/PRST/1999/6).

92 For the records of the meeting, see UN Docs. S/PV.4833 and S/PV.4835.

of the relevant UN work had been ad hoc, it was useful "to address rule of law issues in a systemic and comprehensive way in the Council's work".[93]

This thematic debate was organized in two stages. The first meeting (24 September 2003) was for members of the Security Council, most of them represented at ministerial level. The second meeting (30 September 2003) was organized to allow other members of the UN to present their views on the topic; 25 members used this opportunity. The debate focused primarily on the domestic dimensions of the topic, more specifically on transitional justice issues. When opening the first meeting, Foreign Minister Straw from the United Kingdom referred to the challenges for the UN and the Security Council "of bringing countries out of conflict and into societies based on justice and the rule of law".[94]

However, in the opening words of his address to the Council, Secretary-General Annan also pointed at the international dimension: "[t]his Council has a very heavy responsibility to promote justice and the rule of law in its efforts to maintain international peace and security. This applies both internationally and in rebuilding shattered societies". Even though the purpose of the meeting was to focus on justice and the rule of law at the national level, most representatives also discussed the international dimension. Russia's Foreign Minister Ivanov referred to "the primacy of law in international relations" and stated that "the principle of the rule of law is an imperative for the entire system of international relations".[95] Foreign Minister Li Zhaoxing from China stated:[96]

> Governing a country requires the rule of law, as does managing international relations. To uphold what is right, defend what is just and observe international obligations is the solemn commitment made by the United Nations to the world's people and is the essence of the United Nations Charter. The answer to bringing about a world of peace, stability, justice and the rule of law lies solely in closer international cooperation, a multilateral approach and democracy and the rule of law in international relations.

In addition, Mexico reflected on the meaning of the rule of law for the Security Council itself, and called for "greater clarification of the framework within which it acts".[97] The meeting resulted in the adoption of a brief presidential

93 UN Doc. S/PV.4835, p. 10.
94 UN Doc. S/PV.4833, p. 2.
95 Id., p. 5.
96 Id., p. 8.
97 Id., p. 9.

statement in which the Secretary-General was invited to prepare a report on the issues discussed.[98]

The second meeting of this thematic debate offered an opportunity for UN members that were not represented in the Security Council to present their views. Again, most representatives not only touched upon the national dimension of 'justice and the rule of law', but also discussed the international dimension. For example, the representative of Trinidad and Tobago recalled that "the United Nations was founded after the Second World War with the objective of saving succeeding generations from the scourge of war", but that this objective cannot be assured without observing the fundamental principles of international law.[99]

In August 2004, the Secretary-General presented the report that he was invited to prepare at this first thematic debate on the rule of law.[100] The report is entitled 'The rule of law and transitional justice in conflict and post-conflict societies' and essentially focuses on the national context. However, it also has a wider importance since it provides a definition of the concept of the rule of law, as follows:[101]

> 6. The 'rule of law' is a concept at the very heart of the Organization's mission. It refers to a principle of governance in which all persons, institutions and entities, public and private, including the State itself, are accountable to laws that are publicly promulgated, equally enforced and independently adjudicated, and which are consistent with international human rights norms and standards. It requires, as well, measures to ensure adherence to the principles of supremacy of law, equality before the law, accountability to the law, fairness in the application of the law, separation of powers, participation in decision-making, legal certainty, avoidance of arbitrariness and procedural and legal transparency.

The report notes that norms and standards developed by the UN "also set the normative boundaries of United Nations engagement"; for example, "where we are mandated to undertake executive or judicial functions, United Nations-operated facilities must scrupulously comply with international standards for human rights in the administration of justice".[102] Rule of law standards are not

98 UN Doc. S/PRST/2003/15.
99 UN Doc. S/PV.4835, p. 30.
100 UN Doc. S/2004/616 (23 August 2004).
101 Id., p. 4. The report also defines the concepts of 'justice' and 'transitional justice'.
102 Id., p. 5.

only for others, external to the UN, but also for the UN itself. In short: practice what you preach.

This report received considerable attention and triggered initiatives and discussions, within the UN and elsewhere. At the UN level, the report sparked further thematic debates in the Security Council (discussed below) and deliberations in the context of the General Assembly.[103] In addition, a number of informal consultations were organized; one example is the 'Austrian Initiative'.[104] At the end of 2004, following the presentation of the 2004 rule of law report by the Secretary-General, the Permanent Mission of Austria to the UN organized a series of seven panel discussions together with the New York University School of Law, to examine 'the Role of the Security Council in Strengthening a Rules-Based International System'. A retreat was organized in Austria in 2007 and a New York based advisory group was established that later became a 'group of friends of the rule of law' composed of a number of permanent representatives of UN member states and high-level officials of the UN Secretariat.[105] This Austrian initiative resulted in a report with 17 recommendations.[106]

Focusing now on further developments within the Security Council, the 2004 report by the Secretary-General became the basis for a second thematic debate, held on 6 October that same year, also at the initiative of the United Kingdom. Most statements in this debate concentrated on the rule of law at the national level and the adopted presidential statement almost exclusively concerns justice and the rule of law at the national level, in conflict and post-conflict national societies. One sentence refers to the international dimension: "[t]he Security Council recalls that justice and rule of law at the international level are of key importance for promoting and maintaining peace, stability and development in the world".[107]

103 See further S. Barriga and A. Alday, 'The General Assembly and the Rule of Law: Daring to Succeed? – The Perspective of Member States', *12 Max Planck Yearbook of United Nations Law (2008)*, pp. 381–408.

104 On this initiative, see K.G. Bühler, 'The Austrian Rule of Law Initiative 2004–2008', *12 Max Planck Yearbook of United Nations Law (2008)*, pp. 409–446.

105 Id.

106 *The UN Security Council and the Rule of Law*, prepared by S. Chesterman (2008), also published as UN Doc. A/63/69-S/2008/270. The recommendations include both specific proposals to improve sanction procedures and request advisory opinions from the ICJ as well as the general recommendation for the Council to ensure "that its own decisions are firmly rooted in [international law], including the Charter of the United Nations, general principles of law, international human rights law, international humanitarian law, and international criminal law" (Recommendation 1).

107 UN Doc. S/PRST/2004/34.

5.2.2 The 2006 and 2010 Thematic Debates: the Rule of Law at the International Level

A third thematic debate on the rule of law took place in 2006 at the initiative of Denmark. This time, the title of the agenda item was 'Strengthening international law: rule of law and maintenance of international peace and security'. In a discussion paper for the meeting, Denmark defined as the objective of the debate "to consider the Security Council's particular role in promoting international law".[108] As stated in the paper, "[t]he Security Council operates within the framework of international law in all its functions".[109] Denmark outlined three topics to which the meeting could give special attention: the promotion of the rule of law in conflict and post-conflict situations, ending impunity for international crimes, and enhancing the efficiency and credibility of United Nations sanctions regimes. In its opening statement at the meeting, Denmark added a fourth topic, peaceful settlement of disputes.[110] During the general debate of 22 June 2006, the Security Council was addressed by a number of states, members and non-members of the Security Council. In addition, Legal Counsel Michel of the UN (speaking on behalf of the Secretary-General) and President Higgins of the International Court of Justice presented statements.

At the end of this thematic debate, the Security Council adopted a presidential statement, which did not only contain conclusions regarding the specific topics suggested by Denmark, but also a more general conclusion:[111]

> The Security Council reaffirms its commitment to the Charter of the United Nations and international law, which are indispensable foundations of a more peaceful, prosperous and just world. The Council underscores its conviction that international law plays a critical role in fostering stability and order in international relations and in providing a framework for cooperation among States in addressing common challenges, thus contributing to the maintenance of international peace and security.

Security Council conclusions such as this one are necessarily of a rather general nature, since they must reflect (often widely) diverging views of the members.

108 UN Doc. S/2006/367.

109 Id., p. 2. Legal Counsel Michel concluded his address to the Security Council during the meeting (S/PV.5474, p. 5) by quoting this.

110 UN Doc. S/PV.5474, p. 3. In its intervention, Denmark emphasized the general, thematic nature of the debate by referring to the aim of the meeting "to take a step back from the daily business of the Council" (id.).

111 UN Doc. S/PRST/2006/28, first para.

A brief impression of some of the statements made during this debate shows that the activism of the Security Council and the euphoria of the 1990s also triggered rule of law concerns. This was not unlike what had happened during the 1945 San Francisco negotiations related to the purpose of the UN laid down in Article 1 of the Charter.

In their statements during the meeting, almost all representatives addressed not only the specific issues suggested by Denmark, but also made some general comments on the rule of law and the maintenance of international peace and security by the Security Council. A few of the statements interpreted the rule of law as almost synonymous to international law. A number of representatives referred to the August 2004 report by the Secretary-General on the rule of law and transitional justice, mentioned above, and to his September 2004 address to the General Assembly.[112] This address was fully dedicated to the rule of law, "in each country and in the world". It mentioned principles of justice laid down in Hammurabi's code of laws of ancient Mesopotamia, "recognized, if seldom fully implemented, by almost every human society since his time" (including, for example, "restraints on the strong, so that they cannot oppress the weak"). It concluded: "[t]hat code was a landmark in mankind's struggle to build an order where, instead of might making right, right would make might. Many nations represented in this chamber can proudly point to founding documents of their own that embody that simple concept. And this Organization – your United Nations – is founded on the same simple principle".[113]

Almost all the general comments on the rule of law and the maintenance of international peace and security by the Security Council shared the view that the Security Council operates within the framework of international law.[114] More specifically, a number of states emphasized that the Security Council itself should fully respect international law and the rule of law.[115] In doing so, some quoted the Secretary-General, who stated in his above-mentioned September 2004 address to the General Assembly: "[t]hose who seek to bestow

112 E.g. Mexico (id., p. 29) and Austria (id., p. 32).

113 UN Doc. A/59/PV.3 (21 September 2004), pp. 2–4.

114 E.g. statements by Peru (UN Doc. S/PV/5474, p. 15) and China (id., p. 26 ("[a]s the major United Nations organ responsible for the maintenance of international peace and security, the Security Council not only performs its functions within the framework of international law, but also plays an important role in strengthening international law") and p. 27 ("international law is important as the foundation of the Security Council's work in the maintenance of international peace and security")).

115 E.g. Egypt (S/PV.5474 (Resumption 1), p. 4).

legitimacy must themselves embody it; and those who invoke international law must themselves submit to it".[116] Liechtenstein stated:[117]

> In our view, the best way for the Security Council to promote international law and the rule of law is to lead by example. During this debate we do not want to venture into the legal question of the extent to which the Council is bound by rules of international law. We would, however, submit that it is a wise policy choice for the Council to respect and promote international law [...].

Switzerland stated:[118]

> As one of the principal organs of the United Nations, the Security Council has important responsibilities with regard to the promotion of the rule of law. On the one hand, the Council must respect the rule of law in its own actions at all times, and on the other, we expect the Council to promote the rule of law in all areas of its activities.

South Africa:[119]

> Any credible debate on the role of the Security Council in strengthening international law, the rule of law and the maintenance of international peace and security ought to begin with an assessment of the performance of the Security Council itself. The Security Council bears the primary responsibility for the maintenance of international peace and security and for saving succeeding generations from the scourge of war. The question that therefore arises is whether the Security Council, in its current form, is representative of the United Nations membership and is willing and able to carry out its Charter responsibilities.

Finally, the long and substantive statement by Mexico deserves particular attention.[120] It focused on the use by the Security Council of its powers and the need to keep this within the limits of law. In doing so, it echoed the spirit of interventions by other Latin American countries (Panama, Uruguay) during

116 UN Doc. A/59/PV.3 (21 September 2004), p.3.
117 UN Doc. S/PV.5474 (Resumption 1), p. 9.
118 Id., p. 10.
119 Id., p. 13.
120 UN Doc. S/PV.5474, pp. 29–31.

the 1945 San Francisco conference (see paragraph 3.4 above). Mexico referred to the September 2004 address to the General Assembly by Secretary-General Annan ("[w]here enforcement capacity does exist, as in the Security Council, many feel it is not always used fairly or effectively"), indicating "that that is the issue that needs to be addressed today".[121] Mexico criticized the Security Council's "excessive recourse to Chapter VII and certain abuses of the notion of a threat to peace".[122] In particular, "when determining whether there has been a breach of the peace or an act of aggression, the Council should be able to rely on the international legal rule that has been violated and base its decisions in international law. Peace as an end in itself cannot justify any action".[123]

This very last sentence echoed precisely the concern of other Latin American countries in 1945 in San Francisco, when Professor Alfaro representing Panama stated: " [...] justice and obedience to the law are the fundamental elements of any organized society".[124] "[W]e all want [...] a peace founded upon justice and nothing but justice, a peace that will be on no occasion a peace of expediency, a peace of force, a peace of appeasement. It must be a peace of justice".[125] In the same spirit, Professor Payssé from Uruguay stated in 1945: "[w]e firmly support a drastic system of effective security measures, but we conceive it only on the basis of justice and in conformity with the rules of international law".[126]

Therefore, according to Mexico, not only Security Council determinations of the existence of a threat to the peace, breach of the peace or act of aggression, but also the measures subsequently taken should be "grounded in and motivated by international law. The Security Council is bound to discharge its duties in accordance with the purposes and principles of the United Nations, as set out in Article 24, paragraph 2, of the Charter". The last few words seem to suggest that grounding its Chapter VII decisions in international law is required by the text of the Charter. This would be true if the Egyptian amendment to the proposed text for Article 1 of the Charter had been adopted. However, as discussed in paragraph 3.4, this amendment failed to receive the necessary two-third majority support. As a result, only Security Council measures taken on the basis of Chapter VI, not those taken under Chapter VII must be "in conformity with the principles of justice and international law".[127]

121 Id., p. 29.
122 Id., p. 30.
123 Id.
124 UNCIO, Vol. VI, p. 28.
125 Id.
126 UNCIO, Vol. VI, p. 33.
127 UN Charter, Art. 1(1).

Coincidence or not, it was also Mexico that took the initiative for a fourth thematic debate on these issues, held four years later. The agenda item was now named 'The promotion and strengthening of the rule of law in the maintenance of international peace and security'. It did no longer contain a reference to international law, therefore focusing fully on the heart of the issues discussed in this Chapter. In a "concept note" for the meeting, Mexico suggested to discuss three specific topics within the larger theme: the promotion of the rule of law in conflict and post-conflict situations, international justice and the peaceful settlement of disputes, and the efficiency and credibility of sanctions regimes.[128]

This fourth thematic debate devoted to the rule of law was somewhat similar to the 2006 debate. The presidential statement adopted at the end contained more or less the same general conclusion as the one four years before:[129]

> The Security Council reaffirms its commitment to the Charter of the United Nations and international law, and to an international order based on the rule of law and international law, which is essential for peaceful coexistence and cooperation among States in addressing common challenges, thus contributing to the maintenance of international peace and security.

The main difference with the 2006 presidential statement is the specific reference to "an international order based on the rule of law and international law". Mexico mentioned this at the end of its opening statement during this meeting, when it referred to

> the brilliant jurist Hersch Lauterpacht, who reminded us that the principal function of international law is "the subjection of the totality of international relations to the rule of law". By promoting compliance with international law through its actions and decisions and by functioning within the framework of international law, the Security Council helps to fulfil its primary responsibility.[130]

In addition, the 2010 Presidential Statement reflected to some extent the need 'to practice what you preach', or, in the earlier quoted words of Secretary-General Annan "[t]hose who seek to bestow legitimacy must themselves embody it; and those who invoke international law must themselves submit to

128 UN Doc. S/2010/322.

129 UN Doc. S/PRST/2010/11.

130 UN Doc. S/PV.6347, p. 8.

it".[131] The reference to this in the 2010 Presidential Statement is far less clear (but at least it is there, while it was still lacking in the 2006 Presidential Statement): "[t]he Security Council expresses its commitment to ensure that all United Nations efforts to restore peace and security themselves respect and promote the rule of law".[132]

The statements made during this 2010 thematic debate mostly paid attention both to the general theme of the rule of law in the work of the Security Council and to the three more specific topics mentioned in Mexico's concept note. The references to the general theme were mostly somewhat similar to those already made in the 2006 thematic debate. Perhaps South Africa captured the spirit of the meeting by beginning its statement by saying:[133]

> We move from the premise, as does your concept note, that the old debate about whether the Security Council functions above international law is truly passé and that, notwithstanding the primary role of the Security Council in the maintenance of international peace and security, the Security Council operates within the framework of international law in all its functions.

Indeed, as the United Kingdom stated, "[t]here is now widespread recognition that the rule of law is a principle that applies much more broadly across the spectrum of issues dealt with by the United Nations, and by the Security Council in particular".[134] Lebanon stated: "the basis for maintaining international peace and security [...] is the might of the law and not the law of might".[135] Other states mentioned the same fundamental idea.[136] The emphasis in most

131 As stated by Secretary-General Annan in his September 2004 address to the General Assembly, UN Doc. A/59/PV.3, p.3.

132 UN Doc. S/PRST/2010/11.

133 UN Doc. S/PV.6347, p. 15.

134 Id., p. 18.

135 Id., p. 21.

136 For example Japan (id., p. 23), Denmark (S/PV.6347 (Resumption 1), p. 2), Australia (S/PV.6347 (Resumption 1), p. 8), Norway (S/PV.6347 (Resumption 1), p. 12), Liechtenstein (S/PV.6347 (Resumption 1), pp. 6–7; at p. 6: "the best way for the Security Council to promote international law and the rule of law is to lead by example. [...] The Council is legally bound by the applicable rules of the Charter and of international law".). Botswana wrongly interpreted Art. 1(1) of the Charter (as if the 1945 Egyptian amendment to the draft for that provision had been adopted), by saying: "Article 1 of the Charter of the United Nations recognizes that the collective measures employed by the United Nations in the prevention and removal of threats to peace should be underpinned by the principles of justice and international law" (S/PV.6347 (Resumption 1), p. 21).

statements was more on the specific topics suggested by Mexico, demonstrating to some extent how the Security Council in its practice followed the rule of law.

5.2.3 Subsequent Thematic Debates on the Rule of Law

A fifth thematic debate on the rule of law took place in January 2012, on the basis of a report by the Secretary-General on 'the rule of law and transitional justice in conflict and post-conflict societies'.[137] This report focuses almost exclusively on rule of law issues at the national level. It included the ways in which the UN could provide assistance, just as almost a decade earlier during the first thematic debate on the rule of law. Only in one paragraph, the international dimension is mentioned:[138]

> 13. It is important for the Security Council to adhere to basic rule of law principles to ensure the legitimacy of its actions. The establishment of the international criminal tribunals and the maintenance of complex sanctions regimes, among other initiatives, have raised questions as to the binding nature of international law on the Council. The expansion of the mandate of the Ombudsperson under the Al-Qaida sanctions regime, pursuant to Council resolution 1989 (2011), and the increased use of the International Court of Justice to clarify legal elements of international disputes, are steps that can strengthen the legitimacy of Council actions. The Court's role in the maintenance of international peace and security is further enhanced where Member States accept its compulsory jurisdiction.

In line with this report, the statements made during the meeting focused almost exclusively on the rule of law at the national level.[139] Only a few states made brief observations on the rule of law and the Security Council, in particular the need for the Council to apply international law in its work, or, as some states put it, "to lead by example".[140] The presidential statement adopted

---

137 UN Doc. S/2011/634.

138 Id., p. 5.

139 For the reports of the meeting, see UN Docs. S/PV.6705 and S/PV.6705 (Resumption 1).

140 See the statements by Pakistan (UN Doc. S/PV.6705, p. 17) and Liechtenstein (id., p. 27). The same idea was mentioned in other statements, see e.g. those by Mexico (id., p. 24), Costa Rica (id., p. 29), Austria (id., p. 31) and Norway (UN Doc. S/PV.6705 (Resumption 1), p. 11).

at this thematic debate contains one sentence devoted to this international dimension:[141]

> The Security Council reaffirms its commitment to international law and the Charter of the United Nations, and to an international order based on the rule of law and international law, which are essential for cooperation among States in addressing common challenges, thus contributing to the maintenance of international peace and security.

Later in 2012, another rule of law thematic debate took place at the initiative of Guatemala.[142] This debate was devoted to the relationship between the Security Council and the International Criminal Court. It did not result in the adoption of a presidential statement. The statements made during the meeting regarded the relationship between peace and justice, and the connections between the work of the Security Council and that of the ICC.[143] Only exceptionally reference was made to the application of international law by the Security Council.[144]

The next thematic debate of the Security Council devoted to the rule of law took place during in February 2014, at the initiative of Lithuania.[145] Its focus was on assistance by the UN to the strengthening of national rule of law institutions, in the context of the UN's peacekeeping and peacebuilding activities. Most statements mentioned what the UN should or should not do in this regard (e.g. tasks of the UN Secretariat, mandates of UN missions). Only a few observations addressed the way in which the UN was performing its functions,

---

141 UN Doc. S/PRST/2012/1. The text is almost fully copied from the 2010 Presidential Statement quoted above.

142 See the concept note prepared for the meeting by Guatemala, UN Doc. S/2012/731.

143 See UN Docs. S/PV.6849 and S/PV.6849 (Resumption 1), meeting of 17 October 2012.

144 See in particular the statement by the Russian Federation: "[o]wing to its role and mandate under the Charter, the Security Council has a special part to play in strengthening the legal foundation of international relations. The Council makes an extremely important contribution to developing the system of international relations based on the rule of international law. That means that the Council itself must serve as an example in strengthening the authority of international law. It is extremely important that decisions by the Council rely on the provisions of the Charter and take into account the rules of international humanitarian law and universally recognized human rights standards. The Council cannot afford to take hasty decisions that are not well founded or to manipulate Chapter VII of the Charter. It cannot allow irresponsible actions, dictated by short-sighted interests, to lead to the disintegration of the entire system of international law" (S/PV.6849, p. 19).

145 See the concept note prepared for the meeting by Lithuania, UN Doc. S/2014/75.

i.e. that it should fully apply international law in its work. Specific examples mentioned included the UN's zero tolerance policy for sexual exploitation and abuse and the UN's due diligence policy on human rights.[146] Similar to previous thematic debates, Mexico emphasized that "[i]t is crucial for the decisions of the Security Council to respect and strengthen the principles of the rule of law in order to guarantee legitimacy for their actions, and also, of course, for the Security Council to comply with international law".[147] The presidential statement adopted at the end of the debate reproduced the provision from the January 2012 Presidential Statement (quoted above), in which the Security Council reaffirmed "its commitment to international law and the Charter of the United Nations, and to an international order based on the rule of law and international law".[148]

5.2.4 The Security Council as a Model for the Rule of Law?

Since 2014, the Security Council has not devoted any further thematic debates to the rule of law relevant for the topic analyzed in this Chapter. There have been thematic debates on international law and the maintenance of international peace and security, but these concerned almost exclusively the application and observance of international law by states.[149] As Fassbender has observed: the Security Council returned "to a more conventional perspective".[150]

---

146 E.g. the statement by France, referring to "the exemplary nature of peacekeeping operations and more broadly of the Organization in the field of the rule of law" (UN Doc. S/PV.7113, p. 7). See also the statement by Liechtenstein (id. p. 29).

147 UN Doc. S/PV.7113, pp. 40–41.

148 UN Doc. S/PRST/2014/5 (21 February 2014).

149 A general debate took place on 21 February 2018 at the initiative of Kuwait (see Kuwait's concept note for the meeting, UN Doc. S/2018/85). The item on the agenda was entitled 'Maintenance of international peace and security – purposes and principles of the Charter of the United Nations in the maintenance of international peace and security'. Both Secretary-General Guterres and former Secretary-General Ban Ki-moon delivered addresses. For the records of this meeting, see UN Doc. S/PV.8185. Three months later, on 17 May 2018, another thematic debate took place at the initiative of Poland. See Poland's concept note for the meeting, UN Doc. S/2018/417/Rev.1. For the records of the meeting, see UN Doc. S/PV.8262. On 9 November 2018, at the initiative of China the Security Council met to discuss 'strengthening multilateralism and the role of the UN' (S/PV.8395). On 13 August 2019, a meeting took place under the agenda item 'The promotion and strengthening of the rule of law in the maintenance of international peace and security', on the occasion of the 70th anniversary of the Geneva Conventions (UN Doc. S/PV.8596). In January 2020, following the killing of General Suleimani of Iran in Iraq by the US on 3 January, the Security Council had a three-day meeting devoted to the topic 'Upholding the United Nations Charter' (S/PV.8699; S/PV.8699 (Resumption 1), S/PV.8699 (Resumption 2)), and adopted Presidential Statement PRST/2020/1.

150 Fassbender, op. cit. note 22, p. 783.

In a number of statements, UN members not only reaffirmed their commitment to international law but also accused each other of violations of international law. Hardly any observations were made regarding the application of international law by the UN, more specifically the Security Council. However, the main exception has been the address to the Council on 17 May 2018 by President Meron of the President of the International Residual Mechanism for Criminal Tribunals (the successor of the Yugoslav and Rwanda Tribunals). Judge Meron opened his address by referring to his personal background:[151]

> This is not simply a professional matter. I was 9 years old when Nazi Germany invaded Poland, the country of my birth. Overnight, we became refugees, and most of my family were killed by the Nazis because we were Jews. When the war ended, I emerged lucky to be alive but profoundly affected by my experiences.

It is useful to cite part of his address to the Security Council in full, as it put the essence on the table of the Security Council:[152]

> the Security Council is not only a leading voice in upholding accountability and the rule of law. It must also serve as a model itself. In some respects that is a challenging task. Given that the Council is an inherently political body, it is perhaps to be expected that the different situations coming before the Council may receive differing degrees of attention, be resolved in different ways or be made subject to varying priorities. Yet the rule of law depends on consistency and equality of enforcement, and abhors selectivity. If one situation involving alleged atrocity crimes is treated with all due attention and another is disregarded or left to linger in a decision-making limbo, does that not fundamentally undermine the values at the core of the principle of the rule of law? How can the Council's identity as a political body and its role as a champion of the rule of law be reconciled?
>
> One possibility would be for the Council to develop and publicly adopt objective criteria to assess and, where appropriate, steps to be deployed with respect to, all credible allegations of international crimes that come before it passing a certain threshold. Agreement in the abstract on such an approach would not only enhance equality of enforcement and reduce perceptions as to the ad hoc and arguably inconsistent nature of the Council's

151 UN Doc. S/PV.8262, p. 8.

152 Id., p. 10. In the second paragraph quoted below a word seems to be missing (before "steps").

> actions when confronted with reported atrocity crimes. It would also reduce the degree to which subjective or political considerations weigh on, and potentially delay or divert, the ultimate decision-making process.
>
> Another possibility would be for the Council to reflect on its role not simply as a political body but as a representative political body. In accordance with Article 24 of the Charter, the Members of the United Nations have conferred on the Council primary responsibility for the maintenance of international peace and security and have agreed that, in carrying out its duties in that regard, the Council acts on their behalf. Given that, is it too idealistic to suggest that members of the Council are duty-bound to act on behalf of the broader international community - that they must, when reaching decisions on issues of accountability in the context of peace and security, serve the interests of the United Nations membership as a whole rather than prioritizing their own interests or those of strategic allies?

This statement is particularly relevant, because Judge Meron not only mentions dilemmas inherent in acting in accordance with the rule of law as a political body, but also suggests two ways to deal with such dilemmas. Firstly, the Security Council could adopt criteria for dealing with international crimes that come before it. Secondly, Security Council members should act more on behalf of all UN members rather than doing what is only in the national interest.

As to the first suggestion, from a rule of law perspective the adoption of criteria for dealing with international crimes would certainly address some of the criticism that the Security Council is selective. In this way, the Council would commit itself to a certain normative framework within which it would operate. Such a framework should guide the Council itself, and it would provide criteria for the outside world to assess the Council's action and inaction. Obviously, such criteria still would need to be interpreted on a case-by-case basis, but at least they would offer a common standard for making such interpretations. It could be questioned however, whether it would not be more appropriate for the General Assembly to adopt such criteria. Even though there is no *trias politica* within the UN, its principal organs perform different functions that they need to mutually respect. When the Declaration on the Rule of Law was adopted by the General Assembly, Secretary-General Ban Ki-moon stated:[153]

> The Charter of the United Nations – the "constitution" of the international community – provides indispensable tools to deepen the rule of

153 UN Doc. A/67/PV.3, p. 2.

> law: the universal standard-setting power of the General Assembly, the enforcement power of the Security Council and the judicial power of the International Court of Justice.

If standard-setting is indeed for the General Assembly, it would be more appropriate for this principal organ in which all member states are represented to adopt criteria for action when atrocity crimes are committed, as guidance for the Security Council, just as it has done on other occasions.[154]

A similar suggestion has been made in 2004, by the High-level Panel on Threats, Challenges and Change, with regard to Security Council decisions on the use of force.[155] This Panel proposed the adoption of a set of guidelines ("five basic criteria of legitimacy") for decisions relating to the use of force.[156] The purpose of such guidelines would be to improve the quality of such decisions, to ensure that they are "better made, better substantiated and better communicated", and that they are made "on solid evidentiary grounds, and for the right reasons".[157] Such guidelines would not dictate outcomes when applied to individual situations. As the Panel stated:

> The guidelines we propose will not produce agreed conclusions with pushbutton predictability. The point of adopting them is not to guarantee that the objectively best outcome will always prevail. It is rather to maximize the possibility of achieving Security Council consensus around when it is appropriate or not to use coercive action, including armed force; to maximize international support for whatever the Security Council decides; and to minimize the possibility of individual Member States bypassing the Security Council.

The Panel advised that these guidelines "should be embodied in declaratory resolutions of the Security Council and General Assembly".[158] While Secretary-General Annan supported this approach in his 2005 report 'In Larger Freedom', he recommended that only the Security Council (not the General Assembly) would "adopt a resolution setting out these principles and expressing its

154 For example when the General Assembly adopted the definition of aggression in 1974, GA Res. 3314 (XXIX). The Assembly indicated in para. 4 of this resolution that its definition was intended as "guidance" for the Security Council.

155 UN Doc. A/59/565.

156 These five basic criteria of legitimacy are: seriousness of threat, proper purpose, last resort, proportional means and balance of consequences (id., at 57–58).

157 Id., p. 57.

158 Id., p. 58.

intention to be guided by them when deciding whether to authorize or mandate the use of force".[159] However, the subsequent World Summit Outcome Resolution of the General Assembly did not follow this advice. It merely somewhat ritually "reiterated" Charter purposes and principles and a commitment to multilateralism, and it "reaffirmed" relevant Charter provisions and the responsibilities of both the Security Council and the General Assembly.[160]

Meron wonders whether his second suggestion (Security Council members should act more on behalf of all UN members rather than doing what is only in the national interest) is "too idealistic". In the light of practice, it is realistic to ask this question. However, it is decisive that acting on behalf of UN membership as a whole is a Charter obligation, as Meron mentions. In addition, this obligation was not only written in the Charter in 1945, in times when a strong sense of what is in the common interest prevailed, it was also regularly reaffirmed in UN practice, for example in the 2005 World Summit Outcome resolution of the General Assembly.[161] Even the United States during the Trump administration ('America first') has indirectly confirmed in the Security Council that members of the Council do not only act in their capacity as sovereign states acting purely in their national interests, but also in their capacity as members of a collective body, when it stated:[162]

> all too often Member States invoke the United Nations Charter not to inspire us to act, but to excuse their lack of action. And so we see the Security Council frequently failing to act at the times it is most important to defend the principles of the Charter. However, the United Nations is not simply a collection of nations. The United Nations Charter gives this organ an identity and a meaning of its own.

Nevertheless, practice has demonstrated that members, in particular permanent members, struggle to act in the Security Council not only as sovereign states but also as representatives of UN membership at large, both in taking initiatives for Security Council action and in refraining from blocking such action.

∴

159 UN Doc. A/59/2005, p. 33.

160 GA Res. 60/1, paras. 77–80.

161 Id., para. 152: "We reaffirm that Member States have conferred on the Security Council primary responsibility for the maintenance of international peace and security, acting on their behalf, as provided for by the Charter".

162 On 21 February 2018 (UN Doc. S/PV.8185, p. 12).

This overview of thematic debates of the Security Council on the rule of law demonstrates that the focus has mostly been on the rule of law at the national level, including the ways in which the UN should assist national authorities in strengthening the rule of law. The international dimension was mostly discussed in the 2006 and 2010 thematic debates. This international dimension essentially covered two aspects: states must act within the law and the UN, including the Security Council, must do so as well. It is in particular the latter aspect that is analyzed in this Chapter.

Within the Security Council, both permanent members and the ten elected members have been active in organizing thematic debates and making substantive contributions to developing a collective view on the meaning of the rule of law for the work of the Council, manifested in the respective presidential statements. For example, the United Kingdom took the initiative for the first two thematic debates; elected members Denmark, Mexico, Guatemala, South Africa and Lithuania for others.[163] Of the permanent members, China in particular made general references to the relevance of the rule of law for the Security Council.[164] During open debates, also many non-members of the Security Council participated actively in the discussions.

A number of member states that participated in the thematic debates expressed the view that the Security Council is bound by international law. Others however did not mention this explicitly or only stated that the Council is bound by the Charter (including Article 1(1)). As a result, the language used in the relevant presidential statements is somewhat general. Whereas a wide

163 See in particular A. Rodiles, 'Non-Permanent Members of the United Nations Security Council and the Promotion of the International Rule of Law', 5 *Goettingen Journal of International Law* (2013), pp. 333–373; A. Rodiles, 'What Kind of Rule of Law Should Elected Members Promote?', in N. Schrijver and N. Blokker (eds.), *Elected Members of the Security Council* (2020), pp. 183–196. According to Rodiles (2020), "[w]hile the P5 tend to favour the thicker version of the rule of law, the E10 are more concerned with the thinner one"(id., p. 187).

164 See S/PV.6347 (2010), p. 21: "The Security Council's fulfillment of its primary responsibility to maintain international peace and security within the framework of international law is of great significance in strengthening international law and furthering the process of strengthening the rule of law in international relations"; in a similar way in S/PV.5474 (2006), p. 26. See also the statement by the Russian Federation in S/PV.5474 (2006), p. 16: "In the course of the last decade and a half, we have seen the Security Council play an increased role and make greater use of its potential. It faces more difficult tasks in meeting old and new threats and challenges, primarily those posed by international terrorism. In line with that trend, the means at its disposal are also evolving. It is for that very reason of considerably increased responsibility that the Security Council should pay particular attention to reasserting the principle of the rule of law, in both its own work and its relations with other United Nations bodies, organizations and States".

variety of states is ready to explicitly state that the UN or the Charter are based on the idea 'the rule of law, not the rule of power',[165] there is no full consensus (just as it was absent in 1945) on whether the Security Council, in performing its functions, must act in conformity with the principles of justice and international law. However, there was consensus on the more general text contained in the 2006 and 2010 Presidential Statements. The 2010 Presidential Statement may be compared to the opening paragraphs of the 2012 Rule of Law Declaration of the General Assembly.

The 2010 Presidential Statement:

> The Security Council reaffirms its commitment to the Charter of the United Nations and international law, and to an international order based on the rule of law and international law, which is essential for peaceful coexistence and cooperation among States in addressing common challenges, thus contributing to the maintenance of international peace and security.

The 2012 General Assembly Declaration:

1. We reaffirm our solemn commitment to the purposes and principles of the Charter of the United Nations, international law and justice, and to an international order based on the rule of law, which are indispensable foundations for a more peaceful, prosperous and just world.
2. We recognize that the rule of law applies to all States equally, and to international organizations, including the United Nations and its principal organs, and that respect for and promotion of the rule of law and justice should guide all of their activities and accord predictability and legitimacy to their actions. We also recognize

165 Examples include the following: "[t]he foundation of multilateralism is international law. The rule of law is in its DNA, as opposed to the law of the strongest and the law of the jungle. Respect for the law is at the heart of the Charter of the United Nations, […]" (France, S/PV.8395, p. 19); "[t]he United Nations is the ultimate expression of the rule of law at the international level" (Liechtenstein, id., p. 30); "[t]he Charter, the foundation stone of the Organization, recognizes that the rule of law must be at the heart of our shared efforts to create a peaceful world" (Ireland, S/PV.8262, p. 45); "the Security Council operates within the framework of international law in all its functions" (South Africa, S/PV.6347, p.15); "the basis for maintaining international peace and security […] is the might of the law and not the law of might" (Lebanon, id., p. 21). More in general: "[t]rue multilateralism is founded on inclusion instead of exclusion; cooperation in place of confrontation; equality rather than inequality; the rule of law instead of the rule of power; […]" (Iran, S/PV.8395, p. 40).

> that all persons, institutions and entities, public and private, including the State itself, are accountable to just, fair and equitable laws and are entitled without any discrimination to equal protection of the law.

It is clear that the General Assembly Declaration uses much of the text of the Presidential Statement adopted two years earlier by the Security Council. Both the Assembly and the Council are committed to the Charter, to international law and to an international order based on the rule of law. However, there are also differences. In the General Assembly Declaration, the member states not only commit themselves to international law but also to the broader notion of justice. Moreover, on the basis of paragraph 2 of the Declaration, the rule of law applies to the Security Council; in addition, respect for and promotion of the rule of law and justice should guide all of its activities and accord predictability and legitimacy to its actions (the Presidential Statement does not say this). The 2012 Declaration therefore goes beyond Article 1(1) of the Charter in connecting the Security Council to international law, in particular because it does not exclude Chapter VII measures.

The next Section will briefly examine how the Security Council is applying its general rule of law position in practice, by analyzing how it has dealt with two specific topics often mentioned in the thematic rule of law debates: international criminal justice and individual sanctions. These topics have been prominent on the agenda of the Security Council since the 1990s.

5.3 *Two Specific Topics: International Criminal Justice and Individual Sanctions*

5.3.1 Introduction

As discussed above, the Security Council has held several general debates on the rule of law since 2003. At the same time, those general debates were closely connected to more specific items on the agenda of the Council. When concept notes prepared for thematic debates suggested to focus on such more specific items, many statements made in the Council also referred to the notion of the rule of law in general. When a thematic debate was intended to be of a more general nature, many statements focused on specific items. It is therefore appropriate, in addition to the preceding overview of general debates, to examine specific topics on the agenda of the Security Council within the broader rule of law theme. It would be too ambitious and not necessary to cover all topics that are relevant in this regard. Therefore, two prominent examples have been selected: international criminal justice and individual sanctions.

5.3.2 The Rise and Fall of International Criminal Justice in the Security Council

Two specific topics will be briefly examined here, specifically through a rule of law lens: the establishment of ad hoc criminal tribunals by the Security Council and referrals of 'situations' by the Council to the International Criminal Court.

International criminal justice is an area fraught with rule of law challenges. Well-established principles of (national) criminal law, such as the principles of legality and equality before the law, have been more difficult to implement and guarantee at the international level. As Cryer wrote, "[i]nternational criminal law is more susceptible to claims of selectivity than domestic law".[166] Since the 1990s, the Security Council (a political organ with superpowers as prominent permanent members) has used international criminal justice measures when it found that the commission of international crimes amounted to a threat to the peace. It was to be expected that such use could be at odds with principles of criminal law and that rule of law questions and criticism would emerge. A few examples should suffice; the list could easily be expanded. In light of this experience and for other reasons (e.g. the costs involved), after the heyday of the 1990s the pendulum swung the other way. It has even been observed that today, "talking about international criminal justice in the Security Council is something of a taboo".[167]

5.3.2.1 *The Establishment of Ad Hoc Criminal Tribunals*

The collapse of the Soviet Union and the end of the Cold War facilitated not only the (re-) emergence of internal conflicts in a number of states (e.g. Yugoslavia, Somalia, Angola, Georgia), but also the ability of the Security Council to actively contribute to their resolution. Soon after the beginning of the armed conflict in the former Yugoslavia, an increasing number of sources reported about mass killings, ethnic cleansing and other violations of international humanitarian law. In 1992, the Security Council requested the Secretary-General to establish a Committee of Experts to examine and analyze information about such violations.[168] Early in 1993, this Committee presented an interim report, in which it not only found extensive evidence of grave violations of

166 R. Cryer, *Prosecuting International Crimes: Selectivity and the International Criminal Law Regime* (2005), p. 198. This is partly "because international criminal law is more selectively enforced than domestic law".

167 G. Nesi, 'Non-Permanent Members of the Security Council and International Criminal Justice: A Proposal for Revitalization', in Schrijver and Blokker, op. cit. note 163, pp. 267–278, at p. 267.

168 SC Res. 780 (6 October 1992).

international humanitarian law, but also, at the very end of its report, "was led to discuss the idea of the establishment of an ad hoc international tribunal. In its opinion, it would be for the Security Council or another competent body of the United Nations to establish such a tribunal in relation to events in the territory of the former Yugoslavia".[169]

Subsequently, the Security Council decided to establish the proposed ad hoc criminal tribunal, in two steps. First, it took the decision of principle that such a tribunal "shall be established" and it asked the Secretary-General to prepare a report "on all aspects of this matter".[170] In this report, the Secretary-General essentially proposed most details of the future tribunal, including its Statute.[171] Next, in a second resolution, the Security Council approved this report, established the tribunal and adopted its Statute.[172]

While there was broad agreement in the international community about the need for an ad hoc tribunal in this case, there was considerable disagreement about how to establish it. Essentially three options were on the table: the creation of the tribunal by a multilateral treaty, by the General Assembly or by the Security Council. It was generally agreed that the first option was to be preferred. The main question was whether the other options were legitimate and acceptable under the circumstances, as an exceptional measure and because it was widely perceived that it would take too long before a treaty could be concluded and would enter into force. These discussions about the proper legal basis for the tribunal are reflected in the report by the Secretary-General and in the reports of the two relevant Security Council meetings.

While both Security Council resolutions were adopted unanimously, doubts about the creation of the tribunal by a Security Council resolution were expressed in particular by Brazil, and to some extent by China.[173] Brazil questioned whether it was within the powers of the Security Council to establish an ad hoc criminal tribunal. In its statement in the Security Council in February 1993, it concluded:[174]

> In this rapidly changing world, we consider it increasingly important to promote the rule of law, in international relations by acting to ensure

169 UN Doc. S/25274 (10 February 1993).
170 SC Res. 808 (22 February 1993).
171 un Doc. S/25704 (3 May 1993).
172 SC Res. 827 (25 May 1993).
173 China stated that its support for the resolution did not "prejudge China's position on future Security Council actions on the subject" (UN Doc. S/PV.3175, p. 7).
174 UN Doc. S/PV.3175, p. 7.

> strict respect for the provisions of our Charter and other norms of international law.

More specifically, Brazil explained its 'rule of law criticism' in the following way:[175]

> It is of particular importance that the international tribunal to be established rest on a solid legal foundation, which will ensure the effectiveness of its actions. [...]
>
> As regards the definition of the best method for the establishment of an ad hoc international criminal tribunal, it should be borne in mind that the authority of the Security Council is not self-constituted but originates from a delegation of powers by the whole membership of the Organization. It is never too much to recall that the Security Council, in the exercise of its responsibilities, acts on behalf of the States Members of the United Nations, in accordance with Article 24, paragraph 1, of the Charter.
>
> Just as the authority of the Council does not spring from the Council itself but derives from the fact that certain responsibilities have been conferred upon it by all the Members of the United Nations, the powers of the Council cannot be created, recreated or reinterpreted creatively by decisions of the Council itself, but must be based invariably on specific Charter provisions.
>
> [...] Especially when the Council is being increasingly called upon to fully exercise the considerable powers entrusted to it, the definition of such powers must be construed strictly on the basis of the text of the relevant Charter provisions. To go beyond that would be legally inconsistent and politically unwise.

Subsequently, Brazil repeated its 'rule of law' criticism in a letter to the UN Secretary-General[176] and during the Security Council meeting of 25 May 1993, when the Statute of the tribunal was adopted.[177] Also China expressed its reservations: "to adopt by a Security Council resolution the Statute of the International Tribunal which gives the Tribunal both preferential and exclusive jurisdiction is not in compliance with the principle of State judicial sovereignty".[178]

---

175 Id., pp. 6–7.

176 UN Doc. A/47/922 – S/25540 (6 April 1993).

177 UN Doc. S/PV.3217. In this meeting, Brazil stated that it "did not favour" the creation of the tribunal by the Security Council (p. 37).

178 Id., p. 33.

Therefore, this "can only be an ad hoc arrangement suited only to the special circumstances of the former Yugoslavia and shall not constitute any precedent".[179] Other members of the Security Council also referred to the rule of law, but in a different meaning.[180]

In the Security Council, the 'rule of law criticism' expressed by Brazil was addressed in particular by Spain, by referring to 'rule of law provisions' in the Preamble of the UN Charter:[181]

> In the final analysis, the Council, by adopting resolution 827 (1993) is seeking to make a reality of the determination contained in the preamble of the Charter to reaffirm faith in fundamental human rights, in the dignity and worth of the human person, and indeed to establish conditions for the maintenance of justice and respect for international law in so tragic a situation as that unfortunately still being experienced by the peoples of the former Yugoslavia.

The unanimous adoption of the Security Council resolutions establishing the Yugoslavia Tribunal did not silence the 'rule of law criticism' voiced in particular by Brazil. Two years later, in the first case before the tribunal, counsel for the defence of Duško Tadić argued that the tribunal lacked jurisdiction, *inter alia* because it was improperly established. The tribunal rejected this preliminary defence motion. According to its Appeals Chamber, the tribunal was "lawfully established as a measure under Chapter VII of the Charter".[182] In addition, the same 'rule of law criticism' was expressed when in 1994 the Security Council created a second ad hoc tribunal, the Rwanda Tribunal.[183]

179 Id., p. 34.

180 France and the United States emphasized that the creation of the tribunal would contribute to re-establishing the rule of law in the former Yugoslavia. According to France, establishing the tribunal demonstrated the UN's "common resolve not to tolerate infamy and to assert the rule of law". The US emphasized that the tribunal would establish the truth, and "truth is the cornerstone of the rule of law" (id., p. 12). Morocco stated that the tribunal "will promote the justice to which we all aspire and will strengthen the rule of law in international relations" (id., p. 27).

181 Id., p. 41.

182 ICTY, Prosecutor v. Dusko Tadic a/k/a/ "Dule", Decision on the Defence Motion for the Interlocutory Appeal on Jurisdiction, 2 October 1995, para. 40.

183 SC Res. 955 (8 November 1994). During the meeting in which this resolution was adopted, Brazil stated: "Exceptional ad hoc initiatives by the Council may not be the best way to promote the consistent, balanced and effective application of international humanitarian law or to create an environment conducive to the enhancement of the rule of law in international public order. The Security Council's responsibilities lie not in the judicial or institution-building field, but in the maintenance of international peace and security.

There is not some 'rule of law principle of equality' obliging the Security Council to establish a criminal tribunal for Rwanda to prosecute international crimes just like it established a criminal tribunal to deal with international crimes committed on the territory of the former Yugoslavia.[184] Nevertheless, inside and outside the chambers of the Security Council, criticism of selectivity and double standards lurked everywhere, as well as arguments of fairness and justice. Why criminal justice for the former Yugoslavia, not for Rwanda? It was emphasized by many that the Security Council should respond in the same way to the genocide in Rwanda as it had done one year before when it established the Yugoslavia Tribunal.[185]

More recently, the establishment of the Lebanon Tribunal was also criticized within the Security Council, not explicitly in rule of law terms, but mainly because the Council used its Chapter VII powers to decide that the agreement concluded between the United Nations and Lebanon would enter into force on 10 June 2007, even if the Lebanese government would not ratify it before that date.[186] Earlier, the establishment of the Special Court for Sierra Leone in 2002 did not raise similar rule of law concerns.[187] The agreement concluded between the United Nations and Sierra Leone on which this court was based, entered into force in 2002 following the ratification by Sierra Leone.

The creation of these ad hoc tribunals by the Security Council bolstered the preparations for establishment of a permanent international criminal court. When the Council created the Rwanda Tribunal, France stated, "it is only because such a court does not exist that the Security Council has had to make use of its powers to establish a first and then a second ad hoc international tribunal".[188] Indeed, during the preparations for such a court by the International

---

Therefore, the invocation of Chapter VII of the Charter for the purpose of establishing an international tribunal goes, in our view, beyond the competence of the Council as clearly defined in the Charter" (UN Doc. S/PV.3453, p. 9). China expressed similar criticism as when the Yugoslavia Tribunal was created (id., p. 11), also earlier (UN Doc. S/PV.3400, p. 7).

184 Cf. Cryer, op. cit. note 166, p. 211.

185 See e.g. UN Doc. S/PV.3400 (1 July 1994), p. 6: "the Security Council took steps to ensure that persons suspected of committing war crimes in the former Yugoslavia can be brought to justice. We can be no less concerned about the commission of such offences in Rwanda" (New Zealand). See in particular the statements made during the meeting when the Security Council established the Rwanda Tribunal, UN Doc. S/PV.3453 (8 November 1994).

186 See the records of the relevant Security Council meeting, UN Doc. S/PV.5685.

187 SC Resolutions 1315 (2000) and 1400 (2002).

188 UN Doc. S/PV/3453, p. 4. The Russian Federation stated: "the history of the establishment of international tribunals, first in the former Yugoslavia and now in Rwanda, reinforces our conviction that a permanent international criminal court must be established in the near future" (id., pp. 2–3).

Law Commission, its member Crawford stated with regard to draft article 23 (providing for a Security Council referral to the future permanent court): "[a]s to article 23, it would be most undesirable if the Security Council were compelled, owing to the absence of a provision such as that which appeared in article 23, paragraph 1, to create further ad hoc courts, as it had been forced to do at great expense in the case of the former Yugoslavia, without even knowing in advance whether the court in question would ever have to hear a case".[189] A few years later, the possibility for the Security Council to refer a situation to the ICC became a reality, when the Rome Statute entered into force. This "gift to the Security Council" will now be discussed.[190]

5.3.2.2 *Referrals to the International Criminal Court*

The 1998 Rome Statute of the International Criminal Court provides that one of the ways in which the Court may exercise jurisdiction is if a situation in which one or more of the Statute crimes "appears to have been committed is referred to the Prosecutor by the Security Council acting under Chapter VII of the Charter of the United Nations".[191] When the Statute was signed, it seemed unlikely that the Security Council would soon make such a referral. It was expected that it would first of all take a considerable number of years before the Statute would enter into force, given the 60 ratifications requirement. Secondly, it was expected that permanent members would veto a proposed referral, in particular the United States because of its opposition to the ICC. However, the Statute entered into force within four years (on 1 July 2002), much faster than expected. And when a proposal was made to refer the situation in Darfur (Sudan) to the Court, the Security Council agreed in March 2005, after initial resistance by the United States.[192]

It took some months before the first referral resolution could be adopted. The voting result and the records of the relevant Security Council meeting show that not only the US but also other members had considerable doubts and concerns. The resolution was adopted by 11 votes in favour and four abstentions (Algeria, Brazil, China, United States). The United States maintained its fundamental objections to the ICC, but its conviction finally prevailed that "justice must be served in Darfur" and that "the international community

189 Yearbook of the ILC 1994, Vol. I (UN Doc. A/CN.4/SER.A/1994), p. 229, para. 78.

190 The expression is from L. Condorelli and S. Villalpando, 'Can the Security Council Extend the ICC's Jurisdiction?', in A. Cassese, P. Gaeta, J. Jones (eds.), *The Rome Statute of the ICC: A Commentary* (2002), pp. 571–583, at p. 572.

191 ICC Statute, Art. 13(b).

192 SC Res. 1593 (31 March 2005).

[should] speak with one voice in order to help promote effective accountability".[193] Algeria abstained because it was more in favour of finding a solution for the situation in Sudan with the African Union.[194] China abstained in view of the absence of consent from the Sudanese government to the exercise of jurisdiction by the ICC; China "cannot accept any exercise of the ICC's jurisdiction against the will of non-State parties".[195] Brazil decided to abstain because it disagreed with the price that had to be paid for the adoption of the resolution, in particular the exemption from the jurisdiction of the Court of nationals of non-state parties.[196]

In 2011 the Security Council made a second referral to the ICC: the situation in Libya.[197] This time the referral resolution was adopted unanimously.[198] For the approval of some members, it was important that the permanent representative of Libya to the UN no longer supported his government and had called for a referral in a letter to the President of the Security Council.

Three years later another referral was proposed, concerning the situation in Syria, but this time the Security Council was unable to come to an agreement: while 13 members voted in favour, China and the Russian Federation used their vetoes.[199] The meeting of the Security Council in which the vetoes were cast, demonstrated repressed anger, frustration and above all deep disunity amongst the members.[200] A large majority was frustrated by the impasse in the peace negotiations, the long absence of any perspective for the much-needed political agreement about the future of Syria, to end the war and the suffering. They wanted to use the ICC for what it was created: to put an end to impunity for the perpetrators of the most serious crimes of concern to the international community.[201] Russia and China - not parties to the Rome Statute - criticized the other members for not continuing to work for an overall political solution and believed the adoption of a referral would make it more difficult to achieve peace. Both the majority and the two veto-users criticized each other for not doing more to achieve the unity without which the Council cannot act.

193 UN Doc. S/PV.5158, p. 3.
194 Id., pp. 4–5.
195 Id., p. 5.
196 Id., p. 11.
197 SC Res. 1970.
198 UN Doc. S/PV.6491, p. 2.
199 See for the text of the draft resolution, sponsored by no less than 65 UN member states: UN Doc. S/2014/348.
200 See UN Doc. S/PV.7180.
201 See the Preamble of the Rome Statute.

Before the referral resolution was presented to the Security Council, in 2013 the Commission of Inquiry on Syria recommended to the Security Council that it should refer the situation in Syria "to justice, possibly to the International Criminal Court".[202] The High Commissioner for Human Rights urged the Security Council to refer the situation in Syria to the ICC.[203] At the beginning of the meeting of the Security Council in which the two vetoes were cast, Deputy Secretary-General Eliasson delivered a statement on behalf of the Secretary-General, in which he openly criticized the Security Council for its inability to act:[204]

> For more than three years, the Security Council has been unable to agree on measures that could bring an end to this extraordinarily brutal war, which has deeply affected and damaged not only millions of Syrian civilians but also the entire region. If members of the Council continue to be unable to agree even on a measure that could provide some accountability for the ongoing crimes, the credibility of this body and of the entire Organization will continue to suffer.

After the vote, a number of members expressed their support for existing initiatives recommending the permanent members not to use their vetoes when decisions are taken concerning large-scale atrocities.[205] From the rule of law perspective of this chapter, in particular the interventions by Argentine and the United States are relevant. Argentine addressed the question of selective justice:[206]

> On the one hand, it would seem that once again we are to accept as normal the exercise of selective justice. We should not be surprised that in comparable situations where heinous crimes are committed, some are considered appropriate to be referred to the Court while others are not. On the other hand, there seems to be an attempt to make us believe that undermining the integrity of legal instruments in no way hinders the

202 UN Doc. A/HRC/22/59 (5 February 2013), Report of the Independent international commission of inquiry on the Syrian Arab Republic (established by the UN Human Rights Council), para. 180(b).

203 See https://www.reuters.com/article/us-syria-crisis-un-rights/u-n-rights-chief-says-syria-government-abuses-far-outweigh-rebels-idUSBREA371UM20140408.

204 UN Doc. S/PV.7180, p. 2.

205 For example France, Rwanda, Jordan, Luxembourg (see id., pp. 4, 6–8).

206 Id., p. 10. Unsurprisingly, the representative of Syria also criticized the Security Council for applying double standards (id., p. 16).

> objective of achieving justice. In some cases, transcendent values are invoked, whereas in others sophisticated arguments are brought into play, although they mainly lean on the pragmatic principle that the end justifies the means.

The United States, represented by ambassador Samantha Power, expressed rule of law criticism of the Security Council and its two permanent members that had used their vetoes:[207]

> Today is about accountability for Syria, but it is also about accountability for the Security Council. [...] Why should the International Criminal Court pursue accountability for the atrocities in Africa but not those in Syria, where the worst horrors of our time are being perpetrated? For those who have asked the Security Council that very reasonable question, today they have their answer – the Russian and Chinese vetoes. [...] While there may be no accountability before the ICC today for the horrific crimes being carried out against the Syrian people, there should be accountability for those members of the Council that have prevented such accountability.

The situation in Syria is not the only example where a Security Council referral was proposed. Other examples include the situations in North Korea, Myanmar and Yemen.[208] It is difficult to compare degrees of evil, different violations of human rights, international criminal law and international humanitarian law. Yet the ICC was created to make such comparisons. As the Rome Statute's Preamble states, "the most serious crimes of concern to the international community as a whole must not go unpunished". The Rome Statute defines such crimes and lays down the conditions under which they can be prosecuted. As the Preamble states, during the 20th century there have been "unimaginable atrocities that deeply shock the conscience of humanity", and "such grave crimes threaten the peace, security and well-being of the world". Being threats to the peace explains why one of the mechanisms to trigger the jurisdiction of the Court is a referral by the Security Council acting under Chapter VII of the Charter. While it is for the Prosecutor to decide whether someone should be

207 Id., pp. 4–5.

208 North Korea: see GA Res. 70/172 (17 December 2015). Myanmar: see International Commission of Jurists, https://www.icj.org/myanmar-why-an-iiim-and-security-council-referral-are-needed-despite-the-icc-ruling-relating-to-bangladesh/ (13 September 2018). Yemen: European Parliament Resolution 2018/2853(RSP) (4 October 2018).

charged with the commission of crimes within the jurisdiction of the Court, on the basis of criteria provided by the Statute, it is for the Security Council to decide whether a situation "in which one or more of such crimes appears to have been committed" is to be referred to the Prosecutor.[209] Unlike the Prosecutor, the Security Council does not have criteria for taking referral decisions. It is a political organ, in which the rule of power prevails. At the same time, as was illustrated above, the need is felt to have some guidance in taking these decisions, to make such decisions fairer, more legitimate and less prone to double standards reproaches. In short: to promote the rule of law in this field.

∴

This brief overview has demonstrated how rule of law considerations have led the Security Council to get involved in international criminal justice and have influenced the way in which it has treaded these new paths. First of all, its wish prevailed to end impunity in the countries and regions of the world affected by large-scale violence and atrocities, to re-establish the rule of law at the national level. However, secondly, rule of law considerations have also played a role in proceeding in this *terra incognita*. Originally there were doubts, particularly from Brazil and China, as to whether the establishment of ad hoc criminal tribunals by the Security Council was within its powers. However, such doubts did not prevent these members to support this or abstain from using the veto. There is now considerable practice in favour of the view that it is within the Security Council's powers to be involved in the creation of ad hoc criminal tribunals. This is still true today, even now that the Council may also decide to refer a situation to the ICC. Practice has nonetheless demonstrated, that the road of a referral is not always accessible, for example because the crimes concerned predate the ICC (Special Court for Sierra Leone) or are not part of the ICC's jurisdiction (Special Tribunal for Lebanon). As far as referrals are concerned, the key question is not whether the Council may follow this road but when it should do so.

On 11 July 1994, Prime Minister Balladur of France addressed the Security Council after the Council had authorized *Opération Turquoise* in Rwanda.[210] Balladur referred to Rwanda's call for international assistance in dealing with the genocide on its territory, and stated:

209 ICC Statute, Art. 13(b).

210 SC Res. 929 (22 June 1994).

> If we can respond to its appeal to us for justice and solidarity, our international community will have taken a further step towards an international society in which the rule of law is respected - towards a more just society.

From the perspective of today, is this what happened at the time, also after the Rwanda Tribunal was created a few months after Prime Minister Balladur made his statement? Did the international community take a further step towards "an international society in which the rule of law is respected"?

As more often, the glass is half full and half empty. It is half full, because since 1993 and 1994 international criminal justice is on the agenda of the Security Council; before it was not. It is now generally accepted that the international criminal justice measures are at its disposal when it has determined that there is a threat to the peace somewhere in the world. The Council *may* take such measures. However, the glass is also half empty. The way in which the Security Council proceeds in this area, or does not proceed, has been widely criticized as being selective, applying double standards, following the political whims of the day. Whether or not the Security Council will create an ad hoc tribunal or will refer a situation to the ICC, is highly uncertain and mainly depends on the rule of power.[211] There is no beginning of a collective sense of obligation that the Council *must* take such measures under certain circumstances, for example in a 'Rwanda situation'.

Decisions taken by a political organ as the Security Council in the field of international criminal justice will never be 'pushbutton decisions', i.e. decisions taken almost automatically once international crimes have been committed somewhere in the world, similar in gravity and scale to those on the territory of the former Yugoslavia or in Rwanda. On the other hand, rule of law arguments of fairness, justice and legitimacy require that the Security Council should demonstrate a minimum of consistency, a minimum of adherence to the rule of law.

211 As Cryer has observed: "Where there is agreement on the acceptability of a tribunal among the permanent five members of the Security Council, the possibility of an international tribunal is there. Where it is not, either because there is insufficient interest to make proposals for a Tribunal or if the interests of any one of those powers is implicated, then quite simply there will not be a Tribunal. In terms of the gravity of offences, like incidents are not being treated alike, and as such, the *ad hoc* nature of the Tribunals leaves them open to charges of exceptionalism" (op. cit. note 166, p. 211).

5.3.3 Reviewing Individual Sanctions

The adoption of targeted sanctions against individuals is another example of Security Council measures raising questions of legality and legitimacy. Unlike the creation of ad hoc criminal tribunals, these questions did not concern the power of the Security Council to impose individual sanctions as such. This power is indeed explicitly attributed to the Council in the Charter.[212] Most criticism focused on the procedures for delisting (removing targeted individuals from a sanctions list) and the lack of any remedies for the individuals concerned. Whereas the right to a remedy is generally recognized, in particular in international human rights treaties, it was questioned whether the Security Council could simply abrogate it for those individuals against whom it imposed targeted sanctions, in the context of its resolve to take robust Chapter VII measures in its fight against international terrorism.

During the Cold War, the Security Council only exceptionally imposed economic sanctions and other "measures not involving the use of armed force".[213] This changed in the 1990s, when the Council adopted comprehensive economic sanctions against a number of states, for example the Federal Republic of Yugoslavia, Libya, Haiti and Iraq. A disadvantage of such comprehensive sanction regimes was that they affected entire populations of the countries concerned, including many innocent people, and were therefore less effective or even counterproductive. The Security Council therefore increasingly took recourse to 'targeted' or 'smart' sanctions, directed at individual leaders whose conduct the Council wanted to change. Examples of such sanctions are travel restrictions for leaders and/or senior officials[214] and the prohibition of the import of diamonds.[215] Most relevant here is the wide range of specific measures taken in the context of the fight against terrorism.

In 1999, the Security Council decided that all states had to freeze funds and other financial resources from the Taliban.[216] These sanctions were later extended to individuals and entities associated with Al-Qaida and Usama bin Laden, in particular after the attacks of 11 September 2001 when hundreds of individuals and entities were targeted.[217] The names of these individuals and

212 UN Charter, Art. 41. What follows is mostly reproduced from H.G. Schermers & N.M. Blokker, *International Institutional Law* (6th ed. 2018), pp. 975–977.

213 Id.

214 E.g. SC Res. 1127 (Angola); SC Res. 1970 (Libya).

215 E.g. SC Res. 1173 (Angola); SC Res. 1306 (Sierra Leone).

216 SC Res. 1267.

217 E.g. SC Res. 1333, SC. Res. 1390. More recently, these sanctions have also been extended to individuals and entities associated with the Islamic State of Iraq and the Levant (ISIL), see SC Res. 2170 and SC Res. 2368.

entities were included in a 'consolidated list' by a sanctions committee, a subsidiary organ of the Security Council.[218] However, some individuals included in this list denied any connection to Al-Qaida. They faced considerable difficulties in having their names removed from the list.[219] The relevant Security Council resolutions do not provide for any form of judicial protection for the individuals concerned. A listed individual who wanted to be delisted (because he claimed to be innocent or for other reasons) had no alternative but to submit a request to the same sanctions committee that had decided to put him on the list; there was no review by any other body. A number of other elements of the sanction procedures have also been criticized, including the lack of transparency and the almost Kafkaesque way in which individuals were listed, all justified by the need to fight terrorism.

This lack of due process was not immediately noted as a major shortcoming, when the first individual sanctions were imposed. Only after a few years, this 'rule of law criticism' was expressed in academic writings,[220] by the UN Secretary-General,[221] by national courts[222] and by the Court of Justice of

218 This sanctions committee was originally called the '1267 Sanctions Committee'. Since the adoption of SC Res. 1989 (2011) it was called the Al Qaida Sanctions Committee, and following the decision to include also individuals associated to ISIL, it is called the ISIL (Da'esh) and Al-Qaida Sanctions Committee.

219 See e.g. the *Sayadi* case, which was brought before the Human Rights Committee (Communication No. 1472/2006). See for the Views of the Human Rights Committee in this case UN Doc. CCPR/C/94/D/1472/2006.

220 See e.g. J.M. Farrall, *United Nations Sanctions and the Rule of Law* (2007); M. Bothe, 'Security Council's Targeted Sanctions Against Presumed Terrorists: The Need to Comply with Human Rights Standards', 6 *Journal of International Criminal Justice* (2008), pp. 541–555. See also B. Fassbender, *Targeted Sanctions Imposed by the UN Security Council and Due Process Rights* (A Study Commissioned by the UN Office of Legal Affairs and Follow-up by the United Nations), reproduced in 3 *International Organizations Law Review* (2006), pp. 437–485; T. Biersteker and S. Eckert, *Addressing Challenges to Targeted Sanctions: An Update of the 'Watson Report'* (2009).

221 Letter dated 15 June 2006 by UN Secretary-General Kofi Annan to the President of the Security Council. Attached to this letter is an informal paper. This paper is confidential, but its main conclusions are included in the statement by the UN Legal Counsel to the Security Council on 22 June 2006 (Fassbender, op. cit. note 220). The Legal Counsel stated, *inter alia*: "[s]uch a person has the right to review by an effective review mechanism. The effectiveness of this mechanism will depend on its impartiality, degree of independence, and ability to provide an effective remedy, including the lifting of the measure and/or, under specific conditions to be determined, compensation" (UN Doc. S/PV.5474, p. 5); see also *United Nations Juridical Yearbook 2006*, pp. 481–484.

222 E.g. the June 2009 judgment by a Canadian federal court in *Abdelrazik v. Canada (Minister of Foreign Affairs)*, 2009 FC 580, [2010] 1 F.C.R. 267, in which it was observed that "[t]he 1267 Committee regime is [...] a situation for a listed person not unlike that of Josef K. in

the European Union.[223] Next, it took a few years before the Security Council agreed to gradually improve the sanction procedures. Only in 2009 a first substantial step was taken towards remedying this deficiency when it created the Ombudsperson.[224] The Ombudsperson is independent. Appointed by the UN Secretary-General, (s)he has to deal with requests from listed individuals to be removed from the ISIL & Al Qaida sanctions list ('delisting requests'). On the one hand, the creation of this Ombudsperson is a major step forward in this highly sensitive policy field. Seen against the background of the absence of any possibility of judicial review of decisions of the Security Council, this is a remarkable development, even though the decisions in question are very specific decisions taken by a subsidiary organ of the Security Council. On the other hand, from a legal perspective, it is obvious that the creation of the Ombudsperson has not solved the judicial protection problem. The Ombudsperson only has the power to make (non-legally binding) "observations".[225] In addition, the functioning of the Ombudsperson is limited to the Al-Qaida/ISIL sanctions. For other individual sanctions lists, requests for delisting continue to be decided by the same body that initially decided to put the individual concerned on the list (the relevant sanctions committee), without any role for the Ombudsperson. This situation will continue to provoke criticism, both by academics and by national and international courts, as it is at variance with basic due process norms. Whether and to what extent further improvements will be made in these targeted sanctions regimes will mainly depend on the political will to maintain these instruments in the arsenal of measures of the Security Council, and to make the necessary due process adaptations.

From a strictly legal perspective, it may be concluded that imposing individual sanctions without any remedies on the basis of Chapter VII of the Charter does not violate international law. It may be argued that it is for the Security

---

Kafka's *The Trial*, who awakes one morning and, for reasons never revealed to him or the reader, is arrested and prosecuted for an unspecified crime" (para. 53).

223 Joined Cases C-402/05 P (*Kadi*) & C-415/05 P (*Al Barakaat*), ECLI:EU:C:2008:461, in which the Court observes that the de-listing procedure existing at the time "does not offer the guarantees of judicial protection" and "is still in essence diplomatic and intergovernmental" (paras. 322–323). On this judgment, see the wide variety of opinions in 5 *International Organizations Law Review* (2008), pp. 323–379, in 6 *International Organizations Law Review* (2009), pp. 257–298 and in 28 *Yearbook of European Law* (2009), pp. 533–697. See also the two judgments in the 'Kadi-2 case': T-85/09 (Kadi-II), ECLI:EU:T:2010:418, and Joined Cases C-584/10 P, C-593 P and C-595/10 P (Kadi-II)), ECLI:EU:C:2013:518.

224 SC Res. 1904.

225 Id., Annex II, para. 7(c).

Council to determine what is necessary to deal with threats to international peace and security (such as terrorism), and to balance this with fundamental human rights. The resulting Security Council decisions are binding and prevail over other treaty obligations of UN member states (including those in human rights treaties, except when they are part of *jus cogens*).[226] Such a view is in accordance with the outcome of the 1945 San Francisco negotiations regarding Article 1 of the UN Charter, as discussed in paragraph 4. If national and international courts would be entitled not to comply with Security Council resolutions (or their implementing measures), even for understandable human rights reasons, would this not in the end undermine the UN legal order and the primacy of the Security Council?

However, what may be lawful is not always perceived as legitimate. Gradually more support was given to the view that delisting procedures should be improved, at least for the ISIL & Al Qaida sanctions, and that some independent review of listings should be introduced. It took some time before this view gained more support, perhaps because terrorist attacks affected many countries and the view prevailed that the aim of fighting terrorism justified the means. However, when the criticism started to build up, by human rights organizations, academics, courts, and subsequently also states and international organizations, developments in favour of creating some form of remedial mechanism moved quickly. Perhaps this is also because the criticism came at the time of strong pressure for Security Council reform, and because the individual sanctions concerned were becoming less effective when courts expressed fundamental disapproval. In the absence of any independent review mechanism, should national and international courts fully comply with Security Council resolutions (or their implementing measures), even if such resolutions are at odds with constitutional principles that these courts must respect?

The governance of (what is now called) the ISIL & Al-Qaida sanctions regime has moved from the rule of power (Security Council primacy) in a rule of law direction (the right to a remedy). Although the protection offered by the Ombudsperson is not equal to fully fledged judicial protection at the national (or regional) level, much of the earlier criticism has been addressed. At the same time, similar protection is not offered in other Security Council sanction regimes and criticism of selective justice is therefore not unfounded.

226 UN Charter, Art. 103.

6 Concluding Observations

According to Bingham, it is the rule of law that makes the difference between good and bad government.[227] At the international level, this might be translated into: the rule of law makes the difference between good and bad governance. If this is true, one may wonder why the UN Charter does not explicitly mention it. The United Nations was established to perform a number of governance functions, including in particular the maintenance of international peace and security. The member states decided that they would no longer be allowed to freely use armed force in international relations, since long an important attribute of government (good or bad). A farewell to such an important attribute was only possible by giving a derived governance function - the primary responsibility for the maintenance of international peace and security - to the Security Council. If the rule of law makes the difference between good and bad governance, the question is pertinent why the UN Charter does not explicitly refer to the rule of law. There may be different answers.

Firstly, while the Charter does not explicitly mention the rule of law as such, it contains some of its substance. The Preamble refers to fundamental human rights, the dignity and worth of the human person, equal rights of men and women and of nations large and small. It also emphasizes the determination "to establish conditions under which justice and respect for the obligations arising from treaties and other sources of international law can be maintained". The reference in Article 1 to "principles of justice and international law", the provisions on the pacific settlement of disputes and the functions given to the International Court of Justice are all examples of rule of law elements justifying to a considerable extent the observation made by many, in 1945 and in UN practice, that the United Nations is based on the rule of law.

Secondly, when the Charter was negotiated, a key question was whether enforcement action by its most powerful organ would have to be in conformity with the principles of justice and international law. Article 1(1) of the Charter demonstrates that in 1945 a negative answer was given to this question. Has this been a missed opportunity to establish the right conditions for good governance, could this even foreshadow bad governance? While such questions were asked in 1945, at the end of the day the wish prevailed to give the Security Council much leeway, in view of "the dangers of a repetition of the so-called 'appeasement policy' " of the 1930s.[228]

227 Bingham, op. cit. note 13, p. 174.

228 UNCIO, Vol. VI, p. 13.

Thirdly, from a somewhat broader perspective, a fundamental idea underlying the rule of law principle, the containment of power, is to a certain degree implemented in the Charter. The power of the five permanent members of the Security Council, put at the disposal of the new world organization, was contained in several ways, even though they have the prerogative of the veto. The permanent members are bound by the same rules of the Charter as all other members of the UN. They are not the only members of the Security Council and need the support of at least four non-permanent members for the adoption of resolutions. In addition, the Security Council has very broad but not unlimited powers. Therefore, the permanent members cannot infinitely exploit the Council for their own ends. Finally, the Security Council is not a self-standing treaty body; it is embedded in the UN. While the Charter does not establish something like a balance of power, it attributes powers to other UN organs, in particular the General Assembly, the International Court of Justice and the Secretariat. This is relevant for the Security Council and to some extent controls the exercise of its powers. Thus, Thucydides' famous words ("the strong do what they can and the weak suffer what they must") might be true for the position of the Athenians in the Peloponnesian war more than 24 centuries ago, in the context of the Security Council it is a cynical overstatement, not an accurate description of the position of the permanent members in the UN.

However, even though the Egyptian amendment was not adopted in 1945 in San Francisco, 'water always finds its way'.[229] This Chapter has shown that the outcome of the 1945 negotiations regarding Article 1 of the Charter has not been the end of the discussion. Unlike water, the rule of law does not find its way automatically, by following the laws of nature. It requires man-made decisions, by those in power. In particular when the Security Council became more active since the 1990s, the question whether its actions were lawful and/or legitimate was posed in specific cases. A much more active Security Council entails greater risks of inconsistent decisions, depending on the political whims of the day, and criticism of double standards. This chapter has demonstrated how rule of law considerations have influenced the work of the Council. Thematic debates were initiated to discuss rule of law issues more generally. International criminal justice measures have been prominent on the agenda of the Security Council since the 1990s. At the same time, the use of such measures is strongly influenced by the rule of power. Individual sanctions are now more in accordance with rule of law requirements than when they were first created.

229 Van Schaack, op. cit. note 81.

At the same time such improvements have so far not been made across the board, but only for the ISIL & Al-Qaida sanctions regime.

This Chapter has again illustrated that the Security Council is not a self-standing body, but is part of the United Nations. The work of other UN organs regarding the rule of law has affected the way in which the Security Council dealt with it, both generally and in specific cases. Secretary-General Annan provided a broad definition of the rule of law in 2004 that also covered the activities of the Security Council. The 2012 General Assembly Declaration on the Rule of Law recognized "that the rule of law applies to all States equally, and to international organizations, including the United Nations and its principal organs, and that respect for and promotion of the rule of law and justice should guide all of their activities and accord predictability and legitimacy to their actions". So far, the Security Council itself has not made similar statements. Instead, it has "[reaffirmed] its commitment to international law and the Charter of the United Nations"[230] and has "[expressed] its commitment to ensure that all United Nations efforts to restore peace and security themselves respect and promote the rule of law".[231] The Security Council's "commitment to international law" was tested in specific cases, for example when it imposed individual sanctions. Following severe criticism of the original sanction procedures, the ISIL & Al-Qaida sanctions regime has moved from the rule of power (Security Council primacy) into a rule of law direction (the right to a remedy).

Establishing the rule of law at the international level does not happen automatically. It is a lengthy process requiring long-term efforts. This is already clear if we remember Dicey's definition. He distinguished as one of the meanings of the rule of law, the one most relevant for this book, the principle that no one is above the law, and everyone is subject to the jurisdiction of the ordinary tribunals. The first strand of this principle (no one is above the law) is generally recognized and well-established at the international level. *Pacta sunt servanda* is a fundamental principle of international law. No state denies that it is bound by treaties to which it is a party and by this fundamental principle. In contrast, the second strand (everyone is subject to the jurisdiction of ordinary tribunals) is as uncommon in international law as it is common at the national level. States are only subject to the jurisdiction of the International Court of Justice if they have accepted it. They are only subject to the jurisdiction of other international courts and tribunals if they have agreed to this. As far as the Security Council is concerned, even if it is assumed that it is bound by international law,

230 UN Docs. S/PRST/2006/28 and S/PRST/2010/11.

231 UN Doc. S/PRST/2010/11.

those who claim that the Security Council has violated international law have no remedy. Even though, in some specific instances, Security Council decisions have been brought before national and international courts, these courts may at most do some scrutinizing but cannot review such decisions.

Large discretionary powers were given to the Security Council in 1945, to save succeeding generations from the scourge of war. The question whether 'the rule of power' or the rule of law should govern the exercise of those powers is answered now differently than in 1945, as a result of globalization, interdependence, increased international cooperation and the development of international law. It seems unlikely that the view would still prevail that measures taken by the Security Council under Chapter VII of the Charter would not need to be "in conformity with the principles of justice and international law", as the drafters of Charter agreed in Article 1. As this Chapter has shown, in particular since the 1990s the rule of law has become more integrated in the work of the Security Council, as a principle of governance for the exercise of its powers. In short: the Security Council is now more 'governanced' by the rule of law than prescribed in 1945. This is not only manifested in the rhetoric during its meetings and in general phrases in presidential statements adopted at the end of thematic debates, but also to some extent in concrete practice, for example in the fields of international criminal justice and individual sanctions.

Nevertheless, even though these are significant developments, Security Council practice is still dominated by 'the rule of power', i.e. power politics and the interests of the permanent members, and is therefore prone to criticism of selectivity and the application of double standards. As a matter of principle, this is obvious. After all, the Security Council is a political organ, and for good reasons: 'la justice sans la force est impuissante'. At the same time, it is necessary to promote the further integration of the rule of law in the Council's practice, for 'la force sans la justice est tyrannique'. The forces of globalization and the need for international cooperation require that the Security Council will exercise its powers in accordance with the rule of law. While this key principle is now accepted, its further implementation in practice is likely to be a long-term, a very long-term process, calling for the efforts and commitment "of men and women and of nations large and small".[232]

232 UN Charter, Preamble, 2nd paragraph.

CHAPTER 4

The Need for a Second Enlargement of the Security Council

1 Introduction

The previous chapters have discussed the creation of the United Nations, the reasons why it was provided with a strong enforcement mechanism and key features of this mechanism. In 1945, the Security Council was established as a powerful part of the new world organization. The united strength of the five principal allied powers was to be continued after the war, embedded in the Security Council. Their military and political force was to protect the entire UN membership. They were willing to accept this global responsibility on the condition of permanent membership of the Security Council with the right of veto. Taking into account the lessons of the League of Nations, this new, centralized collective security system was fully prepared during the Second World War. The Charter was signed before the war came to an end. It was a second attempt to save succeeding generations from the scourge of war.

The Charter reflects the compromises made in San Francisco in 1945. The United Nations was established in the collective interest of the 50 negotiating states, as a dynamic framework for cooperation that should be able to admit new member states. The Charter created an independent secretariat. It laid down a number of fundamental obligations for the member states and far-reaching discretionary powers of the Security Council to deal with future threats to the peace, breaches of the peace and acts of aggression.

The future is by definition uncertain. The UN was therefore created as a flexible mechanism to meet future challenges in the best possible way. At the same time, it was anticipated from the outset that the flexibilities offered by the Charter might be insufficient to cope with future needs, and that it might therefore be necessary to update this mechanism by amending the Charter. As President Truman observed in his statement at the closing plenary session of the San Francisco Conference:[1]

1 UNCIO Vol. I, p. 23.

 | DOI:10.1163/9789004443921_006

> This Charter, like our own Constitution, will be expanded and improved as time goes on. No one claims that it is now a final or a perfect instrument. It has not been poured into a fixed mold. Changing world conditions will require readjustments – but they will be readjustments of peace and not of war.

Article 108 of the Charter imposes strict conditions for the entry into force of Charter amendments. Amendments first of all need a two-thirds majority in the General Assembly. Secondly, after being adopted by the Assembly they must be ratified by two-thirds of the members of the UN. The agreement of the five permanent members of the Security Council is not required at the first stage, only during the second.

One of the "changing world conditions" to which President Truman referred in 1945 is the large increase of the number of members of the UN. Since the Security Council must be representative of UN membership as a whole, the need arose to enlarge the Council. As the number of members, permanent and non-permanent, is laid down in the Charter, an amendment of the Charter is required to increase this number.

This Chapter will analyze the need to enlarge the Security Council.[2] First, paragraph 2 will discuss the 1963 enlargement. Paragraph 3 will argue that a second enlargement is necessary, and paragraph 4 will consider this against the background of questions of effectiveness and representativeness. Paragraph 5 aims to put the discussion about a second enlargement of the Security Council in perspective, by comparing the size of the Council to that of non-plenary organs of other universal organizations. Paragraph 6 will examine the proposals by the 2004 High-level Panel on Threats, Challenges and Change. Some concluding observations will be made in paragraph 7.

2 The Inevitability of the First Enlargement

The most appropriate size and composition of an international organ depends on its task. As stated in Article 24(1) of the UN Charter, "[i]n order to ensure prompt and effective action by the United Nations, *its Members* confer on the Security Council primary responsibility for the maintenance of international peace and security, and agree that in carrying out its duties under this

2 This chapter is largely based on N. Blokker, 'More Non-Permanent Members? On the Need for a Second Enlargement of the Security Council', in N. Schrijver and N. Blokker (eds.), *Elected Members of the Security Council* (2020), pp. 71–82.

responsibility the Security Council acts *on their behalf*" (italics added). The requirement of "prompt and effective action" explains why the Security Council was created as a non-plenary organ. This requirement could be an argument in favour of a very small Security Council, having a few members only, for example the five permanent members.[3] However, it is clear that the Council should have a certain minimum number of members, because UN members agreed that it should act "on their behalf". The Security Council must represent the entire UN membership. It would be difficult to see how it could do so if it would have, for example, only three, five or even seven members. While such a small number of members would probably make it easier to take "prompt and effective action", it would be much more difficult for all members of the UN to recognize themselves in the decisions of the Council, to feel that it is acting on behalf of all of them.

At the creation of the UN in 1945, the agreed size of the Council (11 members) amounted to 22 per cent of the total number of states that signed the Charter. The "changing world conditions" to which President Truman referred in 1945,[4] presented themselves when many states were admitted as new members of the UN, in particular following decolonization. Membership doubled within 15 years after the creation of the UN. As a result, it was inevitable to expand two of the UN's non-plenary organs, ECOSOC and the Security Council. Since the number of members of non-plenary UN organs is explicitly mentioned in the Charter, the only way to change these numbers is to amend the Charter. The urgency of such Charter amendments in the early 1960s was demonstrated when, in spite of the strict conditions of Article 108 and the unfavorable context of the Cold War, agreement was reached to enlarge the Security Council and the Economic and Social Council.

On 17 December 1963, the General Assembly adopted Resolution 1991A, in which it increased the number of members of the Security Council to 15, by adding four non-permanent members. This resolution considered that "the present composition of the Security Council is inequitable and unbalanced", and recognized "that the increase in the membership of the United Nations makes it necessary to enlarge the membership of the Security Council, thus providing for a more adequate geographical representation of non-permanent members and making it a more effective organ for carrying out its functions under the Charter of the United Nations".[5] The amendment entered into force on 31 Augustus 1965. Following the elections for the four new seats, the Security

3 See also Chapter 3, para. 3.3.
4 See above, para. 4.1.
5 GA Res. 1991A (XVIII), Preamble.

Council met for the first time with 15 members in January 1966.[6] The number of members of the Economic and Social Council increased from 18 to 27. However, while the increase to 15 members made the Security Council more representative, seen as a percentage of total UN membership, this increase did not at all make the Council 'as representative' as it was in 1945. At the creation of the UN, 11 members amounted to 22 per cent of the total number of states that signed the Charter, whereas 15 members amounted to only 13 per cent of all UN members in 1963.

3 The Urgency of Another Enlargement

Following these first Charter amendments, UN membership continued to increase, reaching 150 in 1977 and 193 in 2011. Therefore, again, the non-plenary organs of the UN have gradually become less representative. Agreement was reached on a second increase of the membership of the Economic and Social Council in 1971 (from 27 to 54 members). In contrast, no agreement has been reached on a second enlargement of the Security Council.

Such an enlargement has become even more urgent since the 1990s, when the Security Council became much more active than in the preceding 45 years of its existence. It has frequently used its extensive powers under the Charter. In many resolutions the Council has demonstrated its ability to agree on the use of force when necessary. This is one of the reasons why many governments and academics concluded that - leaving aside important exceptions such as the failure to prevent the genocide in Rwanda - the Security Council generally performed its functions in the 1990s and the early years of the 21st century better than before.[7] While the functioning of the Council has become more cumbersome in recent years, as demonstrated by the frequent use of the veto with regard to resolutions proposed to deal with the war in Syria, the Council is still much more active than it used to be during the Cold War era.

The vigorous role played by the Council in particular since 1990 has amplified earlier calls for enlarging its membership. Its legitimacy was increasingly questioned, and this necessarily affected the performance of its functions. Those in favour of enlargement claim that, now that the Council has become much more active, there is a corresponding greater urgency to make it more representative of UN membership as a whole and perform its functions with

6 B. Simma et al (eds.), *The Charter of the United Nations* (2012), p. 2218.

7 E.g. the government of the Netherlands in a letter to Parliament, 1 June 2004, Doc. TK 2003-2004, 24832, no. 5, p. 6.

the requisite legitimacy. In 1992, the General Assembly referred to the following reasons for such greater urgency: "the increasingly crucial role of the Security Council in maintaining international peace and security" and "the changed international situation and the substantial increase in the membership of the United Nations".[8] In 1993, the Assembly decided to establish the Open-ended Working Group on the Question of Equitable Representation on and Increase in the Membership of the Security Council, "to consider all aspects of the question of increase in the membership of the Security Council, and other matters related to the Security Council".[9] The working group was unable to reach agreement.[10]

In 2008, the General Assembly decided, building on the work of the Open-ended Working Group, "to commence intergovernmental negotiations in informal plenary of the General Assembly [...], based on proposals by Member States, in good faith, with mutual respect and in an open, inclusive and transparent manner, on the question of equitable representation on and increase in the membership of the Security Council and other matters related to the Council, seeking a solution that can garner the widest possible political acceptance by Member States".[11] So far, these intergovernmental negotiations (IGN) have not resulted in a text that could be used as the basis for negotiations. There are no official records of the IGN meetings (in spite of the decision of the General Assembly to conduct negotiations "in an open, inclusive and transparent manner"). Until now, the positions of the member states have been too far apart. For example, Brazil, Germany, India and Japan would like to become future permanent members (without the right of veto), the African Union countries would like to have two permanent seats with the right of veto for two African states,[12] and there are others who favour an increase in the number of both

8 GA Res. 47/62.

9 GA Res. 48/26.

10 See the annual reports by the Working Group to the General Assembly, e.g. UN Doc. A/53/47 (1999), UN Doc. A/56/47 (2002), A/62/47 (2008). See further O. Fleurence, *La réforme du Conseil de sécurité – L'état du débat depuis la fin de la guerre froide* (2000); B. Fassbender, *UN Security Council Reform and the Right of Veto – A Constitutional Perspective* (1998); Simma et al (eds.), op. cit. note 6, pp. 756–60; R. Higgins et al. (eds.), *Oppenheim's International Law – United Nations* (2017), pp. 67–69 (and the literature mentioned at pp. 62–63).

11 GA Decision 62/557. The text of this decision is included in UN Doc. A/62/49 (Vol. III), pp. 106–107.

12 In 2019, Sierra Leone stated in the General Assembly of behalf of the group of African states: "[e]ven though Africa is opposed in principle to the veto, it is of the view that so long as it exists and as a matter of common justice, it should be made available to all permanent members of the Security Council" (UN Doc. A/74/PV.33, p. 3).

permanent and non-permanent seats.[13] Lack of unity amongst UN membership is so far the main reason why there has been no agreement on a reform of the Security Council.[14] There is broad agreement that the number of members of the Security Council should be expanded, but there is no agreement on the specifics of such an expansion (for example the future number of members, whether there should be more permanent seats, with or without the veto, etc.).

In January 2020, outside the IGN context, the Russian Federation proposed a summit meeting of the heads of state of the five permanent members of the Security Council, to celebrate the 75th anniversary of the UN and to seek renewed support for it.[15] President Putin did not mention the issue of Security Council reform, but in the absence of any agreement among UN members on such reform, and given the need for ratification by the permanent members, an initiative from their part would not only pay due respect to their leadership role 75 years ago, but could also assist in achieving a breakthrough in the lengthy and complex negotiations on Security Council reform.

Security Council reform is long, very long overdue. At present, the UN has 193 member states; thus, 75 years after its beginning, membership has almost quadrupled. Its Security Council still has 15 members, which is now only some eight per cent of UN membership as a whole. While it is obvious that there is no rule of any nature saying that non-plenary organs of international organizations must have at least a certain percentage of all the members of the organization, it is clear that a reduction from 22 per cent in 1945 to 13 in 1963 and to eight at present is significant and that the long-standing calls for expanding Security Council membership are justifiable.

The current political climate may be unfavourable to achieve an agreement on a reform. At the same time, this was also true when agreement was reached on the first enlargement of the Security Council in the 1960s, one year after the

13 See further *In Hindsight: Security Council Reform*, prepared by Security Council Report (September 2019). In May 2020, the co-chairs of the IGN negotiations decided "to postpone our scheduled meetings until further notice" when physical meeting were no longer possible in New York due to the corona crisis. See https://economictimes.indiatimes.com/news/defence/unsc-reform-process-negotiations-postponed-until-further-notice-due-to-covid-19/articleshow/75753212.cms and https://www.thehindu.com/news/international/unsc-reform-process-negotiations-postponed-until-further-notice-due-to-covid-19/article31590220.ece.

14 See the reports of the relevant General Assembly meetings for an overview of the positions of UN members on Security Council reform, for example during the 74th regular session: UN Docs. A/74/PV.33 (25 November 2019), A/74/PV.34 (25 November 2019) and A/74/PV.35 (26 November 2019). See also Chapter 2, para. 4.

15 For the text of the speech by President Putin in which this proposal was made, see http://en.kremlin.ru/events/president/news/62646.

Cuban missile crisis. In addition, the question is not only whether the existing political climate is conducive to forging a widely supported compromise, but also whether there is a sufficiently firmly shared conviction that such a reform is imperative. Against this backdrop, it is the aim of the remainder of this chapter to illustrate why a second enlargement of the Security Council is long needed, by putting the above-mentioned figures in perspective. It will do so by comparing the size of the Security Council to that of non-plenary organs of other universal organizations, both looking at the situation in 1945 and how this has changed over time. In addition, it will pay particular attention to the reform proposals that were probably closest to being accepted: those made in the 2004 report of the High-level Panel on Threats, Challenges and Change.[16] This report specifically suggested two different models to increase the number of members of the Security Council.

4 Effective and Representative?

If the present size and composition of the Council no longer adequately reflect UN membership as a whole – also taking into account that 80 new members have been admitted to the UN since agreement was reached in 1963 on the first, and so far only, enlargement of the Council –, the next question is whether increasing Council membership might solve one problem only to create a new one, i.e. by increasing the risk of new stalemates in decision-making within the Council. A concern often expressed centers on those instances where the Security Council failed to act or where its actions were ineffective. Seen exclusively against this background, it would seem hazardous to increase the number of members of the Security Council. If, for example, the Council had had 24 members since 1990, would this not have prevented it from adopting some or many of the resolutions it now has been able to adopt? To the extent that the Council is criticized for not always being able to act, or not acting effectively when necessary, is it not likely that, having 24 members, the Council will be ineffective in more cases? These rhetorical questions are based on the presumption that it is easier to reach agreement with 15 members than with 24.

However, it is generally accepted that the question of the enlargement of the Security Council cannot exclusively be considered from this perspective. The Council must also be (seen to be) legitimate and representative. These

16 *A more secure world: our shared responsibility*, Report of the High-level Panel on Threats, Challenges and Change, UN Doc. A/59/565 (2004).

requirements are important in themselves, but they are also directly related to the requirement of effectiveness. After agreement was reached in 1963 on the expansion of membership of ECOSOC and of the Security Council, Secretary-General U Thant wrote: "[I] am sure that such expansion, which will make it possible to secure more adequate geographical representation in the two Councils, will contribute to *the greater effectiveness* of both bodies".[17] It is more difficult for Security Council resolutions to be fully and swiftly implemented if the Council is widely held to be unrepresentative than if it is perceived to carry the trust of UN membership as a whole.[18] 'More representative' therefore does not necessarily amount to 'less effective'. A larger Security Council may also be a more effective Security Council, if the enlargement restores the legitimacy the Council needs to perform its functions.

These questions of effectiveness and representativeness have previously been raised. This happened only to a rather limited extent at the creation of the UN. The text of the Dumbarton Oaks proposals (1944) already referred to five permanent and six non-permanent members.[19] At the 1945 San Francisco Conference a number of delegations, in particular those from Latin America, tabled amendments to the Dumbarton Oaks proposals. These amendments either proposed to increase the total number of members of the Council (varying from 12 to 15 seats, instead of 11), or suggested a larger number of non-permanent members (nine or 10, instead of six). However, at the end of the day these suggestions did not receive sufficient support.[20]

Next, the issue of enlarging Security Council membership was discussed for years before agreement was reached in 1963 to increase the original number of 11 members to the present 15. Since 1956 in particular, Latin American and Western European countries have favoured an increase. The Soviet Union and its allies initially rejected this, mainly because the Chinese communist government was not accepted as the representative of China in the UN. Only in

17 Introduction to the annual report of the Secretary-General on the work of the Organization, UN Doc. A/5801/Add.1 (1964), p. 11 (italics added).

18 As stated in 2004 by the High-level Panel on Threats, Challenges and Change, "the paucity of representation from the broad membership diminishes support for Security Council decisions" (report of the Panel, op. cit. note 16, para. 245).

19 Proposals for the establishment of a general international organization, adopted by China, the Soviet Union, the UK and the US at Dumbarton Oaks, 7 October 1944 (reproduced in *Yearbook of the United Nations 1946–47* (1947), pp. 4–9). See in particular Chapter VI, Section A of these proposals.

20 UNCIO Documents, Vol. XI (1945), p. 762. See also *Het Ontstaan der Verenigde Naties*, Publication No. 23 of the Dutch Ministry of Foreign Affairs (July 1950), pp. 57–60.

1963 did the negotiations gain momentum when African and Asian countries – having been admitted to the UN in previous years and feeling particularly underrepresented in the Security Council – strongly pressed for a larger Council. In December 1963 the General Assembly adopted Resolution 1991A, increasing the number of members to 15.[21] This resolution was adopted notwithstanding considerable opposition from four permanent members of the Council: the Soviet Union and France voted against, the UK and the US abstained. The Soviet Union was against any increase of Security Council membership. The US could agree only to an increase with two members, indicating that – as reported in the *UN Yearbook* – "[i]n the interest of its effectiveness the Security Council should be kept as small as possible".[22]

This dilemma of sailing the best course between the Scylla of effectiveness and the Charybdis of representativeness is by no means unique to the Security Council. Essentially all universal international organizations have faced and are facing this dilemma with regard to the size and composition of their non-plenary, executive organs. It may therefore be helpful, in order to put these Security Council discussions in a wider perspective, to briefly examine how other organizations have dealt with this dilemma.

One preliminary objection to such a comparison may be that the Security Council is a unique body. The primary responsibility to maintain international peace and security can hardly be compared to the work of non-plenary organs in the area of health or civil aviation. This responsibility is of paramount importance. It calls for the strictest possible requirements regarding effectiveness and therefore justifies a relatively small size. Therefore, it is in the collective interest of UN membership as a whole to have a small-sized Security Council. However, while this may be true, the importance of its tasks to all states, perhaps even more for small states than for superpowers, makes it equally or even more important for this organ as compared to others to be representative. Furthermore, the tendency of the Council to now also sometimes perform a quasi-legislative role (e.g. Resolutions 1373 and 1540) makes it more important to be representative. In addition, is it really correct to assume that the Security Council would need to meet a higher standard of effectiveness than other non-plenary organs of universal organizations?

---

21 See for a brief overview of the negotiations preceding the adoption of this resolution: *Yearbook of the United Nations 1963*, pp. 80–87. Voting results: 97 in favour, 11 against (Soviet Union and its allies, France), 4 abstentions (Portugal, South Africa, UK and US).

22 *Yearbook of the United Nations 1963*, p. 82.

5 A Comparison

Table 1 below shows the number of members of the principal non-plenary organs of universal organizations in the early postwar period and at present.[23]

TABLE 1 Size of non-plenary organs of organizations of the UN family

Organization[a]	Organ	Early postwar size	Present Size
ITU (193)	Council	18	48
UPU (192)	Council[b]	20	41
ILO (187)	Governing Body	32 (16 + 8 + 8)	56 (28 + 14 + 14)[c]
FAO (195)	Council	15	49
IBRD (189)	Executive Directors	12	25
IMF (189)	Executive Board	12	24
ICAO (193)	Council	21	36
UNESCO (193)	Executive Board	18	58
WHO (194)	Executive Board	18	34
IMO (174)	Council	16	40
WMO (193)	Executive Council	14	37
IAEA (171)	Board of Governors	23	35
IDA (173)	Executive Directors	12[d]	25
IFC (185)	Board of Directors	15	25

[a] The present number of members of the organizations is included in brackets.
[b] Now named Council of Administration, formerly the Executive Council.
[c] In 1986 amendments were adopted to the ILO Constitution, according to which the number of members of the Governing Body would be doubled. However, this amendment is not expected to enter into force.
[d] See *Yearbook of the United Nations 1960*, 652–53.

Table 2 below shows the number of members of the principal non-plenary organs of other universal organizations, either specialized agencies created after the early UN years or selected other universal organizations. The World Trade Organization (WTO) is not included in this list because it does not have a non-plenary policy-making organ. This is mainly explained by the wish of the

23 Figures for the early postwar period have been taken from the first *Yearbook of the United Nations* (1946–1947) and from H.G. Schermers, *De gespecialiseerde organisaties – Hun bouw en inrichting* (1957). Figures at present reflect the situation as on 1 June 2020.

TABLE 2 Size of non-plenary organs of younger organizations of the UN family and other universal IOs

Specialized agencies	Organ	Initial size	Present size
WIPO (193)	Coordination Committee	27 (1970)[a]	83
UNWTO (159)	Executive Council	33 (1975)	35
UNIDO (170)	Industrial Development Board	53 (1985)	53
IFAD (177)	Executive Board	18 (1977)	18

[a] See *Industrial Property* (Monthly Review of the United International Bureaux for the Protection of Intellectual Property (BIRPI)), 9th year, No. 11, November 1970, p. 361.

Other Universal IOs	Organ	Initial size	Present Size
IOM (173)	Executive Committee	9 (1951)	33 (until 2013)[a]
OPCW (193)	Executive Council	41 (1997)	41
CTBTO (184)	Executive Council	(51)	(Constitution has not yet entered into force)
IRENA (161)	Council	21 (2011)	21

[a] IOM's Executive Committee was abolished in 2013 (because it was considered largely redundant).

US during the *travaux préparatoires* for the WTO (mid 1990s) to ensure that the WTO remained a member-driven organization where all key decisions would be taken by consensus from all the members.[24]

24 V. VanGrasstek, *The History and Future of the World Trade Organization* (2013), pp. 65–73. According to Kuijper, "[t]he damage that the absence of this organ [- a non-plenary organ -] that exists in all other world-wide organizations with broad membership does to the organization and to the role of the Director-General and the Secretariat is one of the taboos of the organizational culture of the WTO" (P.J. Kuijper, 'The Sutherland Report and the WTO's Institutional Law – Do Parallels with other International Organizations Help?' (2005) 2 *International Organizations Law Review*, pp. 191–99 (quotation at p. 196)).

The figures in Tables 1 and 2 are useful to put into perspective the number of members of the Security Council: 11 since its first meeting in 1946, 15 since 1966. The original number of 11 members is *small but not exceptional* when compared to the original number of members of the non-plenary organs mentioned in Table 1. The World Bank had 12 Executive Directors and the IMF Board had 12 members. The non-plenary organs of FAO, WMO and IMO originally were also rather small-sized.

However, if the figures of the present membership of these non-plenary organs are compared, the difference between the size of the Security Council and that of these other non-plenary organs is much more significant. Seen from this perspective, the present number of members of the Security Council is *exceptionally small*. Since 1945, all constitutions of the organizations mentioned in Table 1 have been amended to increase the number of members of their principal non-plenary organs. In most cases, these numbers have been doubled or tripled, reflecting the large inflow of new members into these organizations. At present – as was the case in the early postwar period – the smallest non-plenary organs in this list are those of the IMF and of the World Bank. Their present size corresponds to a frequently proposed future size of the Security Council.[25] The overview given in Table 2 leads to similar conclusions. For only two of the organizations mentioned in this Table, IFAD and IRENA, the number of members of the non-plenary organ is small (respectively 18 and 21).

6 The Proposals by the 2004 High-level Panel on Threats, Challenges and Change

The present size of the smallest non-plenary organs in Table 1, those of the financial agencies, also corresponds to proposals made in 2004 by the High-level Panel on Threats, Challenges and Change. While this Panel was unable to agree on one recommendation for a future composition of the Security Council,[26] the two options it presented (Models A and B) both result in a total number of 24 members.[27]

25 The Netherlands government in a letter to Parliament refers to 24 members (op. cit. note 7, p. 6).

26 Which was inviting the question, as Thakur wrote, "if sixteen distinguished world citizens acting as individuals cannot choose between the two models, can 191 separate governments do so? The answer from the 2005 summit was a resounding 'No' ". (R. Thakur, 'High-Level Panels', in J.K. Cogan, I. Hurd, I. Johnstone, *The Oxford Handbook of International Organizations* (2016), pp. 859–880; quotation at p. 870).

27 Report of the High-level Panel, op. cit. note 16, paras. 244-60.

The way in which the proposed number of Security Council members is increased from 15 to 24 is different in Models A and B of the High-level Panel report. Model A provides for six new permanent seats (without the right of veto) and three new two-year term non-permanent seats. Model B does not provide for new permanent seats, but for eight four-year renewable-term seats and one new two-year non-permanent (and non-renewable) seat. The Panel also recommends how the new permanent seats in Model A and the new four-year renewable-term seats in Model B are divided among major regional areas. An important difference between Models A and B is that Model A is more rigid. If in the future one or more of the six new permanent members lose the qualities on the basis of which they became a permanent member, and if it were decided that they therefore should no longer be a permanent member of the Council, the Charter would have to be amended again. Model B is more flexible in this regard, since it does not create new permanent seats. In case a state occupying a four-year renewable-term seat loses the qualities on the basis of which it once was elected to this seat, it would simply not be re-elected if it were decided that it should no longer be on this seat; no Charter amendment would be necessary.

However, perhaps most striking are the similarities between Models A and B. First of all, they do not give the right of veto to other states than the present five permanent members. The Panel explicitly indicates why: "the institution of the veto has an anachronistic character that is unsuitable for the institution in an increasingly democratic age".[28] Secondly, both Models suggest a total number of 24 members. The Panel report does not give any explicit explanation for suggesting this particular number. It only lists four principles that must be respected in reforming the Council. Such reforms:

- should increase the involvement in decision-making of those who contribute most to the UN financially, militarily and diplomatically;
- should bring into the decision-making process countries more representative of the broader membership, especially of the developing world;
- should not impair the effectiveness of the Security Council;
- should increase the democratic and accountable nature of the Council.[29]

Models A and B are suggested by the Panel and therefore in its view respect these principles. A new size of 24 members is seen as the best possible compromise respecting these four principles.

The recommendation by the Panel that the Security Council should have 24 members is in line with the trend in other universal organizations during

28 Id., para. 256.

29 Id., para. 249.

the past decades, to increase membership of their non-plenary organs. The present number of members of the Security Council is exceptionally low if compared to the present size of these organs. There is of course no 'must' whatsoever regarding the implications of this finding: there is no rule prescribing that all non-plenary boards of universal organizations including the UN would now need to have a minimum number of members. However, this comparison offers at least an indication of how the balancing of effectiveness and representation is weighted in other contexts, and puts the debate concerning the enlargement of the Security Council in a wider perspective.

A few months after the publication of the report by the High-level Panel, Secretary-General Annan presented his own report.[30] In this report, he concluded that the Security Council should be reformed, "to make it more broadly representative of the international community as a whole and the geopolitical realities of today, and to expand its membership to meet these goals".[31] He urged Member States:[32]

> to consider the two options, models A and B, proposed in that report [...], or any other viable proposals in terms of size and balance that have emerged on the basis of either model. Member States should agree to take a decision on this important issue before the summit in September 2005. It would be very preferable for Member States to take this vital decision by consensus, but if they are unable to reach consensus this must not become an excuse for postponing action.

However, UN member states failed to come to an agreement on the basis of these proposals. The September 2005 Summit Outcome Resolution of the General Assembly therefore only supported "early reform of the Security Council [...] in order to make it more broadly representative, efficient and transparent and thus to further enhance its effectiveness and the legitimacy and implementation of its decisions".[33] This was 15 years ago. Since then, further consultations have failed to result in new proposals that were seen as a good basis for agreement on Security Council reform.

30 *In Larger Freedom*, UN Doc. A/59/2005 (21 March 2005).
31 Id., p. 60.
32 Id., para. 170.
33 GA Res. 60/1, para. 153.

7 Concluding Observations

Obviously, it is uncertain whether the role of non-permanent members would be similar or different in a 24-member Security Council. On the one hand, if the Security Council would have nine more non-permanent members serving a two-year term, this could reduce the role that each of these 19 non-permanent members could play, for example because they would less often act as President of the Council.[34] On the other hand, if they were united, a larger number of non-permanent members could, perhaps put more pressure on a reluctant permanent member not to use its veto. But this is mere speculation. In the reform proposals suggested by the High-level Panel, both Model A and Model B include suggestions to have additional two-year term non-permanent members: three in Model A, one in Model B. The role that such additional non-permanent members could play might not be unlike that of the current non-permanent members, the main difference being the changed dynamics as a result of the enlargement of the Council.

There is considerable difference between a two-year term for non-permanent members (three in Model A, one in Model B, in addition to the ten current non-permanent members) and the proposed eight four-year renewable-term seats in Model B. A term of four years, with the possibility of one or more further four-year terms, allows the states concerned to build up the necessary Security Council experience and use it much longer than at present. Compared to permanent members, two-year term non-permanent members are to some extent passersby. They may play a useful role (for example benefiting from a certain expertise or focusing on a particular niche).[35] However, no matter how useful, this role is limited to a period of two years. Four years, possibly extended for one or more further terms, would allow non-permanent members – much more than today – to obtain the necessary experience, build some institutional memory, become involved more deeply in the Council's work and thereby improve its functioning.[36]

It is therefore concluded that an enlargement of the Security Council would be fully in line with the (changes in) membership of non-plenary organs of other universal organizations since 1945. Seen from this perspective, the present

34 L. Sievers and S. Daws, *The Procedure of the UN Security Council* (2014), p. 674.

35 See Schrijver and Blokker (eds.), op. cit. note 2.

36 See E.C. Luck, 'The Security Council at Seventy: Ever Changing or Never Changing?', in S. von Einsiedel, D.M. Malone, and B.S. Ugarte (eds.), *The UN Security Council in the 21st Century* (2016), pp. 195–214, in particular at p. 204.

number of members of the Security Council is exceptionally small. The need to enlarge the Security Council and thereby increase its representativeness and its legitimacy outweighs the fear that it might become more difficult to take decisions.

CHAPTER 5

United Nations? *Security* Council?

Concluding Institutional Legal Reflections

This final chapter will offer some concluding reflections. During the Second World War, the allied nations united to win not only the war, but also the peace that was to follow (to use Roosevelt's expression). These united nations signed the 1942 Declaration by United Nations and subsequently prepared the establishment of the United Nations in 1945, to save succeeding generations from the scourge of war. The name of the organization thus symbolized that wartime cooperation was transformed into a permanent new world organization. The Security Council was created within the UN as the teeth of the new world organization, the main organ responsible for providing security. Three generations later, how should the Security Council be evaluated? Critics might conclude that 'Disunited Nations' and 'Insecurity Council' would more aptly describe the record than their official names. Others might say that at least the UN still exists. It has grown much older than its predecessor and has contributed to the prevention of a third world war. The reflections below aim to look back at 75 years of functioning of the Security Council from an institutional legal perspective, on the basis of the preceding chapters.

1 The Creation of the United Nations Revisited

In 1945 in San Francisco, the strong common determination by 50 states to save succeeding generations from the scourge of war generated the momentum for a second leap forward in international organization. The first leap was made 25 years earlier, only one generation before the United Nations was founded, when the horrors of the Great War triggered the establishment of the League of Nations. *Après la mort, le médecin.* Or, as US President Truman stated at the closing plenary session of the 1945 San Francisco Conference: "[i]f we had had this Charter a few years ago – and above all, the will to use it – millions now dead would be alive".[1] The League was a leap forward because it was created as

1 UNCIO Vol I, p. 680. President Truman continued by looking at the future: "[i]f we should falter in the future in our will to use it, millions now living will surely die".

 | DOI:10.1163/9789004443921_007

the first universal international organization to "achieve international peace and security".[2] The United Nations was a second leap forward because it reached the goal of universality that the League never realized, because it abolished the veto for each and every member state, and because of its centralized, supranational nature. Its founders learned lessons from the League. Therefore, no United Nations without the League of Nations.

The Security Council occupies a pivotal position in the organization that was created to save succeeding generations from the scourge of war, as will be further discussed below. However, the United Nations is much more than just the Security Council. Its approach to pursue sustainable peace is more comprehensive than that of its predecessor. Next to its aim to maintain international peace and security, another purpose is to develop friendly relations among nations and to take other appropriate measures to strengthen universal peace.[3] It was also created to achieve economic, social, cultural and humanitarian cooperation, and to promote and encourage respect for human rights. According to the Charter, such cooperation is not only a means to an end (Article 55 refers to "the creation of conditions of stability and well-being which are necessary for peaceful and friendly relations among nations"), it is also an end in itself (it is mentioned among the purposes of the UN, in Article 1(3)). The Charter reflects this comprehensive approach to pursue sustainable peace by establishing an institutional framework for such cooperation, by creating the Economic and Social Council and by bringing into life the UN family with its specialized agencies. It created an institutional framework that comprises much more than the Security Council.

The Charter closely connects the Security Council to other parts of the United Nations. It is far from a loosely embedded 'stand-alone' body within the world organization. The members of the UN confer on the Security Council primary responsibility for the maintenance of international peace and security "[i]n order to ensure prompt and effective action *by the United Nations*".[4] In discharging its duties under this responsibility, "the Security Council shall act in accordance with the Purposes and Principles *of the United Nations*".[5] In addition, the Charter provides for a joint responsibility or for cooperation between the Security Council and other UN organs such as, in particular, the General Assembly, the International Court of Justice and the Secretariat.[6] Therefore, no Security Council without the United Nations.

2 League of Nations Covenant, Preamble, first sentence.
3 UN Charter, Art. 1(2).
4 UN Charter, Art. 24(1) (italics added).
5 UN Charter, Art. 24(2) (italics added).
6 See further Chapter 1, para. 3.1.

A leap forward, this was certainly what many concluded in 1945. Not surprisingly, this conclusion was expressed emphatically at the concluding plenary session of the San Francisco Conference, on 26 June 1945. The Charter was called "the greatest of international experiments" (Wellington Koo, representing China),[7] "one of the most important documents in human history" (Jan Masaryk, Minister for Foreign Affairs of Czechoslovakia),[8] and "a good practical, workmanlike plan for peace – a very real and substantial advance on all previous plans for security against war" (Field Marshal Jan Smuts, Prime Minister of South Africa).[9]

From the perspective of today, 75 years later, it is even more clear that the establishment of the United Nations was a leap forward. In practice, the UN is often disunited. In recent years, voices of nationalism and populism have become much louder. They adhere to a narrow definition of what is in the national interest and have made international cooperation more difficult. Populist governments criticize the UN; some of their leaders have even threatened to withdraw. They regard the Charter as an instrument for globalization, certainly not as a populist document, even though its opening words are "We the peoples of the United Nations". The outbreak of the COVID-19 virus at the end of 2019 has demonstrated that, when push comes to shove, the world is organized in sovereign states, no matter how much it has become a global village. Even in the "ever closer" European Union, the member states largely isolated themselves from the outside world, just as they asked or ordered their citizens to quasi-quarantine themselves. These national reflexes are understandable in times of emergency. Nevertheless, they also allow us to grasp more fully that creating the United Nations during the Second World War was an impressive leap forward, in the enlightened self-interest of all.

The scourge of war generated the unity and sense of purpose amongst 50 states to organize themselves in an unprecedented way. The insight that world peace is indivisible and requires a collective security mechanism was not new. However, learning lessons of history, the League of Nations was replaced by a much stronger world organization with the perspective of becoming truly universal.

7 UNCIO Vol. 1, p. 661.

8 Id., p. 672.

9 Id., p. 678.

2 The Creation of the Security Council Revisited

During the *travaux préparatoires* for the United Nations, there was always a firm consensus that the new world organization would need a strong enforcement body that its predecessor lacked. Therefore, no United Nations without the Security Council. To prevent future aggression and another world war, the idea was to share the strength of the superpowers and put it at the disposal of the Security Council, so that peace and security could be enforced if necessary. This key idea was agreed in 1945 in San Francisco and its general features were elaborated in the Charter. A number of speakers referred to it in the closing plenary session on 26 June. Chairman Gromyko of the delegation of the Soviet Union, the state that had lost the highest number of people during the war,[10] quoted Stalin: in order to prevent aggression and keep it from developing into a big war,[11]

> there is only one means besides the complete disarmament of the aggressor nations: to establish a special organization for defense of peace and insurance of security, from among the representatives of the peace-loving nations; to place at the disposal of the steering body of this Organization the maximum quantity of armed forces sufficient for the suppression of aggression; and to convince this Organization, in case of necessity, to send without any delay these armed forces for the prevention and liquidation of aggression, for the punishment of those guilty of aggression.

The incorporation of a strong enforcement mechanism in the new world organization was a great, centralized leap forward, compared to the weak, decentralized mechanism of the League of Nations, in which enforcement was essentially left to the member states. However, while the new mechanism was strong on paper, much would depend on its implementation in practice. First, the Charter did not lay down the details of the future UN force that would be put at the disposal of the Security Council. Such details had to be agreed later. However, 75 years after San Francisco, this 'later' of the Charter is yet to be

10 It is estimated that some 25 to 27 million Soviet nationals perished during the Second World War (military and civilian), approximately one-third of all victims of that war. According to the current official Russian view, during the war between Germany and the Soviet Union (1941 - 1945), the Soviet Union lost some 26,6 million of its people; around 12 million soldiers and approximately 14,6 million civilians (see https://www.rbth.com/history/330625-soviet-citizens-died-world-war-statistics).

11 UNCIO Vol. I, p. 663.

implemented. The capstone of the UN's collective security system is stillborn.[12] Secondly, the five superpowers agreed that the new enforcement machinery could only work if each of them would agree. While the Security Council as a whole would not need to be unanimous (like its predecessor), such unanimity was required from its five permanent members. While majority voting was accepted for the Security Council as a whole, it was conditioned by the need for the majority to include the five permanent members. In San Francisco, the other 45 states were fully aware of the risks this would entail.[13] This explains why the veto of the future permanent members was the most difficult issue during the Charter negotiations.

Creating a Security Council without the right of veto for the five permanent members was a bridge too far in 1945. The superpowers made it clear that their right of veto was a *conditio sine qua non* for their participation in the UN. For the other 45 states, it was clear that a UN without such participation would be pointless; it would never be able to save succeeding generations from the scourge of war. This is how the new world organization on the one hand was backed by the necessary power and the potential to use strong military force against a future aggressor, but on the other hand for its effective functioning completely relied on the unity amongst the permanent members. While the creation of the Security Council was a great, centralized leap forward after the 'Great Experiment' of the League of Nations, it was also imperfect, a halfway house on the road towards a more solid, a more certain collective security organization, not fully dependent on the unchecked wills of five of its members. Without the teeth of the Security Council, the United Nations would have been a much weaker world organization. As Pascal wrote, "la justice sans la force est impuissante". However, the uncertainties surrounding the deployment of "la force" by the Security Council, an unavoidable built-in flaw of the Charter, have made the pursuit of justice less "puissante".

12 As the President of the Security Council stated during its first meeting, 17 January 1946, in London: only "[w]hen this process [- of concluding agreements under Art. 43, by which armed forces would be made available to the Security Council -] is complete, the Security Council will be fully equipped to perform a function which is unique in the history of international organization – the direction of collective action for the maintenance of peace, justice, and the rule of law" (UN Doc. SCOR, first year, first series, first meeting, p. 6).

13 See, e.g., several statements made at the closing plenary session of the San Francisco Conference: UNCIO Vol. 1, p. 663 and p. 665 (Soviet Union), p. 669 (France), p. 675 (Mexico).

3 The United Nations in 75 Years of Practice

There are many ways to evaluate the performance of the United Nations and its Security Council over the last 75 years. It is perhaps somewhat of a platitude to do so using the image of a glass that is half empty or half full. Nevertheless, platitudes may carry something true or wise and may be useful for a better understanding. That is certainly true when it comes to making a nuanced assessment of the work of the UN. Any such assessment must take into account the ups and downs of the first 75 years of the life of the world organization.

This book has mainly focused on the Security Council and has done so essentially from an institutional legal perspective. However, before offering some final reflections on the veto, the rule of law and the reform of the Security Council, some very brief more general observations should serve to put these reflections into the larger perspective of the functioning of the UN. An appreciation of the Security Council is incomplete without at least some evaluation of the larger framework of which it is part. How did the world organization and its members fare in pursuing the aim of saving succeeding generations from the scourge of war? What has been achieved as to membership and the evolution of the UN as an organization?

First, while it is true that there have been a number of international and non-international armed conflicts since 1945, genocides, mass killings and mass annihilations,[14] there has not been a World War III and the UN still exists. Some three generations have lived without experiencing a war similar to the two world wars. This is the aspiration laid down in the very first sentence of the UN Charter. At the same time, it may be questioned to what extent the UN may be credited for this, or to what extent there are other explanations. If the League of Nations should not be blamed for not having prevented the Second World War, why should the United Nations be given credit for being more successful in averting another world war? The answer lies in the fundamentally different nature of the two world organizations. While the League of Nations represented a leap forward in world organization, it was a first experiment. The emphasis of the Covenant is on obligations of the member states. Only some limited powers were attributed to the two main organs of the League, whose powers were literally the same. Most decisions were taken unanimously; hence, every

14 See the examples mentioned in Chapter 1, para. 1.

member had a right of veto. The Covenant did not explicitly determine that the League's Secretariat should be independent from the member states. Above all, the League lacked the enforcement teeth necessary to discipline the members. The United Nations Charter reflects the lessons from the League experience. Because the new world organization was provided with its own supranational powers, an independent Secretariat and the possibility of majority voting, failures and successes of the UN should not only be attributed to its member states but also to the organization. The prevention of a World War III and the continuing existence of the UN today must partly be attributed to the organization and the people who have served it.

∵

Second, when evaluating the UN's first 75 years, two membership aspects must be taken into account, participation of the most powerful states and the large increase in the number of members. On the one hand, the world's most powerful states have always been members of the UN (with an important nuance relating to the representation of China until 1971). While the US never joined the League of Nations, it was the first to notify its ratification of the UN Charter, in August 1945, even before the end of World War Two. The Soviet Union became a member of the League only in 1934, but was expelled five years later. Membership of the most powerful states is a prerequisite for an effective world organization; this condition has always been fulfilled in the UN. On the other hand, the near quadruplicating of its membership must be taken into account. Such an expansion of membership has significant effects on any international organization that can hardly be overestimated – the European Union is an example in this respect. The world organization has adapted itself to this fundamental change, for example by the two Charter amendments, by giving more priority to concerns of its new members (self-determination, decolonization, development issues, anti-apartheid) and by the development of decision-making by consensus in the General Assembly. Newly emerging states perceived the United Nations as an organization to join, not to stay out of. These two membership aspects - almost universal membership including the most powerful states – should not be taken for granted. Members, including superpowers, may take the sovereign decision to leave, no matter how much this seems to be against their own interest. Keeping them does not happen automatically. It may therefore be concluded not only that this is an important achievement, but also that the UN and its members cannot rest on these laurels and must continue to engage in permanent 'membership maintenance'.

∵

Third, the United Nations was created as an independent legal person, more than the sum of its members. It would have been hardly any more than the sum of its members if its only purpose would be to be a forum, "a centre for harmonizing the actions of nations".[15] To be such a centre is certainly an important function of the UN, as is visible during the General Assembly's annual ministerial week. However, the world organization is much more than that. It was deliberately established as a powerhouse of the international community, having its own identity based on the common interest of its members.

In 1961, one month before he died in a never fully resolved plane crash, Secretary-General Dag Hammarskjold contrasted two concepts of the world organization. In the introduction to his annual report on the work of the UN, he wrote that debates and events during the past year "have brought to the fore different concepts of the United Nations, the character of the Organization, its authority and structure".[16] In Hammarskjold's own words:[17]

> On the one side, it has in various ways become clear that certain Members conceive of the Organization as a static conference machinery for resolving conflicts of interests and ideologies with a view to peaceful co-existence, within the Charter, to be served by a Secretariat which is to be regarded not as fully internationalized but as representing within its ranks those very interests and ideologies.
>
> Other Members have made it clear that they conceive of the Organization primarily as a dynamic instrument of Governments through which they, jointly and for the same purpose, should seek such reconciliation but through which they should also try to develop forms of executive action, undertaken on behalf of all Members, and aiming at forestalling conflicts and resolving them, once they have arisen, by appropriate diplomatic or political means, in a spirit of objectivity and in implementation of the principles and purposes of the Charter.

The second concept is nearest to what the founders of the UN envisioned in the Charter. In his introduction, Hammarskjold discusses the purposes and principles of the Charter. In his view, they reflect three "basic democratic principles" (or: "basic rules of international ethics") that to a large extent follow "standards accepted as binding for life within states".[18] These three democratic

15 UN Charter, Art. 1(4).
16 UN Doc. A/4800/Add.1, p. 1.
17 Id.
18 Id.

principles are equal political rights, equal economic opportunities and the rule of law. The rule of law (or "the principle of justice"), further discussed below, "has deep roots in the history of the efforts of man to eliminate from international life the anarchy which he had already much earlier overcome on the national level".[19] It is closely connected to the second concept of world organization mentioned above, a United Nations that is more than a passive forum and that has its own functions and identity, inspired by the purposes and principles of the Charter, in the common interest of its member states.

While the founding states had in mind the second concept of world organization at the time of its creation, it did not take long before some of them started to question this and no longer supported it. The United States and the Soviet Union failed to respect the independence of the UN Secretariat. As a result of the Cold War, the Security Council could not fully perform its functions. The Soviet Union used its veto excessively. Under these circumstances, the organization created by the Charter was tested. To what extent could its organs use their powers to implement the words of the Charter? More specifically, how has their practice affected the functioning of the Security Council? The next few observations will briefly discuss the functioning of the General Assembly, the International Court of Justice and the Secretariat.

∴

Fourth, the General Assembly has at times actively contributed to the UN purpose of maintaining international peace and security. The Security Council has a primary responsibility in this field. However, when the Council was often unable to take decisions, to what extent could the General Assembly step in? The main boundary between the powers of the Council and the Assembly is well defined in the Charter: enforcement action in this field can only be taken by the Security Council. It was left to practice to further define specific limits. In this regard, the General Assembly has at times tried to use its own powers to the maximum; according to some members, it overstepped the limits of its powers. Five years after the entry into force of the Charter, the General Assembly adopted its Uniting for Peace Resolution. The Soviet Union referred to this resolution as 'Disuniting for War'. In 1956, during the Suez crisis, the Assembly used the procedure mentioned in this resolution in order to take action where the Security Council could not act. It established the first UN peacekeeping operation, the United Nations Emergency Force. In doing so, making intensive

---

19 Id., p. 2.

use of its powers, it took the initiative for a new instrument of the world organization in its arsenal of measures to maintain international peace and security. Peacekeeping is not mentioned in the Charter. Created in practice, this has become one of the most important assets of the United Nations. As mentioned below, the ICJ and in particular the Secretariat have also contributed to the development of this new instrument.

There are more examples where the General Assembly has to some extent stepped in when the Security Council was unable to agree. Examples from recent years include its recognition of Palestine as a state (by giving it the status of a non-member observer state in the Assembly) when the Security Council was unable to adopt a recommendation to admit Palestine to the UN,[20] the adoption of a resolution on Crimea after the Russian Federation vetoed a draft resolution tabled in the Security Council,[21] and the establishment of the International, Impartial and Independent Mechanism for Syria (IIIM) following the paralysis of the Security Council on this issue (including the vetoed proposal to refer the situation in Syria to the ICC).[22] It is obvious that in these cases the General Assembly cannot fully substitute for the Security Council. Its powers are not the same as those of the Council, as was the situation within the League of Nations. The Assembly cannot admit Palestine to the UN without the support of the Security Council. Neither can it take binding enforcement measures against the Russian Federation, nor refer the situation in Syria to the ICC. Nevertheless, it may express the majority view of UN membership at large and in this way 'mobilize shame', or it may undertake some action by creating a subsidiary criminal justice body such as IIIM.

Apart from taking action where the Security Council remains silent, the General Assembly has been directly or indirectly important for the Security Council in performing normative functions, for which it is best equipped being composed of representatives from all member states. Important examples include the 1948 Universal Declaration of Human Rights,[23] the 1960

20 GA Res. 67/19; UN Docs. A/66/371-S/2011/592 and S/2011/705.

21 See UN Doc. S/2014/189 for the draft resolution proposed to the Security Council (vetoed on 15 March 2014), and GA Res. 68/262 (adopted on 27 March 2014 (by 100 votes in favour, 11 against, and 58 abstentions)). Much of the text of the draft resolution and the General Assembly resolution is similar. They both call on states and international organizations not to recognize any change in the status of Crimea and Sevastopol.

22 This Mechanism is established by GA Res. 71/248 (21 December 2016), "to assist in the investigation and prosecution of persons responsible for the most serious crimes under international law committed in the Syrian Arab Republic since March 2011". The proposal to refer the situation in Syria to the ICC was vetoed by China and Russia in 2014 (see above, Chapter 3, para. 5.3.2).

23 GA Res. 217 (III) A.

Decolonization Declaration,[24] the 1970 Declaration on Principles of International Law concerning Friendly Relations and Cooperation among States in accordance with the Charter of the United Nations,[25] the 1974 Definition of Aggression,[26] the 2000 United Nations Millennium Declaration,[27] the 2005 World Summit Outcome,[28] the 2012 Declaration on the Rule of Law at the National and International Levels,[29] and the 2015 Declaration by which it adopted the 2030 Agenda for Sustainable Development (with the 17 Sustainable Development Goals).[30] In addition, the International Law Commission, a subsidiary organ of the general Assembly, has prepared and adopted draft conventions and other legal instruments that are important for the work of the Security Council. Important recent examples of the latter are the Articles on the Responsibility of International Organizations[31] and the Conclusions on Identification of Customary International Law.[32]

Fifth, the International Court of Justice has made a judicial contribution to the development of the UN in practice during the last 75 years and to the functioning of the Security Council. Obviously, its role was limited to the issues that were brought before it. However, the Court has also, sometimes in *obiter dicta*, contributed to the general development of the law of the UN. Important examples of the Court's contribution are the following:

- "[t]he political character of an organ cannot release it from the observance of the treaty provisions established by the Charter when they constitute limitations on its powers or criteria for its judgment";[33]
- the conclusion that the world organization is an international legal person, even though there is no explicit provision to this effect in the Charter;[34]

24 GA Res. 1514 (XV).

25 GA Res. 2625 (XXV).

26 GA Res. 3314 (XXIX).

27 GA Res. 55/2.

28 GA Res. 60/1 (*inter alia*, this resolution introduced the notion Responsibility to Protect and created the Peacebuilding Commission).

29 GA Res. 67/1.

30 GA Res. 70/1.

31 GA Res. 66/100.

32 GA Res. 73/203.

33 *Admission of a State to the United Nations (Charter, Art. 4)*, Advisory Opinion, ICJ Rep. 1948, p. 56 (quotation at p. 64).

34 *Reparation for injuries suffered in the service of the United Nations*, Advisory Opinion, ICJ Rep. 1949, p. 174.

- the decision that the General Assembly had the power to establish an Administrative Tribunal but that it does not have the right to refuse to give effect to an award of compensation made by this tribunal in favour of a UN staff member;[35]
- its support for the General Assembly's initiatives with respect to the first two UN peacekeeping operations (UNEF and ONUC), and its general observation in that context that, "when the Organization takes action which warrants the assertion that it was appropriate for the fulfilment of one of the stated purposes of the United Nations, the presumption is that such action is not *ultra vires* the Organization";[36]
- its observation that constituent instruments of international organizations such as the UN Charter are treaties of a special nature, with implications for the interpretation of such instruments;[37]
- its observations concerning the interpretation of resolutions of the Security Council. Such resolutions "are issued by a single, collective body and are drafted through a very different process than that used for the conclusion of a treaty". [...] Their interpretation "may require the Court to analyze statements by representatives of members of the Security Council made at the time of their adoption, other resolutions of the Security Council on the same issue, as well as the subsequent practice of relevant United Nations organs and of States affected by those given resolutions";[38]
- its use of the notion of 'practice of the organization' as an interpretative device. An example is the only advisory opinion ever requested from the Court by the Security Council, the 1971 Namibia Advisory Opinion. In this Opinion, the Court drew heavily on the Council's practice, when concluding that a voluntary abstention by a permanent member does not constitute a bar to the adoption of resolutions, even though the text of Article 27(3) of the Charter seems to suggest otherwise.[39] Another example is the 2004 Wall

35 *Effect of awards of compensation made by the UN Administrative Tribunal*, Advisory Opinion, ICJ Rep. 1954, p. 47 (in particular at pp. 53, 58–59 and 62).

36 *Certain expenses of the United Nations (Article 17, paragraph 2, of the Charter)*, Advisory Opinion, ICJ Rep. 1962, p. 151 (quotation at p. 168).

37 Id., p. 157; *Legality of the Use by a State of Nuclear Weapons in Armed Conflict*, Advisory Opinion, ICJ Rep. 1996, p. 66 (at p. 75: "[s]uch treaties can raise specific problems of interpretation owing, *inter alia*, to their character which is conventional and at the same time institutional").

38 *Accordance with International Law of the Unilateral Declaration of Independence in Respect of Kosovo*, Advisory Opinion, ICJ Rep. 2010, p. 403 (quotation at p. 442).

39 *Legal Consequences for States of the Continued Presence of South Africa in Namibia (South West Africa) notwithstanding Security Council Resolution 276 (1970)*, Advisory Opinion, ICJ Rep. 1971, p. 16 (in particular at p. 22 (para. 22)). See also above, Chapter 1, para. 3.3.

> Advisory Opinion, concerning the division of powers between the Assembly and the Security Council and the interpretation of Article 12 of the Charter; the Court considered "that the *accepted practice* of the General Assembly, *as it has evolved*, is consistent with Article 12, paragraph 1, of the Charter".[40]

∴

Sixth, the Secretariat is the third principal organ of the UN that has contributed significantly to the bringing into practice of the purposes and principles of the world organization and has supported the work of the Security Council. The Security Council does not have a separate secretariat; the UN Secretariat is the secretariat of the entire UN organization. Using the experience of the League of Nations Secretariat, it was created as an independent organ of the UN, with an international staff under the leadership of the Secretary-General. Although it has more than administrative powers only, it does not play a major political role unlike, for example, the European Commission. While the Charter expects the Secretary-General to play his (or in the future certainly also: her) own political role, this role is less prominent than the one of his colleagues in organizations such as the IMF and NATO. Whereas the head of the secretariat of these two organizations chairs the main policy-making organs, the General Assembly and the Security Council are chaired by one of their members, not by the Secretary-General.

The Charter mentions a number of specific, mainly administrative functions of the Secretariat (such as the preparation of meetings of other UN organs including the Security Council, the preparation of the budget of the UN, the registration and publication of treaties). In addition, it performs tasks given by other organs including the Security Council. Over the years, a major task has been the preparation and implementation of peacekeeping operations. It is beyond the scope of this book to evaluate the functioning of the Secretariat. From an institutional legal perspective, the most important characteristic of the Secretariat is its independence. By creating an independent secretariat, as

---

40 *Legal Consequences of the Construction of a Wall in the Occupied Palestinian Territory*, Advisory Opinion, ICJ Rep. 2004, p. 136 (quotation at p. 150, emphasis added). Before drawing this conclusion, the Court observed "that there has been an increasing tendency over time for the General Assembly and the Security Council to deal in parallel with the same matter concerning the maintenance of international peace and security [...]. It is often the case that, while the Security Council has tended to focus on the aspects of such matters related to international peace and security, the General Assembly has taken a broader view, considering also their humanitarian, social and economic aspects".

a principal organ, the founders of the UN, including the superpowers, not only accepted but also deliberately chose that it would not merely simply follow whatever orders the Security Council would give, but that it should do so in full respect of the Charter.

Article 100 of the Charter contains the two key obligations necessary to establish an independent international civil service. On the one hand, the obligation for the Secretary-General and the staff not to seek or receive instructions from governments or from outside the organization; on the other hand, the obligation for the member states to respect the independence of the Secretary-General and the staff and not to seek to influence them. Many other international organizations have similar obligations. The independence of international civil servant "is an essential guarantee, not only for the civil servants themselves, but also for the proper functioning of international organizations".[41] In practice, Article 100 of the Charter has at times been more honored in the breach than in the observance. The history of the UN is replete with examples of governments influencing in one way or another their nationals in the Secretariat.[42]

The power that comes with independence requires accountability. Unchecked power is unacceptable at the international level just as it is in national societies governed by the rule of law. The UN Secretariat is answerable to the General Assembly; it is to the Assembly that it must present an annual report on the work of the UN.[43] At the same time, the member states may make it difficult for the Secretariat to be more accountable. Through the General Assembly, they should enable the Secretariat to do what they ask it to do, by giving it the necessary means and resources. In addition, tasks given to the Secretariat should be clear and realistic. This may be difficult to achieve, since such tasks and mandates are often the results of hard-won compromises among the members.[44] Even though at times the UN Secretariat has been accountable,[45] probably the most fundamental current criticism at the functioning of the UN Secretariat concerns its lack of accountability and effectiveness. Over the years,

41 Administrative Tribunal of the International Labour Organization, Judgment no. 2232 (*Bustani*), para. 16 (2003).

42 See J. Lemoine, *The International Civil Servant – An Endangered Species* (1995). For a specific example, see A.N. Shevchenko, *Breaking with Moscow* (1985).

43 UN Charter, Art. 98.

44 See further H.G. Schermers and N.M. Blokker, *International Institutional Law* (6th ed. 2018), para. 441.

45 For example, the 1999 evaluations of the fall of Srebrenica (report by the Secretary-General, requested by the General Assembly, UN Doc. A/54/549) and of the genocide in Rwanda (independent inquiry set up by the Secretary-General, UN Doc. S/1999/1257).

the Secretariat has taken a number of measures to improve the situation. For example, better management systems have been introduced (accountability for delivering results, better performance reporting), the internal dispute settlement system was improved, the internal oversight mechanisms have been strengthened, a whistleblower protection policy has been promulgated and a financial disclosure programme is implemented.[46]

The UN Charter assigns a number of specific functions to the Secretary-General. In the context of his relationship with the Security Council, Article 99 is of particular importance. This is the basis not only for bringing to the attention of the Security Council "any matter which in his opinion may threaten the maintenance of international peace and security", but also for the larger political role played by the Secretary-General. For example, he may perform good offices, carry out mediations and create commissions of inquiry, at the request of member states, the Security Council, the General Assembly, or at his own initiative. During the past 75 years, the nine successive Secretaries-General have developed their own role in these functions, depending on the political context and their personal qualities, but have also gradually built up considerable practice and have made the position of Secretary-General into what it is today.[47]

Trygve Lie, the first Secretary-General of the UN has famously characterized this position as "the most impossible job on earth", when meeting his successor Dag Hammarskjold at New York's Idlewild (now JFK) Airport on 9 April 1953.[48] This was at a time when Lie had lost the support of the Soviet Union (following his criticism of North Korea during the Korea crisis), was reappointed in spite of a Soviet veto in the Security Council,[49] and was under harsh US pressure to dismiss American UN staff accused of being communist, in the era of McCarthyism.[50] The independence of the Secretary-General was severely put

46 See UN Doc. A/64/640 (with references to earlier reports).

47 For a brief overview, see B. Reinalda, 'Institutional Development of the United Nations Secretariat', 26 *Global Governance* (2020), pp. 325–339.

48 United Nations Press Release 'Statement at a General Meeting of the Staff', SG/299 (1 May 1953); see also https://www.un.org/Depts/dhl/dag/time1953.htm. Three weeks later, at a farewell meeting with the staff organized for Lie, Hammarskjold addressed him saying that, if this is the most impossible job on earth, "you have done the impossible" (quoted in B. Urquhart, *Hammarskjold* (1972), p. 54).

49 See E. Luard, *A History of the United Nations Volume 1: The Years of Western Domination, 1945–1955* (1982), pp. 349–360; B. Simma et al., *The Charter of the United Nations – A Commentary* (3rd ed. 2012), pp. 1996–1997. See GA Res. 492(V) ("Continuation in office of the Secretary-General of the United Nations"), adopted 1 November 1950.

50 See A. Megzari, *The Internal Justice of the United Nations – A Critical History 1945 – 2015* (2015), in particular Chapters 6 and 7 (pp. 129 – 206).

to the test. Three days after Lie announced his resignation, UN Legal Counsel Abraham Feller committed suicide.[51] As Cockayne and Malone have written:[52]

> The Secretary-General must walk a fine line between effective cooperation and apparent collusion with the Security Council in particular. Past incumbents have all learned – the hard way – when they have either crossed the limits of tolerance of one of the permanent members of the Council, or cleaved so close that they have sacrificed legitimacy in the eyes of their broader constituency among the member states.

All Secretaries-General have given their own interpretation of the responsibilities of this most impossible job. Although difficult to compare, perhaps Dag Hammarskjold and Kofi Annan have most impressively walked the fine line to which Cockayne and Malone refer.

The *locus classicus* illustration of Hammarskjold's independent attitude towards the Security Council and its permanent members is his "declaration" in the Security Council on 31 October 1956, during the Suez crisis. After he had already almost called for a meeting of the Security Council before the US took this initiative, and considering the military operation by France and the United Kingdom a threat to international peace and security, Hammarskjold made a principled statement in which he described himself as a servant of the principles of the Charter, implicitly criticized France and the United Kingdom for violating their Charter obligations and urged the Security Council to perform its task.[53] Following this declaration, Security Council members (including

51 Id., p. 138.

52 J. Cockayne and D.M. Malone, 'Relations with the Security Council', in S. Chesterman, *Secretary or General? The UN Secretary-General in World Politics* (2007), pp. 69–85 (quotation at p. 69).

53 Security Council Official Records, 751st meeting, UN Doc. S/PV.751, pp. 1–2: "The principles of the Charter are, by far, greater than the Organization in which they are embodied, and the aims which they are to safeguard are holier than the policies of any single nation or people. As a servant of the Organization, the Secretary-General has the duty to maintain his usefulness by avoiding public stands on conflicts between Member nations unless and until such an action might help to resolve the conflict. However, the discretion and impartiality thus imposed on the Secretary-General by the character of his immediate task may not degenerate into a policy of expediency. He must also be a servant of the principles of the Charter, and its aims must ultimately determine what for him is right and wrong. For that he must stand. A Secretary-General cannot serve on any other assumption than that [...] all Member nations honour their pledge to observe all Articles of the Charter. He should also be able to assume that those organs which are charged with the task of upholding the Charter will be in a position to fulfil their task".

France and the United Kingdom) immediately gave their full support to the Secretary-General. The Council decided (France and the United Kingdom voting against, but the veto did not apply to this procedural resolution) to convene the General Assembly in an emergency special session. Within a few days, the Assembly established the first UN peacekeeping force.[54]

In a different era, Kofi Annan also obtained significant authority during his tenure, as has already been illustrated above in Chapters 2 and 3. A good example is his 'fork in the road' speech for the General Assembly, following the US-led invasion of Iraq in 2003, without specific Security Council authorization.[55] This speech reflected deep concerns over this Iraq war within the UN Secretariat.[56] Although this finally did not result in an agreement on a reform of the Security Council, it reminded member states of their Charter obligations. Here, Annan also proved to be a servant of the principles of the Charter, but reached the limits of what he could do in his position. This episode in the history of the UN demonstrated the broad scope as well as the inherent limitations of the powers of the Secretary-General.

All in all, after 75 years the United Nations still exists. The edifice built 75 years ago is still performing its functions. When evaluating its performance, it seems fair to conclude that the glass is half full rather than half empty. It is difficult, if not impossible to say whether another type of world organization – whether more intergovernmental or more supranational than the UN – would have performed better or worse. Of its six principal organs, the Trusteeship Council has long completed its task. The Economic and Social Council has been much criticized. Proposals to upgrade it to an Economic Security Council lacked the necessary support. Other principal organs have also often been criticized, and many proposals for reform have been made. The history of proposals for reforming the UN is almost as old as the UN itself.[57] A distinction

54 See Urquhart, op. cit. note 48, Chapter 7 (pp. 159–194), for an inside overview of this important episode in the history of the UN.

55 See above, Chapter 2, para. 4.

56 See R. Zacklin, *The United Nations Secretariat and the Use of Force in a Unipolar World – Power v. Principle* (2010).

57 For a brief overview, see Simma, op. cit. note 49, pp. 25–69. For an extensive chronologic overview of proposals for UN reform in general, see J. Müller, *Reforming the United Nations* (1997, 2001, 2006, 2010). For a collection of documents on Security Council reform, see B. Fassbender (ed.), *Key documents on the Reform of the UN Security Council 1991–2019* (2020).

must be made between reforms that need an amendment of the Charter and reforms that do not require such an amendment. Reforms by Charter amendment have been rare. However, over the years, many reforms have been agreed and implemented without such amendment. 'Revitalization of the General Assembly' has been on the agenda of the Assembly since 1991, with the aim of enhanced efficiency and effectiveness. The numerous amendments to the Assembly's rules of procedure offer illustrations. The UN Secretariat is almost permanently subject to reform.

While the functioning in practice of the General Assembly, the International Court of Justice and the Secretariat has not triggered many calls for change through Charter amendment, this is different for the Security Council. For some three decades, it has been widely recognized that, of all principal UN organs, the Security Council is by far most in need of constitutional change. While it has adapted to the times in some respects by a number of smaller institutional changes, the calls for more fundamental, constitutional reform have long remained unanswered. This is where the edifice built in 1945 is now most vulnerable. In the aftermath of the 2003 Iraq war, Secretary-General Annan therefore rightly not only sought a recommitment to the UN's collective security system but also an agreement on Security Council reform. The recommitment was given,[58] but the reform attempt failed.[59] Fifteen years later, it is still for the member states to act, and to transform the widely agreed need for reform into a compromise solution, to enable the UN to save future generations from the scourge of war.

The veto was already strongly criticized in 1945. It has dominated the functioning of the Security Council during its first 45 years and is now seen by many as anachronistic, as will be discussed in the next few reflections.

---

58 GA Res. 60/1, para. 2: "We reaffirm our faith in the United Nations and our commitment to the purposes and principles of the Charter of the United Nations and international law, which are indispensable foundations of a more peaceful, prosperous and just world, and reiterate our determination to foster strict respect for them".

59 The failure to agree was translated as follows in the World Summit Outcome resolution (id., para. 153): "We support early reform of the Security Council - an essential element of our overall effort to reform the United Nations - in order to make it more broadly representative, efficient and transparent and thus to further enhance its effectiveness and the legitimacy and implementation of its decisions. We commit ourselves to continuing our efforts to achieve a decision to this end and request the General Assembly to review progress on the reform set out above by the end of 2005".

4 The Veto in Practice

Chapter 2 has given an overview of the use of the veto. The veto has been crucial for the functioning of the Security Council during its first 45 years. Originally almost exclusively used by the Soviet Union, since the 1970s other permanent members took recourse to their special prerogative as well. The practice in the Cold War period has been a far cry from what the US stated in 1945 in San Francisco, "far from frequently used, the veto would seldom, if ever, be exercised. Far from being used perniciously, it would be used by the great powers, [...] not for their own selfish interests but in the interests of the world Organization".[60] This changed with the end of the Cold War. During the last decade of the 20th century, the veto was cast on nine occasions only. In total, 638 resolutions were adopted in the 1990s – thus, 638 cases in which the veto was not used. Half a century after the Charter was signed, the Security Council finally seemed to act in the spirit of San Francisco. The patterns of the 1990s continued to some extent in the new millennium, although the veto was cast again more often. The record of the Security Council in dealing with major crises involving permanent members (such as 9/11, the 2003 Iraq war, and the civil wars in Libya and Syria) showed varying success (in diplomatic terms) or fell far short of the ideals of the Charter and the needs of the peoples concerned. Disagreement amongst the permanent members prevented the Security Council from performing its functions meaningfully in Syria during the last decade, by stopping the killing of hundreds of thousands of people and the exodus of millions of refugees. It may seem unlikely that this human catastrophe would not have happened had the veto been abolished. However, the impotence of the Security Council in light of the long recognized need for its reform at least fuels the idea that a modernized Security Council could have yielded better results.

The most recent rounds of high-level discussions and negotiations involving Security Council reform did not mention the veto, or touched upon it only superficially. In the Millennium Declaration adopted in 2000, UN members resolved, "to intensify our efforts to achieve a comprehensive reform of the Security Council in all its aspects".[61] The attempt to reform the Council in 2005 failed. The 'World Summit Outcome' Resolution did no more than – again – expressing its support for "early reform".[62] It did not mention the veto. This was only raised during the run-up to this resolution, in the 2004 report of the High-level Panel on Threats, Challenges and Change. The Panel was as critical

60 UNCIO, Vol. XI, p. 493 (12 June 1945).

61 Id., para. 30.

62 GA Res. 60/1, para. 153.

of the right of veto as the vast majority of states in 1945, and referred to its "anachronistic character".[63] However, just as this vast majority in 1945 had no choice but to accept the veto, the Panel saw "no practical way of changing the existing members' veto powers".[64] Realism prevailed. The Panel only made two recommendations to the permanent members to limit their use of the veto. In addition, it recommended not to give the veto to any possible future permanent members and suggested to introduce a system of indicative voting, "to increase the accountability of the veto function".[65] Since then, no progress has been made in the negotiations on Security Council reform. The records of the relevant meetings of the General Assembly demonstrate that, even though the veto is criticized as before, it is not considered realistic to even try to abolish it.

Against this backdrop, Chapter 2 has concluded that in the long run, the challenge is to find a compromise solution that would, on the one hand, remove the right of veto from the decision-making of the Security Council, but that would also, on the other hand, still fully commit the most powerful to the purposes of the UN and the functions of the Security Council. In developing such a compromise solution, the decision-making rules and practice of other international organizations may provide some inspiration. Examples are the 'consensus minus one' rule (OSCE), weighted voting (financial organizations) and qualified majority voting in the European Union. The most powerful should continue to have a dominant, very strong position in the decision-making of the Security Council, but no longer an individual veto. In principle, the most powerful should not be opposed to Security Council decisions, but this should no longer be an absolute principle. Exceptionally, it should be possible to overrule a permanent member, to neutralize its veto. The challenge is to find a formula, according to which the Security Council would still be able to take decisions, even after it does not seem possible to secure the support of all permanent members. The mere existence of a possibility to bypass opposition of a permanent member will encourage this member to accept a compromise decision, knowing that otherwise an alternative decision might be taken that it would find less preferable.

Until the time is ripe for such a compromise solution, the veto will apply. As mentioned in Chapter 2, there are two in-built deficiencies in how the veto has been implemented in the Charter. As long as the veto exists, remedies may be sought for such deficiencies, no matter how difficult this is and how unlikely it may seem that an agreement can be reached. First, as discussed above, it is

63 UN Doc. A/59/565, para. 256.

64 Id.

65 Id., para. 257. See Chapter 2, para. 4.

almost impossible to change the composition of group of veto holders. This is a deficiency because it must be assumed that power relations in the world are subject to change. Even though it is difficult to measure such changes in detail, it is obvious that there have been significant shifts in power during the past 75 years. However, the very *raison d'être* of the veto is the need that decisions and action by the UN to maintain or restore international peace and security are backed by (super)power. What if such (super)power is no longer adequately represented in the Security Council? The rules on amendment of the Charter, effectively freezing the 1945 global power structures, are at odds with the *raison d'être* of the veto.

A second deficiency of the current veto rules is that they do not offer a 'fall back scenario' when the five permanent members fail to agree in cases in which it is generally considered that the Security Council should act. It is true that the General Assembly may step in and act as a substitute. This is what has happened at times, in particular during the Cold War (the Uniting for Peace Resolution; peacekeeping) but also in recent years, as mentioned above. However, there are clear political and legal limitations to an extensive subsidiary role of the General Assembly. In addition, organizations outside the UN may step in, such as the Organization on the Prohibition of Chemical Weapons when it declared its Secretariat competent to identify "those who were the perpetrators, organizers, sponsors or otherwise involved" in the use of chemical weapons.[66] The only remaining alternative is unilateral action, by states individually or in smaller groupings or organizations such as NATO. However, such unilateral action undermines the UN collective security system and the very reason why the UN was created in the first place.

During the last 75 years, the veto has been a fact of political life. Even though it is criticized as much now as in 1945, its abolishment as part of a future Security Council reform is widely considered unrealistic. It would be somewhat less ambitious – although still very difficult to achieve – to remedy the above mentioned two deficiencies, by Charter amendments that would remove the 'veto' of the permanent members in Article 108 and that would provide better 'fall back options' in cases of Security Council inaction than currently exist.

All future discussions and negotiations regarding the veto not only concern possible changes in the decision-making of the Security Council. They also relate to the underlying need to fully involve the most powerful states in the work of the Council. What were the most powerful states in 1945 was written into the

66 OPCW Conference Decision C-SS-4/Dec.3, par. 19, adopted by 82 in favour, 24 against (27 June 2018).

Charter, but is not cast in stone and changes over time. However, the Charter has not been changed in this respect, even though the need to involve the most powerful will continue, as a permanent prerequisite of an effective collective security organization. President Truman stated at the closing plenary session of the 1945 San Francisco Conference: "[b]y their own example the strong nations of the world should lead the way to international justice. That principle of justice is the foundation stone of this Charter".[67] This is equally true today and in the future. To quote Pascal once more, "la justice sans la force est impuissante". At the same time, the other half of Pascal's proposition is as much true: "la force sans la justice est tyrannique". Against this background, Chapter 3 has examined to what extent the Security Council is not only governed by the rule of power but also by the rule of law.

5 The Security Council and the Rule of Law

At first glance, the question whether, or to what extent, the Security Council is governed by the rule of law does not seem so difficult to answer. Firstly, because the Security Council was established under international law. The UN Charter defines its powers and composition. Secondly, because nowadays this may seem obvious. Helped by the fact that the concept of the rule of law suffers from a certain indeterminacy, it is universally embraced as something good. It will be difficult to find a government that does not accept that it is governed by the rule of law. International organizations in all regions of the word refer to the rule of law in their constitution or decisions.[68] If states embrace the rule of law at the national level, they must be presumed to also follow it at the international level; *in foro interno, in foro externo*.

However, on closer analysis, the question whether, or to what extent, the Security Council is governed by the rule of law is more complex. As was discussed in Chapter 3, the rule of law is generally considered as a fundamental principle of governance, in particular relating to the way in which governmental authority is exercised. According to Bingham, it is the rule of law that makes the difference between good and bad government.[69] At the international level, this

67 UNCIO, Vol. 1, p. 682.

68 NATO Treaty (1949), Preamble; Council of Europe Statute (1949), Preamble and Art. 3; Constitutive Act of the African Union (2000), Preamble, para. 9; OAS, see the Inter-American Democratic Charter, adopted 11 September 2001, Arts. 2–4; ASEAN Charter (2007), Preamble, para. 7, Arts. 1(7) and 2.2(h).

69 T. Bingham, *The Rule of Law* (2010), p. 174.

might be translated into: the rule of law makes the difference between good and bad governance. For the Security Council, this would imply that it would need to operate under the rule of law in order to properly function in security governance. If this is all true, one may wonder why the UN Charter does not explicitly mention it, and why the proposal was rejected in San Francisco that the first mentioned purpose of the UN, to maintain international peace and security, should be pursued "in conformity with the principles of justice and international law".[70] The answer is not that the notion rule of law has only more recently become in vogue. A number of delegations to the San Francisco conference referred to it. For example, Deputy Prime Minister of Australia Francis Forde in his opening statement proposed that the UN Charter could "declare that the organization should exert its powers for the promotion of justice and the rule of law".[71] The answers are to be found elsewhere.

Firstly, while the Charter does not explicitly mention the rule of law as such, it contains some of its substance. The Preamble refers to fundamental human rights, the dignity and worth of the human person, equal rights of men and women and of nations large and small. It also emphasizes the determination "to establish conditions under which justice and respect for the obligations arising from treaties and other sources of international law can be maintained". The reference in Article 1 to "principles of justice and international law" (in the context of the peaceful settlement of disputes), the provisions on the pacific settlement of disputes and the functions given to the International Court of Justice are all examples of rule of law elements justifying to a considerable extent the observation made by many, in 1945 and in practice,[72] that the United Nations is in fact based on the rule of law.

Secondly, when the Charter was negotiated, a key question was whether enforcement action by its most powerful organ would have to be in conformity with the principles of justice and international law. The *travaux préparatoires* and the text of Article 1(1) of the Charter demonstrate that in 1945 a negative answer was given to this question.[73] Has this been a missed opportunity to establish the right conditions for good governance, could this even foreshadow bad governance? While such questions were asked in 1945, at the end of

70 See above, Chapter 3, para. 4.

71 UNCIO, Vol. I, p. 174 (27 April 1945). Later in the conference, Australia proposed to refer to the rule of law in the context of one of the purposes of the UN, to develop friendly relations (Art. 1(2) of the Charter), see UNCIO, Vol. VI, p. 535.

72 E.g. Secretary-General Hammarskjold in the introduction to his 1961 Annual Report on the work of the UN, UN Doc. A/4800/Add. 1.

73 See Chapter 3, para. 4.

the day the wish prevailed to give the Security Council much leeway, in view of "the dangers of a repetition of the so-called 'appeasement policy'" of the 1930s,[74] *inter alia* allowing Hitler to occupy foreign territory (the 1938 Munich Agreement).

Thirdly, from a somewhat broader perspective, a fundamental idea underlying the rule of law principle, the containment of power, is to a certain degree implemented in the Charter. The power of the five permanent members of the Security Council, put at the disposal of the new world organization, was contained in several ways, even though they have the prerogative of the veto. The permanent members are bound by the same rules of the Charter as all other members of the UN. They are not the only members of the Security Council and need the support of at least four non-permanent members for the adoption of resolutions. In addition, the Security Council has very broad but not unlimited powers. Therefore, the permanent members cannot infinitely exploit the Council for their own ends. Finally, the Security Council is not a self-standing treaty body; it is embedded in the UN. While the Charter does not establish something like a balance of power, it attributes powers to other UN organs, in particular the General Assembly, the International Court of Justice and the Secretariat. This is relevant for the Security Council and to some extent controls the exercise of its powers, as is further detailed in Chapter 3. Thus, Thucydides' famous words ("the strong do what they can and the weak suffer what they must") might be true for the position of the Athenians in the Peloponnesian war more than 24 centuries ago, in the context of the Security Council it is a cynical overstatement, not an accurate description of the position of the permanent members.

Therefore, while the rule of law is not explicitly mentioned, key elements of it are included in the Charter. In the 75 years of past practice, these key elements have become particularly relevant since the 1990s, when the Security Council became more active and the question whether its actions were lawful and/or legitimate was posed in specific cases. A much more active Security Council entails greater risks of inconsistent decisions, depending on the political whims of the day, and criticism of double standards. As was demonstrated in Chapter 3, rule of law considerations have influenced the work of the Council. Thematic debates were initiated to discuss rule of law issues more generally. International criminal justice measures have been prominent on the agenda of the Security Council since the 1990s, even though the use of such measures is strongly influenced by the rule of power. Individual targeted sanctions are

74 UNCIO, Vol. VI, p. 13.

now more in accordance with rule of law requirements than when they were first created. At the same time, such improvements have so far not been made across the board, but only for the ISIL & Al-Qaida sanctions regime.

In dealing with the rule of law, practice has demonstrated how much the work of other UN organs in the field of the rule of law has affected the way in which the Security Council dealt with it, both generally and in specific cases. Secretary-General Annan provided a broad definition of the rule of law in 2004 that also covered the activities of the Security Council. The 2012 General Assembly Declaration on the Rule of Law recognized "that the rule of law applies to all States equally, and to international organizations, including the United Nations and its principal organs, and that respect for and promotion of the rule of law and justice should guide all of their activities and accord predictability and legitimacy to their actions".[75] So far, the Security Council itself has not made similar statements. Instead, it has "[reaffirmed] its commitment to international law and the Charter of the United Nations"[76] and has "[expressed] its commitment to ensure that all United Nations efforts to restore peace and security themselves respect and promote the rule of law".[77] The Security Council's "commitment to international law" was tested in specific cases, for example when it imposed individual sanctions. Following severe criticism of the original sanction procedures, the ISIL & Al-Qaida sanctions regime has moved from the rule of power (Security Council primacy) into a rule of law direction (the right to a remedy).

Establishing the rule of law at the international level does not happen automatically. It is a lengthy process requiring long-term efforts. This is already clear if we remember Dicey's definition. He distinguished as one of the meanings of the rule of law, the one most relevant for this book, the principle that no one is above the law, and everyone is subject to the jurisdiction of the ordinary tribunals. The first strand of this principle (no one is above the law) is generally recognized and well-established at the international level. *Pacta sunt servanda* is a fundamental principle of international law. No state denies that it is bound by treaties to which it is a party and by this fundamental principle. In contrast, the second strand (everyone is subject to the jurisdiction of ordinary tribunals) is as uncommon in international law as it is common at the national level. States are only subject to the jurisdiction of the International Court of Justice if they have accepted it. They are only subject to the jurisdiction of other international courts and tribunals if they have agreed to this. As far as the Security

75 GA Res. 67/1, para. 2.

76 UN Docs. S/PRST/2006/28 and S/PRST/2010/11.

77 UN Doc. S/PRST/2010/11.

Council is concerned, even if it is assumed that it is bound by international law, those who claim that the Security Council has violated international law have no remedy. Even though, in some specific instances, Security Council decisions have been brought before national and international courts, these courts may at most do some scrutinizing but cannot review such decisions.

Large discretionary powers were given to the Security Council in 1945, to save succeeding generations from the scourge of war. The question whether the rule of power or the rule of law should govern the exercise of those powers is answered now differently than in 1945, as a result of globalization, interdependence, increased international cooperation and the development of international law. It seems unlikely that the view would still prevail that measures taken by the Security Council under Chapter VII of the Charter would not need to be "in conformity with the principles of justice and international law", as the drafters of Charter agreed in Article 1. In particular since the 1990s, awareness of the rule of law has considerably increased and is becoming more integrated in the work of the Security Council, as a principle of governance for the exercise of its powers. In short: the Security Council is now more 'governanced' by the rule of law than prescribed in 1945. This is not only manifested in the rhetoric during its meetings and in general phrases in presidential statements adopted at the end of thematic debates, but also to some extent in concrete practice, for example in the fields of international criminal justice and individual sanctions.

Nevertheless, even though these are significant developments, Security Council practice is still dominated by the rule of power, i.e. power politics and the interests of the permanent members. It is therefore prone to criticism of selectivity and the application of double standards. As a matter of principle, this is inevitable. After all, the Security Council is a powerful political organ. At the same time, as is true also at the national level and was recognized by the ICJ in its first advisory opinion,[78] even a powerful political organ is not above the law. It is necessary to promote the further integration of the rule of law in the Council's practice. The forces of globalization and the need for international cooperation require that the Security Council will exercise its powers in accordance with the rule of law. While this key principle is now accepted, its further implementation in practice is likely to be a long-term, a very long-term process. In this process, the non-permanent members of the Security Council

---

78 *Admission of a State to the United Nations (Charter, Art. 4)*, Advisory Opinion, ICJ Rep. 1948, p. 56. At p. 64: "[t]he political character of an organ cannot release it from the observance of the treaty provisions established by the Charter when they constitute limitations on its powers or criteria for its judgment".

have a relevant role to play. They have often taken rule of law initiatives in the Security Council, both as regards thematic debates and specific issues on the agenda (e.g. Denmark, Mexico). A future enlargement of the Security Council may fundamentally change its composition, which may in turn affect how it will deal with rule of law issues in the future. The next few reflections concern the possible future increase of the number of members of the Council.

6 On the Need for a Second Enlargement of the Security Council

The necessity of Security Council reform was discussed in particular in Chapters 2 and 4. Since abolishment of the veto was broadly seen as unrealistic, reform discussions since 2005 have mostly focused on another long criticized characteristic of the Council: its present composition, which is no longer seen as a fair representation of UN membership.

The founders of the UN anticipated a future need for reform of the UN by amending the Charter.[79] In his closing speech at the San Francisco Conference, on 26 June 1945, President Truman stated: "[t]his Charter, like our own Constitution, will be expanded and improved as time goes on. No one claims that it is now a final or a perfect instrument. It has not been poured into a fixed mold. Changing world conditions will require readjustments – but they will be the readjustments of peace and not of war".[80] One of the changing world conditions was the process of decolonization. The resulting expansion of UN membership, discussed in Chapter 1, prompted the only two Charter amendments in the 75 years of existence of the world organization. In 1963, it was agreed to enlarge the Security Council and ECOSOC – both principal organs were becoming increasingly unrepresentative of UN membership. In 1971, ECOSOC was enlarged again. Somewhat later, discussions started on a second enlargement of the Security Council, discussed in Chapter 4. The need for an enlargement is generally recognized. It is imperative in view of the "changing world conditions" to which Truman referred in 1945. An agreement on this is long overdue.

One of the objections against Security Council reform is that this may not be the right time for it. At present, it may seem unlikely that a Charter amendment would enter into force, if at all agreement could be reached in the General Assembly. It seems impossible in the current political climate

79 UN Charter, Art. 108.

80 UNCIO, Vol. I, p. 680.

to adopt an amendment that could secure broad support of all UN members as well as ratification by each of the five permanent members. However, from a historical perspective this does not seem to be an insurmountable problem. Agreement on the first enlargement of the Security Council was reached in the middle of the Cold War, one year after the Cuban missile crisis. As mentioned in Chapter 2, when the 1963 agreement to increase Security Council membership was adopted by the General Assembly, two of the five permanent members of the Security Council, France and the Soviet Union, voted against. Two other permanent members, the UK and the US, abstained. However, within two years these four permanent members changed their minds and deposited their ratifications. In addition, the question is not only whether the existing political climate is conducive to forging a widely supported compromise, but also whether there is a sufficiently firmly shared conviction that reform is necessary.

Against this backdrop, Chapter 4 has illustrated why a second enlargement of the Security Council is long needed. It has given an overview of the size of non-plenary organs of the principal universal international organizations, in 1945 and at present. If this is compared to the size of the Security Council, the original number of 11 members in 1945 is small but not exceptional. However, the current difference between the size of the Security Council and that of these other non-plenary organs is much more significant. The present number of members of the Security Council is exceptionally small when compared to these other organs. Since 1945, almost all constitutions of universal international organizations have been amended to increase the number of members of their principal non-plenary organs. In most cases, these numbers have been doubled or tripled, reflecting the large inflow of new members into these organizations. At present - as was the case in the early postwar period - among the smallest non-plenary organs are those of the IMF (24) and of the World Bank (25). Their present size corresponds to a frequently proposed future size of the Security Council. These figures underline the need for reform of the Security Council, to make it more representative.

7 Institutions Matter

Another, more fundamental objection against proposals for Security Council reform is that it is unlikely that such an institutional reform would improve its functioning, as it cannot provide a substitute for the much needed political will, substantive consensus and unity among the five permanent members. This recalls Claude's important observation mentioned in Chapter 1:[81]

> one of the major tasks of twentieth-century statesmanship is to strike a balance between obsessive concern with institutional problems – which makes international organization an end in itself, and exclusive concentration upon substantive issues of current world politics – which neglects the building of an adequate institutional apparatus for international relations.

It is certainly true that an institutional reform of the Security Council as such is far from a shortcut to a better functioning of the Council. As Secretary-General Annan stated in 2003 when he announced his intention to create a high-level panel to examine threats to international peace and security: "institutional reforms alone will not suffice. Even the most perfect instrument will fail, unless people put it to good use".[82] This echoed earlier observations, for example in statements made at the concluding plenary session of the San Francisco conference,[83] or by the United Kingdom government in the first part of a 'final consideration', at the end of its 1945 Commentary on the UN Charter:[84]

> It is not suggested that all this machinery, however impressive it may be, can by itself preserve the peace or increase the welfare of the peoples of the world. That depends upon how governments use such machinery, and their actions in turn will largely depend upon the public opinion of their respective countries as expressed through their legislative and other bodies. This fact cannot be overemphasized.

It is certainly true that political will is necessary to make the institutions work. However, it is equally true that "an adequate institutional apparatus" is required to channel such a political will and to generate the best possible solutions. The

81 I.L. Claude, *Swords into Plowshares*: The Problems and Progress of International Organization (4th ed. 1971), p. 84).

82 Id.

83 One example is: "[g]reat as our achievement is, I feel that more is needed than a mere machine of peace. Unless the spirit to operate it is there, the best plan or machine may fail" (statement by Field Marshall Smuts, the chairman of the delegation of South Africa, UNCIO Vol. I, p. 678).

84 *A Commentary on the Charter of the United Nations*, presented by the Secretary of State for Foreign Affairs to Parliament by Command from His Majesty (Miscellaneous No. 9 (1945), p. 18.

United Kingdom government therefore correctly continued, in the second part of its abovementioned final consideration:[85]

> But it would be misleading to suggest as a kind of corollary, that the nature of the machinery now provided is of secondary importance. On the contrary, if the discussions at San Francisco had resulted in creating an organization which did not take into account the urgent needs and hard facts of the present time, the difficulties in the way of international co-operation would have been enormously increased, however anxious states might be to play their part in it. As it is, a powerful and flexible Organisation will shortly be at their disposal. […].

Institutions matter. This was agreed when after the First World War the League of Nations was founded, even though the Covenant's High Contracting Parties did not explicitly state that they established a new international organization. Secret bilateral treaties and other bilateral arrangements are commonly seen as one of the causes of the Great War. A future war was to be prevented by concluding a multilateral treaty with mutual rights and obligations and by creating an international organization. As Claude wrote, since the League, "collective security is associated with international organization as ham is with eggs".[86]

Institutions matter. This was agreed even more at the end of the Second World War, when 50 states not only "agreed to the present Charter of the United Nations", but also explicitly "do hereby establish an international organization to be known as the United Nations".[87] The common conclusion was *not* that the League experience had demonstrated that establishing an international organization was not the best way to prevent a future war. It was rather the opposite: a much stronger organization was needed, institutionalizing the political will of 50 states "to unite our strength to maintain international peace and security".[88]

In San Francisco in 1945, the common political will prevailed to establish a powerful international organization to save succeeding generations from the scourge of war. However, the United Nations was not established to replace such political will of the participating states, or to make it irrelevant. It was created to put an institution at the disposal of these states, to channel their political will and to assist them in generating the unity necessary to maintain or

85 Id.
86 Claude, op. cit. note 81, p. 246.
87 UN Charter, Preamble, final sentence.
88 UN Charter, Preamble, 6th paragraph.

restore international peace and security. A whole that is greater than the sum of its parts. The unity of the member states ('united nations') is required to allow their organization (the United Nations) to perform its functions. At the same time, this institution needs a minimum of general support from its members. If they do not defend and promote it with the necessary political will, the foundations of the edifice built 75 years ago are in danger of crumbling. If they do not reach agreement on the necessary reforms, they are accountable towards the peoples of the United Nations, whose ancestors were determined to save succeeding generations from the scourge of war.

APPENDIX

Overview of the Use of the Veto (1945 – 2020)

(reproduced from Security Council Report, available at www.securitycouncilreport.org/un-security-council-working-methods/the-veto.php)

SECURITY COUNCIL REPORT
Independent. Impartial. Informative.

The Security Council Veto

Date	Issue	Vote	Veto(es)	Abstention(S)	Affirmative votes	Meeting Record
20 December 2019	The situation in the Middle East (Syria) (S/2019/961)	13-2	China, Russia		Belgium, Côte d'Ivoire, Dominican Republic, Equatorial Guinea, France, Germany, Indonesia, Kuwait, Peru, Poland, South Africa, UK, USA	S/PV.8697
19 September 2019	Middle East (Syria)	12-2-1	China, Russia	Equatorial Guinea	Belgium, Côte d'Ivoire, Dominican Republic, France, Germany, Indonesia, Kuwait, Peru, Poland, UK, South Africa, US	S/PV.8623
28 February 2019	Venezuela (S/2019/186)	9-3-3	China, Russia (South African voted against)	Côte d'Ivoire, Equatorial Guinea, Indonesia	Belgium, Dominican Republic, France, Germany, Kuwait, Peru, Poland, UK, US	S/PV.8476
1 June 2018	The situation in the Middle East, including the Palestinian question (S/2018/516)	10-1-4	US	Ethiopia, Netherlands, Poland and UK	Bolivia, China, Côte d'Ivoire, Equatorial Guinea, France, Kazakhstan, Kuwait, Peru, Russia and Sweden	S/PV.8274
10 April 2018	Middle East (Syria) (S/2018/321)	12-2-1	Russia (Bolivia voted against)	China	Côte d'Ivoire, Equatorial Guinea, Ethiopia, France, Kazakhstan, Kuwait, Netherlands, Peru, Poland, Sweden, UK, US	S/PV.8228
26 February 2018	Yemen: Sanctions Regime (S/2018/156)	11-2-2	Russia (Bolivia voted against)	China, Kazakhstan	Côte d'Ivoire, Equatorial Guinea, Ethiopia, France, Kuwait, Netherlands, Peru, Poland, Sweden, UK, US	S/PV.8190
18 December 2017	Israel/Palestine: reaffirmed that any decisions and actions that purport to have altered the status of Jerusalem have no legal effect, are null and void and must be rescinded (S/2017/1060)	14-1-0	US		China, Bolivia, Egypt, Ethiopia, France, Kazakhstan, Italy, Japan, Russia, Senegal, Sweden, Ukraine, UK, US, Uruguay	S/PV.8139
17 November 2017	Middle East (Syria) (S/2017/970)	12-2-1	Russia (Bolivia voted against)	China	Egypt, Ethiopia, France, Kazakhstan, Italy, Japan, Senegal, Sweden, Ukraine, UK, US, Uruguay	S/PV.8107
16 November 2017	Middle East (Syria) (S/2017/962)	11-2-2	Russia (Bolivia voted against)	China, Egypt	Ethiopia, France, Kazakhstan, Italy, Japan, Senegal, Sweden, Ukraine, UK, US, Uruguay	S/PV.8105
24 October 2017	Middle East (Syria) (S/2017/884)	11-2-2	Russia (Bolivia voted against)	China, Kazakhstan	Egypt, Ethiopia, France, Italy, Japan, Senegal, Sweden, Ukraine, UK, US, Uruguay	S/PV.8073
12 April 2017	Middle East (Syria) (S/2017/315)	10-2-3	Russia (Bolivia voted against)	China, Ethiopia, Kazakhstan	Egypt, France, Italy, Japan, Senegal, Sweden, Ukraine, UK, US, Uruguay	S/PV.7922
28 February 2017	Middle East (Syria) (S/2017/172)	9-3-3	China, Russia (Bolivia voted against)	Egypt, Ethiopia, Kazakhstan	France, Italy, Japan, Senegal, Sweden, Ukraine, UK, US, Uruguay	S/PV.7893

The Security Council Veto

Date	Issue	Vote	Veto(es)	Abstention(S)	Affirmative votes	Meeting Record
5 December 2016	Syria: called for an end to all attacks in Aleppo for 7 days (S/2016/1026)	11-3-1	China, Russia (Venezuela voted against)	Angola	Egypt, France, Japan, Malaysia, New Zealand, Senegal, Spain, Ukraine, UK, US, Uruguay	S/PV.7825
8 October 2016	Middle East (Syria) (S/2016/846)	11-2-2	Russia (Venezuela voted against)	Angola, China	Egypt, France, Japan, Malaysia, New Zealand, Senegal, Spain, Ukraine, UK, US, Uruguay	S/PV.7785
29 July 2015	MH17 Tribunal (S/2015/562)	11-1-3	Russia	Angola, China, Venezuela	Chad, Chile, France, Jordan, Lithuania, Malaysia, New Zealand, Nigeria, Spain, UK, US	S/PV.7498
8 July 2015	Bosnia and Herzegovina: the 20th anniversary of the Srebrenica genocide (S/2015/508)	10-1-4	Russia	Angola, China, Nigeria, Venezuela	Chad, Chile, France, Jordan, Lithuania, Malaysia, New Zealand, Spain, UK, US	S/PV.7481
22 May 2014	Syria: referred Syria to the ICC (S/2014/348)	13-2-0	China, Russia		Argentina, Australia, Chad, Chile, France, Jordan, Lithuania, Luxembourg, Nigeria, Republic of Korea, Rwanda, UK, US	S/PV.7180
15 March 2014	Declared as invalid a referendum in Crimea, Ukraine	13-1-1	Russia	China	Argentina, Australia, Chad, Chile, France, Jordan, Lithuania, Luxembourg, Nigeria, Republic of Korea, Rwanda, UK, US	S/PV.7138
19 July 2012	Syria: endorsed the 30 June 2012 Geneva communiqué on a Syrian-led political transition, renewed UNSMIS for 45 days and threatened sanctions if the Syrian government did not cease the use of heavy weapons and withdraw from population centres within 10 days (S/2012/538)	11-2-2	China, Russia	Pakistan, South Africa	Azerbaijan, Colombia, France, Germany, Guatemala, India, Morocco, Portugal, Togo, UK, US	S/PV.6810
4 February 2012	Syria: condemned human rights violations and supported the Arab League's 22 January 2012 decision for political transition (S/2012/77)	13-2-0	China, Russia		Azerbaijan, Colombia, France, Germany, Guatemala, India, Morocco, Pakistan, Portugal, South Africa, Togo, UK, US	S/PV.6711
4 October 2011	Syria: condemned human rights violations by the Syrian authorities (S/2011/612)	9-2-4	China, Russia	Brazil, India, Lebanon, South Africa	Bosnia and Herzegovina, Colombia, France, Gabon, Germany, Nigeria, Portugal, UK, US	S/PV.6627
18 February 2011	Israel/Palestine: condemned Israeli settlement activities (S/2011/24)	14-1-0	US		Bosnia and Herzegovina, Brazil, China, Colombia, France, Gabon, Germany, India, Lebanon, Nigeria, Portugal, Russia, South Africa, UK	S/PV.6484
2010	No Vetoes					
15 June 2009	Georgia: on the extension of the UN observer mission's mandate in Georgia and Abkhazia (S/2009/310)	10-1-4	Russia	China, Libyan Arab Jamahiriya, Uganda, Viet Nam	Austria, Burkina Faso, Costa Rica, Croatia, France, Japan, Mexico, Turkey, UK, US	S/PV.6143

The Security Council Veto

Date	Issue	Vote	Veto(es)	Abstention(S)	Affirmative votes	Meeting Record
11 July 2008	Zimbabwe: condemned the violence by the Government of Zimbabwe against civilians after the elections of 27 June and demanded an immediate end to attacks against and intimidation of opposition members and supporters (S/2008/447)	9-5-1	China, Russia (Libyan Arab Jamahiriya, South Africa, Viet Nam voted against)	Indonesia	Belgium, Burkina Faso, Costa Rica, Croatia, France, Italy, Panama, UK, US	S/PV.5933
12 January 2007	Myanmar: called on Myanmar to cease military attacks against civilians in ethnic minority regions and to put an end to the associated human rights and humanitarian law violations (S/2007/14)	9-3-3	China, Russia (South Africa voted against)	Congo, Indonesia, Qatar	Belgium, France, Ghana, Italy, Panama, Peru, Slovakia, UK, US	S/PV.5619
11 November 2006	Israel/Palestine: on the Israeli military operations in Gaza, the Palestinian rocket fire into Israel, and called for immediate withdrawal of Israeli forces from within the Gaza Strip to positions prior to 28 June 2006 (S/2006/878)	10-1-4	US	Denmark, Japan, Slovakia, UK	Argentina, China, Congo, France, Ghana, Greece, Peru, Qatar, Russia, United Republic of Tanzania	S/PV.5565
13 July 2006	Israel/Palestine: demanded the unconditional release of an Israeli soldier captured earlier, as well as Israel's immediate withdrawal from Gaza and the release of dozens of Palestinian officials detained by Israel (S/2006/508)	10-1-4	US	Denmark, Peru, Slovakia, UK	Argentina, China, Congo, France, Ghana, Greece, Japan, Qatar, Russia, United Republic of Tanzania	S/PV.5488
2005	No Vetoes					
5 October 2004	Israel/Palestine: demanded Israel halt all military operations in northern Gaza and withdrawal from the area (S/2004/783)	11-1-3	US	Germany, Romania, UK	Algeria, Angola, Benin, Brazil, Chile, China, France, Pakistan, Philippines, Russia, Spain	S/PV.5051
21 April 2004	Cyprus: on the termination of the mandate of UNFICYP and its replacement with UNSIMIC (S/2004/310)	14-1-0	Russia		Algeria, Angola, Benin, Brazil, Chile, China, France, Germany, Pakistan, Philippines, Romania, Spain, UK, US	S/PV.4947
25 March 2004	Israel/Palestine: on the condemnation of the killing of Ahmed Yassin, the leader of the Islamic Resistance Movement, Hamas (S/2004/240)	11-1-3	US	Germany, Romania, UK	Algeria, Angola, Benin, Brazil, Chile, China, France, Pakistan, Philippines, Russia, Spain	S/PV.4934
14 October 2003	Israel/Palestine: on the security wall built by Israel in the West Bank (S/2003/980)	10-1-4	US	Bulgaria, Cameroon, Germany, UK	Angola, Chile, China, France, Guinea, Mexico, Pakistan, Russia, Spain, Syrian Arab Republic	S/PV.4842

The Security Council Veto

Date	Issue	Vote	Veto(es)	Abstention(S)	Affirmative votes	Meeting Record
16 September 2003	Israel/Palestine: on the Israeli decision to "remove" Palestinian Authority leader Yasser Arafat (S/2003/891)	11-1-3	US	Bulgaria, Germany, UK	Angola, Cameroon, Chile, China, France, Guinea, Mexico, Pakistan, Russia, Spain, Syrian Arab Republic	S/PV.4828
20 December 2002	Israel: on the killing by Israeli forces of several UN employees and the destruction of the WFP warehouse (S/2002/1385)	12-1-2	US	Bulgaria, Cameroun	China, Colombia, France, Guinea, Ireland, Mauritius, Mexico, Norway, Russia, Singapore, Syrian Arab Republic, UK	S/PV.4681
30 June 2002	Bosnia: on the renewal of the UN peacekeeping mission in Bosnia and the immunity of US peacekeepers from ICC jurisdiction (S/2002/712)	13-1-1	US	Bulgaria	Cameroon, China, Colombia, France, Guinea, Ireland, Mauritius, Mexico, Norway, Russia, Singapore, Syrian Arab Republic, UK	S/PV.4563
14 December 2001	Israel/Palestine: condemned acts of terror against Palestinian and Israeli civilians (S/2001/1199)	12-1-2	US	Norway, UK	Bangladesh, China, Colombia, France, Ireland, Jamaica, Mali, Mauritius, Russia, Singapore, Tunisia, Ukraine	S/PV.4438
27 March 2001	Israel/Palestine: on establishing a UN observer force to protect Palestinian civilians (S/2001/270)	9-1-4	US	France, Ireland, Norway, UK	Bangladesh, China, Colombia, Jamaica, Mali, Mauritius, Russia, Singapore, Tunisia	S/PV.4305
2000	No Vetoes					
25 February 1999	Former Yugoslav Republic of Macedonia: on the extension of UNPREDEP in the Former Yugoslav Republic of Macedonia (S/1999/201)	13-1-1	China	Russia	Argentina, Bahrain, Brazil, Canada, France, Gabon, Gambia, Malaysia, Namibia, Netherlands, Slovenia, UK, US	S/PV.3982
1998	No Vetoes					
21 March 1997	Israel: demanding Israel's immediate cessation of construction at Jabal Abu Ghneim in East Jerusalem (S/1997/241)	13-1-1	US	Costa Rica	Chile, China, Egypt, France, Guinea-Bissau, Japan, Kenya, Poland, Portugal, Republic of Korea, Russia, Sweden, UK	S/PV.3756
7 March 1997	Israel/Palestine: calling upon Israel to refrain from East Jerusalem settlement activities (S/1997/199)	14-1-0	US		Chile, China, Costa Rica, Egypt, France, Guinea- Bissau, Japan, Kenya, Poland, Portugal, Republic of Korea, Russia, Sweden, UK	S/PV.3747
10 January 1997	Guatemala: authorisation for 155 observers for verification of the agreement on the definite ceasefire in Guatemala (S/1997/18)	14-1-0	China		Chile, Costa Rica, Egypt, France, Guinea Bissau, Japan, Kenya, Poland, Portugal, Republic of Korea, Russia, Sweden, UK, US	S/PV.3730
1996	No Vetoes					

The Security Council Veto

Date	Issue	Vote	Veto(es)	Abstention(S)	Affirmative votes	Meeting Record
17 May 1995	Israel/Palestine: on the occupied Arab Territories (East Jerusalem) (S/1995/394)	14-1-0	US		Argentina, Botswana, China, Czech Republic, France, Germany, Honduras, Indonesia, Italy, Nigeria, Oman, Russia, Rwanda, UK	S/PV.3538
2 December 1994	Bosnia-Herzegovina: on the transport of goods between the former Yugoslavia and Bosnia (S/1994/1358)	13-1-1	Russia	China	Argentina, Brazil, Czech Republic, Djibouti, France, New Zealand, Nigeria, Oman, Pakistan, Rwanda, Spain, UK, US	S/PV.3475
11 May 1993	Cyprus: on financing UNFICYP (S/25693)	14-1-0	Russia		Brazil, Cape Verde, China, Djibouti, France, Hungary, Japan, Morocco, New Zealand, Pakistan, Spain, UK, US, Venezuela	S/PV.3211
1992	No Vetoes					
1991	No Vetoes					
31 May 1990	Israel/Palestine: on the Occupied Arab Territories (S/21326)	14-1-0	US		Canada, China, Colombia, Côte d'Ivoire, Cuba, Ethiopia, Finland, France, Malaysia, Romania, USSR, UK, Yemen, Zaire	S/PV.2926
17 January 1990	Panama: on the violation of Diplomatic Immunities in Panama (S/21084)	13-1-1	US	UK	Canada, China, Colombia, Côte d'Ivoire, Cuba, Democratic Yemen, Ethiopia, Finland, France, Malaysia, Romania, USSR, Zaire	S/PV.2905
23 December 1989	Panama: demanded the withdrawal of the US armed forces from Panama (S/21048)	10-4-1	France, UK, US (Canada voted against)	Finland	Algeria, Brazil, China, Colombia, Ethiopia, Malaysia, Nepal, Senegal, USSR, Yugoslavia	S/PV.2902
7 November 1989	Israel/Palestine: on the Occupied Arab Territories (S/20945/Rev.1)	14-1-0	US		Algeria, Brazil, Canada, China, Colombia, Ethiopia, Finland, France, Malaysia, Nepal, Senegal, USSR, UK, Yugoslavia	S/PV.2889
9 June 1989	Israel/Palestine: on the situation in the Occupied Arab Territories (S/20677)	14-1-0	US		Algeria, Brazil, Canada, China, Colombia, Ethiopia, Finland, France, Malaysia, Nepal, Senegal, USSR, UK, Yugoslavia	S/PV.2867
17 February 1989	Israel/Palestine: on the situation in the Occupied Arab Territories (S/20463)	14-1-0	US		Algeria, Brazil, Canada, China, Colombia, Ethiopia, Finland, France, Malaysia, Nepal, Senegal, USSR, UK, Yugoslavia	S/PV.2850
11 January 1989	Letter from Libya: complaint by Libya against US downing of aircraft (S/20378)	9-4-2	France, UK, US (Canada voted against)	Brazil, Finland	Algeria, China, Colombia, Ethiopia, Malaysia, Nepal, Senegal, USSR, Yugoslavia	S/PV.2841
14 December 1988	Lebanon/Israel: complaint of Lebanon against Israel (S/20322)	14-1-0	US		Algeria, Argentina, Brazil, China, France, Federal Republic of Germany, Italy, Japan, Nepal, Senegal, USSR, UK, Yugoslavia, Zambia	S/PV.2832

The Security Council Veto

Date	Issue	Vote	Veto(es)	Abstention(S)	Affirmative votes	Meeting Record
10 May 1988	Lebanon/Israel: complaint of Lebanon against Israel (S/19868)	14-1-0	US		Algeria, Argentina, Brazil, China, France, Federal Republic of Germany, Italy, Japan, Nepal, Senegal, USSR, UK, Yugoslavia, Zambia	S/PV.2814
15 April 1988	Israel/Palestine: situation in the Occupied Arab Territories (S/19780)	14-1-0	US		Algeria, Argentina, Brazil, China, France, Federal Republic of Germany, Italy, Japan, Nepal, Senegal, USSR, UK, Yugoslavia, Zambia	S/PV.2806
8 March 1988	South Africa: called for sanctions (S/19585)	10-2-3	US, UK	France, Federal Republic of Germany, Japan	Algeria, Argentina, Brazil, China, Italy, Nepal, Senegal, USSR, Yugoslavia, Zambia	S/PV.2797
1 February 1988	Israel/Palestine: on the situation in the Occupied Arab Territories (S/19466)	14-1-0	US		Algeria, Argentina, Brazil, China, France, Federal Republic of Germany, Italy, Japan, Nepal, Senegal, USSR, UK, Yugoslavia, Zambia	S/PV.2790
18 January 1988	Lebanon/Israel: complaint of Lebanon against Israel (S/19434)	13-1-1	US	UK	Algeria, Argentina , Brazil, China, France, Federal Republic of Germany, Italy, Japan, Nepal, Senegal, USSR, Yugoslavia, Zambia	S/PV.2784
9 April 1987	Namibia Question (S/18785)	9-3-3	UK, US (Federal Republic of Germany voted against)	France, Italy, Japan	Argentina, Bulgaria, China, Congo, Ghana, USSR, UAE, Venezuela, Zambia	S/PV.2747
20 February 1987	South Africa: called for sanctions (S/18705)	10-3-2	UK, US (Federal Republic of Germany voted against)	France, Japan	Argentina, Bulgaria, China, Congo, Ghana, Italy, USSR, UAE, Venezuela, Zambia	S/PV.2738
28 October 1986	Letter from Nicaragua: complaint of Nicaragua against the US (ICJ Judgment) (S/18428)	11-1-3	US	France, Thailand, UK	Australia, Bulgaria, China, Congo, Denmark, Ghana, Madagascar, Trinidad and Tobago, USSR, UAE, Venezuela	S/PV.2718
31 July 1986	Letter from Nicaragua: complaint of Nicaragua against the US (ICJ Judgment) (S/18250)	11-1-3	US	France, Thailand, UK	Australia, Bulgaria, China, Congo, Denmark, Ghana, Madagascar, Trinidad and Tobago, USSR, UAE, Venezuela	S/PV.2704
18 June 1986	Complaint by Angola against South Africa (S/18163)	12-2-1	UK, US	France	Australia, Bulgaria, China, Congo, Denmark, Ghana, Madagascar, Thailand, Trinidad and Tobago, USSR, UAE, Venezuela	S/PV.2693 p.48
23 May 1986	Botswana, Zambia and Zimbabwe: complaint against South Africa (S/18087/Rev.1)	12-2-1	UK, US	France	Australia, Bulgaria, China, Congo, Denmark, Ghana, Madagascar, Thailand, Trinidad and Tobago, USSR, UAE, Venezuela	S/PV.2686
21 April 1986	Letter from Libya, Burkina Faso, Syria and Oman: complaint against US attack (S/18016/Rev.1)	9-5-1	France, UK, US (Australia and Denmark voted against)	Venezuela	Bulgaria, China, Congo, Ghana, Madagascar, Thailand, Trinidad and Tobago, USSR, UAE	S/PV.2682

The Security Council Veto

Date	Issue	Vote	Veto(es)	Abstention(S)	Affirmative votes	Meeting Record
6 February 1986	Syria/Israel: Syrian complaint against Israeli interception of Libyan Civilian Aircraft (S/17796/Rev.1)	10-1-4	US	Australia, Denmark, France, UK	Bulgaria, China, Congo, Ghana, Madagascar, Thailand, Trinidad and Tobago, USSR, UAE, Venezuela	S/PV.2655
30 January 1986	Israel/Palestine: violation of Haram Al-Sharif (Jerusalem) (S/17769/Rev.1)	13-1-1	US	Thailand	Australia, Bulgaria, China, Congo, Denmark, France, Ghana, Madagascar, Trinidad and Tobago, USSR, UAE, UK, Venezuela	S/PV.2650
17 January 1986	Lebanon/Israel: complaint by Lebanon against Israeli aggression (S/17730/Rev.2)	11-1-3	US	Australia, Denmark, UK	Bulgaria, China, Congo, France, Ghana, Madagascar, Thailand, Trinidad and Tobago, USSR, UAE, Venezuela	S/PV.2642
15 November 1985	Situation in Namibia (S/17633)	12-2-1	UK, US	France	Australia, Burkina Faso, China, Denmark, Egypt, India, Madagascar, Peru, Thailand, Trinidad and Tobago, Ukrainian Soviet Socialist Republic, USSR	S/PV.2629
13 September 1985	Israel/Palestine: on the situation in the Occupied Arab Territories (S/17459)	10-1-4	US	Australia, Denmark, France, UK	Burkina Faso, China, Egypt, India, Madagascar, Peru, Thailand, Trinidad and Tobago, Ukrainian Soviet Socialist Republic, USSR	S/PV.2605
26 July 1985	South Africa (S/17354/Rev.1)	12-2-1	UK, US	France	Australia, Burkina Faso, China, Denmark, Egypt, India, Madagascar, Peru, Thailand, Trinidad and Tobago, Ukrainian Soviet Socialist Republic, USSR	S/PV.2602
10 May 1985	Complaint by Nicaragua against the US (S/17172/ Para 2)	13-1-1	US	UK	Australia, Burkina Faso, China, Denmark, Egypt, France, India, Madagascar, Peru, Thailand, Trinidad and Tobago, Ukrainian Soviet Socialist Republic, USSR	S/PV.2580 paragraph 268
10 May 1985	Complaint by Nicaragua against the US (S/17172/ Para 1)	11-1-3	US	Egypt, Thailand, UK	Australia, Burkina Faso, China, Denmark, France, India, Madagascar, Peru, Trinidad and Tobago, Ukrainian Soviet Socialist Republic, USSR	S/PV.2580 paragraph 267
10 May 1985	Complaint by Nicaragua against the US (S/17172/ Preamble)	13-1-1	US	UK	Australia, Burkina Faso, China, Denmark, Egypt, France, India, Madagascar, Peru, Thailand, Trinidad and Tobago, Ukrainian Soviet Socialist Republic, USSR	S/PV.2580 paragraph 266
12 March 1985	Situation in the Middle East (Lebanon) (S/17000)	11-1-3	US	Australia, Denmark, UK	Burkina Faso, China, Egypt, France. India, Madagascar, Peru, Thailand, Trinidad and Tobago. Ukrainian Soviet Socialist Republic, USSR	S/PV.2573

The Security Council Veto

Date	Issue	Vote	Veto(es)	Abstention(S)	Affirmative votes	Meeting Record
6 September 1984	Situation in the Middle East (Lebanon) (S/16732)	14-1-0	US		Burkina Faso, China, Egypt, France, India, Malta, Netherlands, Nicaragua, Pakistan, Peru, Ukrainian Soviet Socialist Republic, USSR, UK, Zimbabwe	S/PV.2556 paragraph 49
4 April 1984	Nicaragua-US: complaint by Nicaragua against the US (S/16463)	13-1-1	US	UK	China, Egypt, France, India, Malta, Netherlands. Nicaragua, Pakistan, Peru, Ukrainian Soviet Socialist Republic, USSR, Upper Volta, Zimbabwe	S/PV.2529
29 February 1984	Situation in the Middle East (Lebanon) (S/16351/Rev.2)	13-2-0	USSR (Ukrainian Soviet Socialist Republic voted against)		China, Egypt, France, India, Malta, Netherlands, Nicaragua, Pakistan, Peru, UK, US, Upper Volta, Zimbabwe	S/PV.2519
27 October 1983	Situation in Grenada: invasion of the Republic of Grenada by US troops (S/16077/Rev.1)	11-1-3	US	Togo, UK, Zaire	China, France, Guyana, Jordan, Malta, Netherlands, Nicaragua, Pakistan, Poland, USSR, Zimbabwe	S/PV.2491
12 September 1983	Republic of Korea/USSR: downing of the Korean Airliner (S/15966/Rev.1)	9-2-4	USSR (Poland voted against)	China, Guyana, Nicaragua, Zimbabwe	France, Jordan, Malta, Netherlands, Pakistan, Togo, UK, US, Zaire	S/PV.2476
2 August 1983	Israel/Palestine: situation in the Arab Occupied Territories (S/15895)	13-1-1	US	Zaire	China, France, Guyana, Jordan, Malta, Netherlands, Nicaragua, Pakistan, Poland, Togo, USSR, UK, Zimbabwe	S/PV.2461
6 August 1982	Situation in the Middle East (Lebanon) (S/15347/Rev.1)	11-1-3	US	Togo, UK, Zaire	China, France, Guyana, Ireland, Japan, Jordan, Panama, Poland, Spain, Uganda, USSR	S/PV.2391
26 June 1982	Situation in the Middle East (Lebanon) (S/15255/Rev.2)	14-1-0	US		China, France, Guyana, Ireland, Japan, Jordan, Panama, Poland, Spain, Togo, Uganda, USSR, UK, Zaire	S/PV.2381
8 June 1982	Situation in the Middle East (Lebanon) (S/15185)	14-1-0	US		China, France, Guyana, Ireland, Japan, Jordan, Panama, Poland, Spain, Togo, Uganda, USSR, UK, Zaire	S/PV.2377
4 June 1982	Falkland Islands (Malvinas) (S/15156/Rev.2)	9-2-4	UK, US	France, Guyana, Jordan, Togo	China, Ireland, Japan, Panama, Poland, Spain, Uganda, USSR, Zaire	S/PV.2373
20 April 1982	Situation in the Middle East: the Al-Aqsa Mosque in Jerusalem attack (S/14985)	14-1-0	US		China, France, Guyana, Ireland, Japan, Jordan, Panama, Poland, Spain, Togo, Uganda, USSR, UK, Zaire	S/PV.2357
2 April 1982	Situation in the Middle East: Mayors of Nablus and Ramallah dismissal (S/14943)	13-1-1	US	Zaire	China, France, Guyana, Ireland, Japan, Jordan, Panama, Poland, Spain, Togo, Uganda, USSR, UK	S/PV.2348
2 April 1982	Nicaragua: the situation in Central America (S/14941)	12-1-2	US	UK, Zaire	China, France, Guyana, Ireland, Japan, Jordan, Panama, Poland, Spain, Togo, Uganda, USSR	S/PV.2347

The Security Council Veto

Date	Issue	Vote	Veto(es)	Abstention(S)	Affirmative votes	Meeting Record
20 January 1982	Situation in the Middle East (Golan Heights) (S/14832/Rev.1)	9-1-5	US	France, Ireland, Japan, Panama, UK	China, Guyana, Jordan, Poland, Spain, Togo, Uganda, USSR, Zaire	S/PV.2329
31 August 1981	Complaint by Angola against South Africa (S/14664/Rev.2)	13-1-1	US	UK	China, France, German Democratic Republic, Ireland, Japan, Mexico, Niger, Panama, Philippines, Spain, Tunisia, Uganda, USSR	S/PV.2300
30 April 1981	Question of Namibia (S/14462)	12-3-0	France, UK, US		China, German Democratic Republic, Ireland, Japan, Mexico, Niger, Panama, Philippines, Spain, Tunisia, Uganda, USSR	S/PV.2277 paragraph 27
30 April 1981	Question of Namibia (S/14461)	11-3-1	France, UK, US	Japan	China, German Democratic Republic, Ireland, Mexico, Niger, Panama, Philippines, Spain, Tunisia, Uganda, USSR	S/PV.2277 paragraph 26
30 April 1981	Question of Namibia (S/14460/Rev.1)	9-3-3	France, UK, US	Ireland, Japan, Spain	China, German Democratic Republic, Mexico, Niger, Panama, Philippines, Tunisia, Uganda, USSR	S/PV.2277 paragraph 25
30 April 1981	Question of Namibia (S/14459)	9-3-3	France, UK, US	Ireland, Japan, Spain	China, German Democratic Republic, Mexico, Niger, Panama, Philippines, Tunisia, Uganda, USSR	S/PV.2277 paragraph 24
30 April 1980	Situation in the Middle East: Palestinian rights (S/13911)	10-1-4	US	France, Norway, Portugal, UK	Bangladesh, China, German Democratic Republic, Jamaica, Mexico, Niger, Philippines, Tunisia, USSR, Zambia	S/PV.2220
11-13 January 1980	US and Iran hostage question (S/13735)	10-2-2	USSR (German Democratic Republic voted against)	Bangladesh, Mexico (China did not participate)	France, Jamaica, Niger, Norway, Philippines, Portugal, Tunisia, UK, US, Zambia	S/PV.2191/ Add.1 paragraph 149
7-9 January 1980	Soviet invasion of Afghanistan (S/13729)	13-2-0	USSR (German Democratic Republic voted against)		Bangladesh, China, France, Jamaica, Mexico, Niger, Norway, Philippines, Portugal, Tunisia, UK, US, Zambia	S/PV.2190 Coor.1 + Add.1 paragraph 140
16 March 1979	China and Viet Nam: border dispute in South-East Asia (S/13162)	13-2-0	USSR (Czechoslova-kia voted against)		Bangladesh, Bolivia, China, France, Gabon, Jamaica, Kuwait, Nigeria, Norway, Portugal, UK, US, Zambia	S/PV.2129
15 January 1979	Cambodia and Viet Nam: Viet Nam intervention in Kampuchea (Cambodia) (S/13027)	13-2-0	USSR (Czechoslova kia voted against)		Bangladesh, Bolivia, China, France, Gabon, Jamaica, Kuwait, Nigeria, Norway, Portugal, UK, US, Zambia	S/PV.2112
1978	No Vetoes					
31 October 1977	Situation in South Africa (S/12312/Rev.1)	10-5-0	France, UK, US (Canada and Federal Republic of Germany also voted against)		Benin, China, India, Libyan Arab Jamahiriya, Mauritius, Pakistan, Panama, Romania, USSR, Venezuela	S/PV.2045 paragraph 55

The Security Council Veto

Date	Issue	Vote	Veto(es)	Abstention(S)	Affirmative votes	Meeting Record
31 October 1977	Situation in South Africa (S/12311/Rev.1)	10-5-0	France, UK, US (Canada and Federal Republic of Germany also voted against)		Benin, China, India, Libyan Arab Jamahiriya, Mauritius, Pakistan, Panama, Romania, USSR, Venezuela	S/PV.2045 paragraph 54
31 October 1977	Situation in South Africa and the illegal invasion of Namibia (S/12310/Rev.1)	10-5-0	France, UK, US (Canada and Federal Republic of Germany also voted against)		Benin, China, India, Libyan Arab Jamahiriya, Mauritius, Pakistan, Panama, Romania, USSR, Venezuela	S/PV.2045 paragraph 53
15 November 1976	Admission of New Members: Viet Nam (S/12226)	14-1-0	US		Benin, China, France, Guyana, Italy, Japan, Libyan Arab Republic, Pakistan, Panama, Romania, Sweden, USSR, UK, United Republic of Tanzania	S/PV.1972
19 October 1976	Situation in Namibia (S/12211)	10-3-2	France, UK, US	Italy, Japan	Benin, China, Guyana, Libyan Arab Republic, Pakistan, Panama, Romania, Sweden, USSR, United Republic of Tanzania	S/PV.1963
29 June 1976	Question of the exercise by the Palestinian people of their inalienable rights (S/12119)	10-1-4	US	France, Italy, Sweden, UK	Benin, China, Guyana, Japan, Libyan Arab Republic, Pakistan, Panama, Romania, USSR, United Republic of Tanzania	S/PV.1938
23 June 1976	Admission of New Members: Angola (S/12110)	13-1-0	US	China did not participate	Benin, France, Guyana, Italy, Japan, Libyan Arab Republic, Pakistan, Panama, Romania, Sweden, USSR, UK, United Republic of Tanzania	S/PV.1932
25 March 1976	Israel/Palestine: Jerusalem status (S/12022)	14-1-0	US		Benin, China, France, Guyana, Italy, Japan, Libyan Arab Republic, Pakistan, Panama, Romania, Sweden, USSR, UK, United Republic of Tanzania	S/PV.1899
6 February 1976	Situation in Comoros: dispute between the Comoros and France over Mayotte (S/11967)	11-1-3	France	Italy, UK, US	Benin, China, Guyana, Japan, Libyan Arab Republic, Pakistan, Panama, Romania, Sweden, USSR, United Republic of Tanzania	S/PV.1888
25 January 1976	Israel/Palestine: right of self-determination (S/11940)	9-1-3	US	Italy, Sweden, UK (China and Libya did not participate)	Benin, France, Guyana, Japan, Pakistan, Panama, Romania, USSR, United Republic of Tanzania	S/PV.1879
8 December 1975	Israel/Lebanon: strongly condemning the Government of Israel for its premeditated air attacks against Lebanon (S/11898)	13-1-1	US	Costa Rica	Byelorussian Soviet Socialist Republic, Cameroon, China, France, Guyana, Iraq, Italy, Japan, Mauritania, Sweden, USSR, UK, United Republic of Tanzania	S/PV.1862
30 September 1975	Admission of New Members: North Viet Nam (S/11833)	14-1-0	US		Byelorussian Soviet Socialist Republic, Cameroon, China, Costa Rica, France, Guyana, Iraq, Italy, Japan, Mauritania, Sweden, USSR, UK, United Republic of Tanzania	S/PV.1846 paragraph 42

The Security Council Veto

Date	Issue	Vote	Veto(es)	Abstention(S)	Affirmative votes	Meeting Record
30 September 1975	Admission of New Members: South Viet Nam (S/11832)	14-1-0	US		Byelorussian Soviet Socialist Republic, Cameroon, China, Costa Rica, France, Guyana, Iraq, Italy, Japan, Mauritania, Sweden, USSR, UK, United Republic of Tanzania	S/PV.1846 paragraph 41
11 August 1975	Admission of New Members: North Viet Nam (S/11796)	14-1-0	US	Costa Rica	Byelorussian Soviet Socialist Republic, Cameroon, China, France, Guyana, Iraq, Italy, Japan, Mauritania, Sweden, USSR, UK, United Republic of Tanzania	S/PV.1836
11 August 1975	Admission of New Members: South Viet Nam (S/11795)	13-1-1	US	Costa Rica	Byelorussian Soviet Socialist Republic, Cameroon, China, France, Guyana, Iraq, Italy, Japan, Mauritania, Sweden, USSR, UK, United Republic of Tanzania	S/PV.1836
6 June 1975	Situation in Namibia: on South Africa's occupation of Namibia (S/11713)	10-3-2	France, UK, US	Italy, Japan	Byelorussian Soviet Socialist Republic, Cameroon, China, Costa Rica Guyana, Iraq, Mauritania, Sweden, USSR, United Republic of Tanzania	S/PV.1829
30 October 1974	Expulsion of South Africa from UN Membership (S/11543)	10-3-2	France, UK, US	Austria, Costa Rica	Australia, Byelorussian Soviet Socialist Republic, Cameroon, China, Indonesia, Iraq, Kenya, Mauritania, Peru, USSR, United Republic of Tanzania	S/PV.1808
31 July 1974	Situation in Cyprus (S/11400/Rev.1)	12-2-0	USSR (Byelorussia voted against)	(China did not participate)	Australia, Austria, Cameroon, Costa Rica, France, Indonesia, Iraq, Kenya, Mauritania, Peru, UK, US	S/PV.1788
26 July 1973	Situation in the Middle East: Palestinian Question (S/10974)	13-1-0	US	(China did not participate)	Australia, Austria, France, Guinea, India, Indonesia, Kenya, Panama, Peru, Sudan, USSR, the UK, Yugoslavia	S/PV.1735
22 May 1973	Situation in Rhodesia: on sanctions (S/10928)	11-2-2	UK, US	Austria and France	Australia, China, Guinea, India, Indonesia, Kenya, Panama, Peru, Sudan, USSR, Yugoslavia	S/PV.1716
21 March 1973	Panama Canal Question (S/10931/Rev.1)	13-1-1	US	UK	Australia, Austria, China, France, Guinea, India, Indonesia, Kenya, Panama, Peru, Sudan, USSR, Yugoslavia	S/PV.1704
29 September 1972	Situation in South Rhodesia (S/10805/Rev.1 as amended)	10-1-4	UK	Belgium, France, Italy, US	Argentina, China, Guinea, India, Japan, Panama, Somalia, Sudan, USSR, Yugoslavia	S/PV.1666
29 September 1972	Situation in South Rhodesia (S/10805/Rev.1 op.para 5)	10-1-4	UK	Belgium, France, Italy, US	Argentina, China, Guinea, India, Japan, Panama, Somalia, Sudan, USSR, Yugoslavia	S/PV.1666
29 September 1972	Situation in South Rhodesia (S/10805/Rev.1 op. para 1)	10-1-4	UK	Belgium, France, Italy, US	Argentina, China, Guinea, India, Japan, Panama, Somalia, Sudan, USSR, Yugoslavia	S/PV.1666

The Security Council Veto

Date	Issue	Vote	Veto(es)	Abstention(S)	Affirmative votes	Meeting Record
10 September 1972	Situation in the Middle East: ceasefire 1967 violation (S/10784)	13-1-1	US	Panama	Argentina, Belgium, China, France, Guinea, India, Italy, Japan, Somalia, Sudan, USSR, UK, Yugoslavia	S/PV.1662
10 September 1972	Situation in the Middle East: on the ceasefire 1967 violation (S/10786)	9-6-0	China and USSR (Guinea, Somalia, Sudan and Yugoslavia voted against)		Argentina, Belgium, France, India, Italy, Japan, Panama, UK and the US	S/PV.1662
25 August 1972	Admission of New Members: Bangladesh (S/10771)	11-1-3	China	Guinea, Somalia, Sudan	Argentina, Belgium, France, India, Italy, Japan, Panama, USSR, UK, US, Yugoslavia	S/PV.1660
4 February 1972	Situation in South Rhodesia (S/10606)	9-1-5	UK	Belgium, France, Italy, Japan, US	Argentina, China, Guinea, India, Panama, Somalia, Sudan, USSR, Yugoslavia	S/PV.1639
30 December 1971	Situation in South Rhodesia (S/10489)	9-1-5	UK	Belgium, France, Italy, Japan, US	Argentina, Burundi, China, Nicaragua, Poland, Sierra Leone, Somalia, Syrian Arab Republic, USSR	S/PV.1623
13 December 1971	India-Pakistan: calling for an immediate ceasefire and withdrawal of the troops at the borders (S/10446/Rev.1)	11-2-2	USSR (Poland voted against)	France, UK	Argentina, Belgium, Burundi, China, Italy, Japan, Nicaragua, Sierra Leone, Somalia, Syrian Arab Republic, US	S/PV.1613
5 December 1971	India-Pakistan: urging for a ceasefire at the border and for the return of refugees (S/10423)	11-2-2	USSR (Poland voted against)	France, UK	Argentina, Belgium, Burundi, China, Italy, Japan, Nicaragua, Sierra Leone, Somalia, Syria, US	S/PV.1607
4 December 1971	India-Pakistan: calling for a ceasefire at the border (S/10416)	11-2-2	USSR (Poland voted against)	France, UK	Argentina, Belgium, Burundi, China, Italy, Japan, Nicaragua, Sierra Leone, Somalia, Syria, US	S/PV.1606
10 November 1970	South Rhodesia (Zimbabwe): independence and sanctions (S/9976)	12-1-2	UK	France, US	Burundi, China, Colombia, Finland, Nepal, Nicaragua, Poland, Sierra Leone, Spain, Syria, USSR, Zambia	S/PV.1556
17 March 1970	Zimbabwe: condemning the proclamation of a so-called republic by the racist minority regime in Salisbury (S/9696)	9-2-4	UK, US	Colombia, Finland, France, Nicaragua	Burundi, China, Nepal, Poland, Sierra Leone, Spain, Syria, USSR, Zambia	S/PV.1534
1969	No Vetoes					
22 August 1968	On the complaint by Czechoslovakia: its invasion by USSR and other members of the Warsaw Pact (S/8761)	10-2-3	USSR (Hungary voted against)	Algeria, India, Pakistan	Brazil, Canada, China, Denmark, Ethiopia, France, Paraguay, Senegal, UK, US	S/PV.1443
1967	No Vetoes					
4 November 1966	Syria/Israel: violation of the Armistice Agreement (S/7575/Rev.1)	10-4-1	USSR (Bulgaria, Jordan and Mali voted against)	China	Argentina, France, Japan, Netherlands, New Zealand, Nigeria, Uganda, Uruguay, UK, US	S/PV.1319
1965	No Vetoes					

The Security Council Veto

Date	Issue	Vote	Veto(es)	Abstention(S)	Affirmative votes	Meeting Record
21 December 1964	Syria/Israel: violation of the Armistice Agreement (S/6113)	8-3-0	USSR (Czechoslovakia and Morocco voted against)		Bolivia, Brazil, China, France, Ivory Coast, Norway, UK, US	S/PV.1182
17 September 1964	On the relationship between Malaysia and Indonesia (armed incidents) (S/5973)	9-2-0	USSR (Czechoslovakia voted against)		Bolivia, Brazil, China, France, Ivory Coast, Morocco, Norway, UK, US	S/PV.1152
13 September 1963	Southern Rhodesia (S/5425/Rev.1)	8-1-2	UK	France, US	Brazil, China, Ghana, Morocco, Norway, Philippines, USSR, Venezuela	S/PV.1069
3 September 1963	Syria/Israel: deploring renewal of armed incidents and calling on Israel and Syria to cooperate fully according to the armistice agreement (S/5407)	8-2-1	USSR (Morocco voted against)	Venezuela	Brazil, China, France, Ghana, Norway, Philippines, UK, US	S/PV.1063
22 June 1962	India-Pakistan (S/5134)	7-2-2	USSR (Romania voted against)	Ghana, United Arab Republic	Chile, China, France, Ireland, the UK, US, Venezuela	S/PV.1016
18 December 1961	Calling upon India to withdraw its forces from Goa, Damao and Diu (S/5033)	7-4-0	USSR (Sri Lanka, Liberia and the United Arab Republic voted against)		Chile, China. Ecuador, France, Turkey, UK, US	S/PV.988
30 November 1961	Admission of New Members: Kuwait (S/5006)	10-1-0	USSR		Sri Lanka, Chile, China, Ecuador, France, Liberia, Turkey, United Arab Republic, UK, US	S/PV.985
24 November 1961	Congo Question (S/4989/Rev.2, US amendment on paragraph 11)	9-1-1	USSR	France	Sri Lanka, Chile, China, Ecuador, Liberia, Turkey, United Arab Republic, UK, US	S/PV.982
7 July 1961	Kuwait: on independence and territorial integrity (S/4855)	7-1-3	USSR	Sri Lanka, Ecuador, United Arab Republic	Chile, China, France, Liberia, Turkey, UK, US	S/PV.960
20 February 1961	Situation in the Congo (S/4733/Rev.1 as amended)	7-3-1	USSR (Sri Lanka and the United Arab Republic voted against)	Liberia	Chile, China, Ecuador, France, Turkey, UK, US	S/PV.942
20 February 1961	Situation in Congo (S/4733/Rev.1 as amended)	8-3-0	USSR (Sri Lanka and the United Arab Republic voted against)		Chile, China, Ecuador, France, Liberia, Turkey, UK, US	S/PV.942
13 December 1960	Situation in Congo (S/4578/Rev.1)	7-3-1	USSR (Sri Lanka and Poland voted against)	Tunisia	Argentina, China, Ecuador, France, Italy, UK, US	S/PV.920
4 December 1960	Admission of New Members: Mauritania (S/4567/Rev.1)	8-2-1	USSR (Poland voted against)	Sri Lanka	Argentina, China, Ecuador, France, Italy, Tunisia, UK, US	S/PV.911
17 September 1960	The situation in the Congo (S/4523)	8-2-1	USSR (Poland voted against)	France	Argentina, China, Ecuador, Italy, Tunisia, Sri Lanka, UK, US	S/PV.906
26 July 1960	On the incident in which a US Air Force plane was brought down by Soviet military forces (complaint from USSR) (S/4411)	9-2-0	USSR (Poland voted against)		Argentina, China, Ecuador, France, Italy, Sri Lanka, Tunisia, UK, US	S/PV.883

The Security Council Veto

Date	Issue	Vote	Veto(es)	Abstention(S)	Affirmative votes	Meeting Record
26 July 1960	On the incident in which a US Air Force plane was brought down by Soviet military forces (complaint from USSR) (S/4409/Rev.1)	9-2-0	USSR (Poland voted against)		Argentina, China, Ecuador, France, Italy, Sri Lanka, Tunisia, UK, US	S/PV.883
1959	No Vetoes					
9 December 1958	Admission of New Members: South Viet Nam (S/4130/Rev.1)	8-1-2	USSR	Canada and Iraq	China, Colombia, France, Japan, Panama, Sweden, UK, US	S/PV.843
9 December 1958	Admission of New Members: Republic of Korea (S/4129/Rev.1)	9-1-1	USSR	Iraq	Canada, China, Colombia, France, Japan, Panama, Sweden, UK, US	S/PV.843
22 July 1958	Complaint by Lebanon on the situation arising from interference of the United Arab Republic in the internal affairs of Lebanon (S/4055/Rev.1)	10-1-0	USSR		Canada, China, Colombia, France, Iraq, Japan, Panama, Sweden, UK, US	S/PV.837
18 July 1958	Complaint by Lebanon on the situation arising from interference of the United Arab Republic in the internal affairs of Lebanon (S/4050/Rev.1)	9-1-1	USSR	Sweden	Canada, China, Colombia, France, Iraq, Japan, Panama, UK, US	S/PV.834
2 May 1958	Complaint by USSR: on the incident in which a US Air Force plane was brought down by Soviet military forces (S/3995)	10-1-0	USSR		Canada, China, Colombia, France, Iraq, Japan, Panama, Sweden, UK, US	S/PV.817
9 September 1957	Admission of New Members: Viet Nam (S/3885)	10-1-0	USSR		Australia, China, Colombia, Cuba, France, Iraq, Philippines, Sweden, UK, US	S/PV.790
9 September 1957	Admission of New Members: Republic of Korea (S/3884)	10-1-0	USSR		Australia, China, Colombia, Cuba, France, Iraq, Philippines, Sweden, UK, US	S/PV.790
20 February 1957	India-Pakistan (S/3787)	9-1-1	USSR	Sweden	Australia, China, Colombia, Cuba, France, Iraq, Philippines, UK, US	S/PV.773
4 November 1956	Situation in Hungary (S/3730/Rev.1)	9-1-0	USSR	(Yugoslavia did not participate: present and not voting)	Australia, Belgium, China, Cuba, France, Iran, Peru, UK, US	S/PV.754
30 October 1956	Palestinian Question: on the steps for the immediate cessation of the military action of Israel in Egypt (S/3713/Rev.1)	7-2-2	France, UK	Belgium, US	Australia, China, Cuba, Iran, Peru, USSR, Yugoslavia	S/PV.750
30 October 1956	Palestinian Question: on the steps for the immediate cessation of the military action of Israel in Egypt (S/3710)	7-2-2	France, UK	Australia, Belgium	China, Cuba, Iran, Peru, USSR, US, Yugoslavia	S/PV.749

The Security Council Veto

Date	Issue	Vote	Veto(es)	Abstention(S)	Affirmative votes	Meeting Record
13 October 1956	Situation created by the unilateral action of the Egyptian Government in bringing to an end the system of international operation of the Suez Canal, which was confirmed and completed by the Suez Canal Convention of 1888 (S/3671/Rev.1)	9-2-0	USSR (Yugoslavia voted against)		Australia, Belgium, China, Cuba, France, Iran, Peru, UK, US	S/PV.743
15 December 1955	Admission of New Members: Japan (S/3510)	10-1-0	USSR		Belgium, Brazil, China, France, Iran, New Zealand, Peru, Turkey, UK, US	S/PV.706
14 December 1955	Admission of New Members: Japan (S/3510)	10-1-0	USSR		Belgium, Brazil, China, France, Iran, New Zealand, Peru, Turkey, UK, US	S/PV.705
13 December 1955	Admission of New Members: Spain (S/3502)	9-1-1	USSR	Belgium	Brazil, China, France, Iran, New Zealand, Peru, Turkey, UK, US	S/PV.704
13 December 1955	Admission of New Members: Laos (S/3502)	10-1-0	USSR		Belgium, Brazil, China, France, Iran, New Zealand, Peru, Turkey, UK, US	S/PV.704
13 December 1955	Admission of New Members: Japan (S/3502)	10-1-0	USSR		Belgium, Brazil, China, France, Iran, New Zealand, Peru, Turkey, UK, US	S/PV.704
13 December 1955	Admission of New Members: Cambodia (S/3502)	10-1-0	USSR		Belgium, Brazil, China, France, Iran, New Zealand, Peru, Turkey, UK, US	S/PV.704
13 December 1955	Admission of New Members: Libya (S/3502)	10-1-0	USSR		Belgium, Brazil, China, France, Iran, New Zealand, Peru, Turkey, UK, US	S/PV.704
13 December 1955	Admission of New Members: Nepal (S/3502)	10-1-0	USSR		Belgium, Brazil, China, France, Iran, New Zealand, Peru, Turkey, UK, US	S/PV.704
13 December 1955	Admission of New Members: Sri Lanka (S/3502)	10-1-0	USSR		Belgium, Brazil, China, France, Iran, New Zealand, Peru, Turkey, UK, US	S/PV.704
13 December 1955	Admission of New Members: Finland (S/3502)	10-1-0	USSR		Belgium, Brazil, China, France, Iran, New Zealand, Peru, Turkey, UK, US	S/PV.704
13 December 1955	Admission of New Members: Austria (S/3502)	10-1-0	USSR		Belgium, Brazil, China, France, Iran, New Zealand, Peru, Turkey, UK, US	S/PV.704
13 December 1955	Admission of New Members: Italy (S/3502)	10-1-0	USSR		Belgium, Brazil, China, France, Iran, New Zealand, Peru, Turkey, UK, US	S/PV.704
13 December 1955	Admission of New Members: Portugal (S/3502)	10-1-0	USSR		Belgium, Brazil, China, France, Iran, New Zealand, Peru, Turkey, UK, US	S/PV.704

The Security Council Veto

Date	Issue	Vote	Veto(es)	Abstention(S)	Affirmative votes	Meeting Record
13 December 1955	Admission of New Members: Ireland (S/3502)	10-1-0	USSR		Belgium, Brazil, China, France, Iran, New Zealand, Peru, Turkey, UK, US	S/PV.704
13 December 1955	Admission of New Members: Jordan (S/3502)	10-1-0	USSR		Belgium, Brazil, China, France, Iran, New Zealand, Peru, Turkey, UK, US	S/PV.704
13 December 1955	Admission of New Members: Mongolia (S/3502)	8-1-2	China	Belgium, US	Brazil, France, Iran, New Zealand, Peru, Turkey, UK, USSR	S/PV.704
13 December 1955	Admission of New Members: Viet Nam (S/3502)	9-1-1	USSR	New Zealand	Belgium, Brazil, China, France, Iran, Peru, Turkey, UK, US	S/PV.704
13 December 1955	Admission of New Members: Republic of Korea (S/3502)	9-1-1	USSR	New Zealand	Belgium, Brazil, China, France, Iran, Peru, Turkey, UK, US	S/PV.704
20 June 1954	Complaint by Guatemala (S/3236/Rev.1)	10-1-0	USSR		Brazil, China, Colombia, Denmark, France, Lebanon, New Zealand, Turkey, UK, US	S/PV.675
18 June 1954	Situation in Thailand: on the request for a Peace Observation Commission (S/3229)	9-1-1	USSR	Lebanon	Brazil, China, Colombia. Denmark, France, New Zealand, Turkey, UK, US	S/PV.674
29 March 1954	Palestinian Question: on the Egypt-Israeli dispute over the Suez Canal (S/3188/Corr.1)	8-2-1	USSR (Lebanon voted against)	China	Brazil, Colombia. Denmark, France, New Zealand, Turkey, UK, US	S/PV.664
22 January 1954	Palestinian Question: declares that the General Armistice Agreement between Syria and Israel be observed by the parties (S/3151/Rev.2)	7-2-2	USSR (Lebanon voted against)	Brazil, China	Colombia, Denmark, France, New Zealand, Turkey, UK, US	S/PV.656
1953	No Vetoes					
19 September 1952	Admission of New Members: Cambodia (S/2758)	10-1-0	USSR		Brazil, Chile, China, France, Greece, Netherlands, Pakistan, Turkey, UK, US	S/PV.603
19 September 1952	Admission of New Members: Laos (S/2759)	10-1-0	USSR		Brazil, Chile, China, France, Greece, Netherlands, Pakistan, Turkey, UK, US	S/PV.603
19 September 1952	Admission of New Members: Viet Nam (S/2760)	10-1-0	USSR		Brazil, Chile, China, France, Greece, Netherlands, Pakistan, Turkey, UK, US	S/PV.603
18 September 1952	Admission of New Members: Japan (S/2754)	10-1-0	USSR		Brazil, Chile, China, France, Greece, Netherlands, Pakistan, Turkey, UK, US	S/PV.602
16 September 1952	Admission of New Members: Libya (S/2483)	10-1-0	USSR		Brazil, Chile, China, France, Greece, Netherlands, Pakistan, Turkey, UK, US	S/PV.600
9 July 1952	Request for investigation of alleged bacterial warfare (S/2688)	9-1-1	USSR	Pakistan	Brazil, Chile, China, France, Greece, Netherlands, Turkey, UK, US	S/PV.590

The Security Council Veto

Date	Issue	Vote	Veto(es)	Abstention(S)	Affirmative votes	Meeting Record
3 July 1952	Request for investigation of alleged bacterial warfare (S/2671)	10-1-0	USSR		Brazil, Chile, China, France, Greece, Netherlands, Pakistan, Turkey, UK, US	S/PV.587
6 February 1952	Admission of New Members: Italy (S/2443)	10-1-0	USSR		Brazil, Chile, China, France, Greece, Netherlands, Pakistan, Turkey, UK, US	S/PV.573
1951	No Vetoes					
30 November 1950	Complaint of aggression against Republic of Korea (S/1894)	9-1-0	USSR	(India did not participate in the vote)	China, Cuba, Ecuador, Egypt, France, Norway, UK, US, Yugoslavia	S/PV.530
30 November 1950	Complaint of aggression against Republic of Korea (S/1894)	9-1-0	USSR	(India did not participate in the vote)	China, Cuba, Ecuador, Egypt, France, Norway, UK, US, Yugoslavia	S/PV.530
30 November 1950	Complaint of aggression against Republic of Korea (S/1894)	8-1-1	USSR	Yugoslavia (India did not participate)	China, Cuba, Ecuador, Egypt, France, Norway, UK, US	S/PV.530
12 September 1950	Complaint of bombing by air forces on China's territory (S/1752)	7-1-2	USSR	India, Yugoslavia (China did not participate)	Cuba, Ecuador, Egypt, France, Norway, UK, US	S/PV.501
5 September 1950	Complaint of aggression against Republic of Korea (S/1653)	9-1-1	USSR	Yugoslavia	China, Cuba, Ecuador, Egypt, France, India, Norway, UK, US	S/PV.496
13 December 1949	Indonesian Question: on independence (S/1431)	8-2-1	USSR (the Ukrainian Soviet Socialist Republic also voted against)	Argentina	Canada, China, Cuba, Egypt, France, Norway, UK, US	S/PV.456
13 December 1949	Indonesian Question: on independence (S/1431 first part)	9-2-0	USSR (the Ukrainian Soviet Socialist Republic also voted against)		Argentina, Canada, China, Cuba, Egypt, France, Norway, UK, US	S/PV.456
18 October 1949	Regulation and Reduction of Armaments (S/1408/Rev.1)	8-2-1	USSR (the Ukrainian Soviet Socialist Republic also voted against)	Argentina	Canada, China, Cuba, Egypt, France, Norway, UK, US	S/PV.452
18 October 1949	Proposal of the Commission on Conventional Armaments (S/1399/Rev.1)	9-2-0	USSR (the Ukrainian Soviet Socialist Republic also voted against)		Argentina, Canada, China, Cuba, Egypt, France, Norway, UK, US	S/PV.452
11 October 1949	Proposal of the Commission on Conventional Armaments (S/1398)	9-2-0	USSR (the Ukrainian Soviet Socialist Republic also voted against)		Argentina, Canada, China, Cuba, Egypt, France, Norway, UK, US	S/PV.450
13 September 1949	Admission of New Members: Sri Lanka (S/1337)	9-2-0	USSR (the Ukrainian Soviet Socialist Republic also voted against)		Argentina, Canada, China, Cuba, Egypt, France, Norway, UK, US	S/PV.443
13 September 1949	Admission of New Members: Austria (S/1336)	9-2-0	USSR (the Ukrainian Soviet Socialist Republic also voted against)		Argentina, Canada, China, Cuba, Egypt, France, Norway, UK, US	S/PV.443

The Security Council Veto

Date	Issue	Vote	Veto(es)	Abstention(S)	Affirmative votes	Meeting Record
13 September 1949	Admission of New Members: Ireland (S/1335)	9-2-0	USSR (the Ukrainian Soviet Socialist Republic also voted against)		Argentina, Canada, China, Cuba, Egypt, France, Norway, UK, US	S/PV.443
13 September 1949	Admission of New Members: Finland (S/1334)	9-2-0	USSR (the Ukrainian Soviet Socialist Republic also voted against)		Argentina, Canada, China, Cuba, Egypt, France, Norway, UK, US	S/PV.443
13 September 1949	Admission of New Members: Italy (S/1333)	9-2-0	USSR (the Ukrainian Soviet Socialist Republic also voted against)		Argentina, Canada, China, Cuba, Egypt, France, Norway, UK, US	S/PV.443
13 September 1949	Admission of New Members: Jordan (S/1332)	9-2-0	USSR (the Ukrainian Soviet Socialist Republic also voted against)		Argentina, Canada, China, Cuba, Egypt, France, Norway, UK, US	S/PV.443
13 September 1949	Admission of New Members: Portugal (S/1331)	9-2-0	USSR (the Ukrainian Soviet Socialist Republic also voted against)		Argentina, Canada, China, Cuba, Egypt, France, Norway, UK, US	S/PV.443
7 September 1949	Admission of New Members: Nepal (S/1385)	9-2-0	USSR (The Ukrainian Soviet Socialist Republic also voted against)		Argentina, Canada, China, Cuba, Egypt, France, Norway, UK, US	S/PV.439
8 April 1949	Admission of New Members: Republic of Korea (S/1305)	9-2-0	USSR (the Ukrainian Soviet Socialist Republic also voted against)		Argentina, Canada, China, Cuba, Egypt, France, Norway, UK, US	S/PV.423
15 December 1948	Admission of New Members: Sri Lanka (S/PV.384)	9-2-0	USSR (the Ukrainian Soviet Socialist Republic also voted against)		Argentina, Belgium, Canada, China, Colombia, France, Syria, UK, US	S/PV.384
25 October 1948	Letter from France, the UK and the US: on the Berlin blockade (S/1048)	9-2-0	USSR (the Ukrainian Soviet Socialist Republic also voted against)		Argentina, Belgium, Canada, China, Colombia, France, Syria, UK, US	S/PV.372
18 August 1948	Admission of New Members: Sri Lanka	9-2-0	USSR (the Ukrainian Soviet Socialist Republic also voted against)		Argentina, Belgium, Canada, China, Colombia, France, Syria, UK, US	S/PV.351
22 June 1948	Reports from the Atomic Energy Committee	9-2-0	USSR (the Ukrainian Soviet Socialist Republic also voted against)		Argentina, Belgium, Canada, China, Colombia, France, Syria, UK, US	S/PV.325
24 May 1948	Letter from Chile: on events in Czechoslovakia	9-2-0	USSR (the Ukrainian Soviet Socialist Republic also voted against)		Argentina, Belgium, Canada, China, Colombia, France, Syria, UK, US	S/PV.303
24 May 1948	Letter from Chile: on events in Czechoslovakia (preliminary question)	8-2-1	USSR (the Ukrainian Soviet Socialist Republic also voted against)	France	Argentina, Belgium, Canada, China, Colombia, Syria, UK, US	S/PV.303

The Security Council Veto

Date	Issue	Vote	Veto(es)	Abstention(S)	Affirmative votes	Meeting Record
10 April 1948	Admission of New Members: Italy	9-2-0	USSR (the Ukrainian Soviet Socialist Republic also voted against)		Argentina, Belgium, Canada, China, Colombia, France, Syria, the UK, US	S/PV.279
1 October 1947	Admission of New Members: Finland	9-2-0	USSR (Poland also voted against)		Australia, Belgium, Brazil, China, Colombia, France, Syria, UK, US	S/PV.206
1 October 1947	Admission of New Members: Italy	9-2-0	USSR (Poland also voted against)		Australia, Belgium, Brazil, China, Colombia, France, Syria, UK, US	S/PV.206
15 September 1947	Greek Frontier Incidents (preliminary question)	8-2-1	USSR (Poland also voted against)	Syria	Australia, Belgium, Brazil, China, Colombia, France, UK, US	S/PV.202
15 September 1947	Greek Frontier Incidents	9-2-0	USSR (Poland also voted against)		Australia, Belgium, Brazil, China, Colombia, France, Syria, UK, US	S/PV.202
25 August 1947	Indonesia Question: on the establishment of a Committee of three to assist with the settlement (S/514)	7-2-2	France (Belgium voted against)	China, UK	Australia, Brazil, Colombia, Poland, Syria, USSR, US	S/PV.194
21 August 1947	Admission of New Members: Austria	8-1-2	USSR	France, Poland	Australia, Belgium, Brazil, China, Colombia, Syria, UK, US	S/PV.190
21 August 1947	Admission of New Members: Italy	9-1-1	USSR	Poland	Australia, Belgium, Brazil, China, Colombia, France, Syria, UK, US	S/PV.190
19 August 1947	Greek Frontier Incidents (S/486)	9-2-0	USSR (Poland voted against)		Australia, Belgium, Brazil, China, Colombia, France, Syria, UK, US	S/PV.188
19 August 1947	Greek Frontier Incidents (S/471)	9-2-0	USSR (Poland voted against)		Australia, Belgium, Brazil, China, Colombia, France, Syria, UK, US	S/PV.188
18 August 1947	Admission of New Members: Portugal	9-2-0	USSR (Poland voted against)		Australia, Belgium, Brazil, China, Colombia, France, Syria, UK, US	S/PV.186
18 August 1947	Admission of New Members: Ireland	9-1-1	USSR	Poland	Australia, Belgium, Brazil, China, Colombia, France, Syria, UK, US	S/PV.186
18 August 1947	Admission of New Members: Jordan	9-1-1	USSR	Poland	Australia, Belgium, Brazil, China, Colombia, France, Syria, UK, US	S/PV.186
29 July 1947	Greek Frontier Incidents	9-2-0	USSR (Poland voted against)		Australia, Belgium, Brazil, China, Colombia, France, Syria, UK, US	S/PV.170
25 March 1947	Incidents in the Corfu Channel	7-2-1	USSR (Poland voted against)	Syria (the UK did not participate)	Australia, Belgium, Brazil, China, Colombia, France, US	S/PV.122
20 September 1946	Ukrainian Complaint against Greece	8-2-1	USSR (Poland voted against)	Australia	Brazil, China, Egypt, France, Mexico, Netherlands, UK, US	S/PV.70
29 August 1946	Admission of New Members: Portugal	8-2-1	USSR (Poland voted against)	Australia	Brazil, China, Egypt, France, Mexico, Netherlands, UK, US	S/PV.57
29 August 1946	Admission of New Members: Ireland	9-1-1	USSR	Australia	Brazil, China, Egypt, France, Mexico, Netherlands, Poland, UK, US	S/PV.57
29 August 1946	Admission of New Members: Jordan	8-2-1	USSR (Poland voted against)	Australia	Brazil, China, Egypt, France, Mexico, Netherlands, UK, US	S/PV.57

Security Council Veto

Date	Issue	Vote	Veto(es)	Abstention(S)	Affirmative votes	Meeting Record
26 June 1946	Spanish Question	9-2-0	USSR (Poland voted against)		Australia, Brazil, China, Egypt, France, Mexico, Netherlands, UK, US	S/PV.49
26 June 1946	Spanish Question (preliminary question)	8-2-1	France and USSR	Poland	Australia, Brazil, China, Egypt, Mexico, Netherlands, UK, US	S/PV.49
26 June 1946	Spanish Question	9-2-0	USSR (Poland voted against)		Australia, Brazil, China, Egypt, France, Mexico, Netherlands, UK, US	S/PV.49
18 June 1946	Spanish Question (S/PV.45)	9-1-1	USSR	?	?	S/PV.47
18 June 1946	Spanish Question (S/PV.45)	9-1-1	USSR	?	?	S/PV.47
18 June 1946	Spanish Question (S/PV.45)	9-1-1	USSR	?	?	S/PV.47
18 June 1946	Spanish Question (S/PV.45)	10-1-0	USSR		?	S/PV.47
16 February 1946	Lebanese-Syria (S/PV.22)	7-1-1	USSR	? (France and the UK did not participate)	?	S/PV.23

Index

www.ingramcontent.com/pod-product-compliance
Lightning Source LLC
LaVergne TN
LVHW102227300926
849160LV00005B/55
9789004443914